D0824561

MASTER *of* PERSUASION

MASTER *of* PERSUASION

BRIAN MULRONEY'S
GLOBAL LEGACY

FEN OSLER HAMPSON

SIGNAL
McCLELLAND
& STEWART

Hardcover edition published 2018

Signal and colophon are registered trademarks of McClelland & Stewart

LIBRARY AND ARCHIVES CANADA CATALOGUING IN PUBLICATION
Hampson, Fen Osler, author
    Master of persuasion / Fen Osler Hampson.
Issued in print and electronic formats.
ISBN 978-0-7710-3907-2 (hardcover). —ISBN 978-0-7710-3908-9 (EPUB)
    1. Mulroney, Brian, 1939- —Influence. 2. Prime ministers—Canada—
Biography. 3. Canada—Foreign relations—1945-. I. Title.
FC630.H33 2018   971.064'7   C2017-904789-2
                                              C2017-904790-6

Excerpts on pages 39 and 40 from "Famine in Ethiopia: Suffering and Grace," by David Lamb, published December 30, 1984, copyright © 1984. *Los Angeles Times*. Used with permission.

Interior photographs courtesy of the Rt. Hon. Brian Mulroney, Rt. Hon. Brian Mulroney Fonds, Library & Archives Canada

Published simultaneously in the United States of America by Signal, an imprint of McClelland & Stewart, a division of Penguin Random House Canada Limited, a Penguin Random House Company

Library of Congress Control Number is available upon request

Typeset in Dante by M&S, Toronto
Printed and bound in the USA

Published by Signal,
an imprint of McClelland & Stewart,
a division of Penguin Random House Canada Limited,
a Penguin Random House Company
www.penguinrandomhouse.ca

1 2 3 4 5   22 21 20 19 18

Penguin
Random House
Canada

For my students

CONTENTS

═════════

By James A. Baker III

U NDER BRIAN MULRONEY'S LEADERSHIP CANADA PUNCHED
well above its weight on the world stage. The reasons are spelled
out in this important book on the foreign policy achievements
of Brian Mulroney, which not only describes in rich, compelling detail
the many, singular accomplishments of Canada's 18th prime minister, but
also explores the reasons behind his success.

As Fen Hampson explains, Brian Mulroney understood that one of
the major sources of Canada's global influence rested on building strong
and durable ties with the United States and its leaders. That platform lent
credibility and leverage to Canada's global engagements, but also showed
that Canada could be a major, global player while simultaneously enjoy-
ing positive and constructive relations with its southern neighbour.
Although Brian Mulroney enjoyed remarkably good personal relations
with many world leaders, including German chancellor Helmut Kohl,
South African president Nelson Mandela, French president François
Mitterrand, and Britain's prime minister Margaret Thatcher, it must be
said that his relations with United States president Ronald Reagan and
then-President George Herbert Walker Bush were incomparable in terms
of their depth, breadth, and closeness.

Together with Presidents Reagan and then Bush, Mulroney advanced
a compelling, new vision for North America that would see the removal
of many of the outstanding barriers to trade in goods and services by

constructing the world's biggest and most successful trading bloc, first under the Canada-US Free Trade Agreement (CUSFTA) and then under the North American Free Trade Agreement (NAFTA) with the addition of Mexico. Their collective vision produced millions of new jobs, spurred billions in cross-border investment, and enhanced prosperity and stability in all three countries. Today, the integrated economies of North America have a combined population of half a billion people and a total GDP that is slightly over $21 trillion USD, which is more than double China's GDP.

Despite much of the anti-trade fervour in Washington these days, North America today is a global economic juggernaut. Cooperation among the three NAFTA countries is a source of America's strength, as are the close community and cultural ties that have developed among our three countries. North America is also one of the most competitive regions in the world. NAFTA helped our three countries succeed in a highly competitive world. However, it is also important to remember that this highly beneficial enterprise began with Mulroney's early overtures to President Reagan for a bilateral free trade agreement and Reagan's own immediate enthusiasm for the idea.

Mulroney's friendships with Reagan and Bush were clearly based on warm personal relations, mutual respect, an unwavering commitment to shared political values, and a bedrock of trust. Mulroney was seen by both Presidents as a valuable interlocutor and trusted counsel, often on issues that went well beyond the narrow scope of Canada–US relations. This was especially true in the run up to the first Gulf War when President Bush built a global coalition with Mulroney's help to expel Iraqi leader Saddam Hussein's forces out of Kuwait, which Hussein had illegally invaded. Mulroney's counsel was also helpful as the Berlin Wall came tumbling down and Western allies found themselves divided on the thorny issue of German reunification, which Bush and Mulroney strongly supported. Mulroney had an uncanny grasp of American politics and American politicians which is why his counsel was unfailingly pertinent. He was instrumental in bolstering the trust of other allies on these critical issues. It was truly a momentous time in global affairs and tested the leadership skills of all who were involved.

I was privileged to lead the U.S. team in the final stages of the bilateral free trade negotiation and I believe that the result was one of two major, economic achievements of the Reagan administration; the other being tax reform. At the negotiating table, as I can personally attest, Mulroney was an effective and principled negotiator, as were the members of his team. Although negotiations on trade and acid rain, for example, were sometimes challenging, protracted, and difficult, they never descended into acrimony or bitterness that could have soured relations or poisoned the well for future talks. Mulroney upheld the interests of Canada with a bold vision few would have attempted. But he also understood the importance of securing mutual benefits that would enhance the prosperity and security of North America as a whole. The same is true about Canada's defence and security relations with the United States during Mulroney's tenure: Canada was a reliable security partner that carried its fair share on defence and dutifully deployed its men and women in uniform to help bring peace to the world's troubled hot spots.

The close partnership Canada had with the United States under Brian Mulroney's leadership was a compelling symbol to the rest of the world during a period of geostrategic upheaval and uncertainty following the break-up of the Soviet Union and the disintegration of the Warsaw Pact. It was a partnership that continues to serve as a model to others about how to conduct relations between neighbours. President Reagan, President Bush, and Prime Minister Mulroney were truly visionary and transformative leaders. They recognized that North Americans had to work together to secure their borders, while simultaneously opening their shared borders to promote jobs and prosperity and to preserve our shared environment.

T HIS BOOK WAS WRITTEN TO FILL A VOID: there is no single-authored book on the global legacy of Brian Mulroney. This is more than an oversight given the many tomes that have been written about the foreign policy achievements of Canada's other post-war prime ministers, especially Lester B. Pearson and Pierre Elliott Trudeau. Much, of course, has been written about the history of the Canada–U.S. Free Trade Agreement and the North American Free Trade Agreement, both negotiated under Brian Mulroney's leadership, but there has been no attempt to place these issues on a broader, foreign policy canvas, or to extract lessons that are still highly relevant today for the management of Canada's international relations.

This book tells the story of how a Conservative prime minister promoted Canada's values and national interests on the world stage with a degree of passion, energy, intensity, discipline, and laser-like focus that will come as a surprise to most Canadians, especially those who worry about how Canada's current leadership can reinvigorate the country's diminished global influence and waning brand at a time of major global transition, uncertainty, and turbulence.

One of the main reasons for Mulroney's success on the international stage was that he forged remarkably close personal ties not just with two U.S. presidents but with other world leaders in Africa, the Asia-Pacific, Europe, and Latin America. Mulroney understood better than most that relationships matter and that they can be used to advance Canada's interests when used purposely and productively.

This book tells how, under Brian Mulroney's leadership, Canada scored important wins not just on trade but also on critical problems like acid rain, ozone depletion, and climate change, which threatened the welfare and future of all Canadians. It also tells the story of how Mulroney, along with other key Commonwealth leaders, stood up to Britain's Margaret Thatcher to promote the end of apartheid in South Africa.

The late 1980s were also a time of global upheaval, with the collapse of the Soviet Union and the communist regimes of Eastern Europe. Western leaders feared that anarchy and chaos would ensue in the wake of that collapse. Canada was not a passive bystander, either in managing the difficult transition or in shaping the new global order that emerged as the Cold War ended. Mulroney stood shoulder to shoulder with other key Western leaders to fashion that order and promote global stability through diplomacy, targeted development assistance, and cooperation with security partnerships. At the same time, Mulroney worked assiduously to engage a rising China and the other emerging powers of Asia, Africa, and Latin America. A key platform of that engagement was the development of a series of important, new institutional partnerships that came with Canada's full membership in the Organization of American States and La Francophonie.

What is remarkable is how much was achieved during the course of eight years and 281 days, the time that Brian Mulroney served in office and during which his government was preoccupied with major domestic challenges such as major constitutional reform (Meech Lake) and growing fiscal challenges that had to be addressed by controversial measures such as the introduction of the goods and services tax (GST).

During the course of writing this book, I learned a lot about the depth and reach of Brian Mulroney's relations with other world leaders. No Canadian prime minister before or since Mulroney has ever been called a member of the inner cabinet by an American president, as George H.W. Bush did with Mulroney because he was so respected and trusted.

Mulroney's capacity to maintain generous and courteous contact with legions of friends and their families is legendary and reinforces his skill in developing and sustaining personal relationships, a central theme of this book.

Robin Sears, who worked with Mulroney, reports that Mulroney loves to flaunt both his vast intelligence-gathering capability and the fact that he invariably knows about a breaking piece of news before anyone else. He cites the example of the day that a television journalist shared the breaking news that former Trudeau and Mulroney foreign policy advisor Bob Fowler was about to be released by his kidnappers in Mali.

Mulroney was at that moment hospitalized in Florida with a serious bout of the flu, and Sears asked the hospital if he could share the story with Mulroney before it was announced a few minutes later. Having beaten down the resistance of the clinic switchboard, who had been sternly told not to put through calls for Mulroney, Sears had to overcome the further barricade of the senior nurse before finally being passed to Mila Mulroney, whom he advised that he had some news that he thought would cheer Brian up.

Passing the phone to her husband, Mila said, "Brian, Robin says he has some good news for us . . ." In response to Sears's news about the imminent release of Fowler and his colleague Louis Guay, Mulroney said enthusiastically, "Yes, isn't it marvellous news! I've just sent Mary Fowler some flowers." Sears hung up, once more frustrated at the reach and speed of the Mulroney information-gathering machine.

I could not have written this book without the generous assistance, support, and judicious counsel I received throughout from Derek Burney, Mulroney's chief of staff who went on to serve with great distinction as Canada's ambassador to Washington. Mr. Burney also helped arrange a series of interviews with Mr. Mulroney. Arthur Milnes, a celebrated historian who served as the research assistant on Mulroney's Memoirs, was especially helpful in providing important background materials on Mulroney's efforts to end apartheid in South Africa and sharing other useful documents.

In addition, I am especially grateful to Paul Heinbecker, Stephen Lewis, Jim Mitchell, David Runnalls, Robin Sears, Hugh Segal, James H. Taylor, and Gerald Wright for reviewing the manuscript or select chapters, and for sharing many useful stories with me. James Baxter and Mike Blanchfield deserve special thanks for also reading the manuscript and bringing some key documents to my attention. Stephanie MacLellan and Simon Palamar provided valuable research assistance and were kind enough to read some of the early draft chapters. My Carleton colleagues, Meredith Lilly and Valerie Percival, read and commented on some of the chapters and have been supportive throughout. Jennifer Spencer helped me secure permissions for some of the quotations that appear in the book.

I also wish to thank my colleague Rohinton Medhora, CIGI's president, for providing a generous and supportive research environment at Canada's leading global affairs think-tank, where I also work in addition to being a faculty member at Carleton University in the Faculty of Public Affairs, which is so ably led by Dean André Plourde.

Finally, at Signal/McClelland & Stewart, I wish to thank publisher Doug Pepper for his enthusiastic and unwavering support for this project from beginning to end, and Kimberlee Hesas for expertly shepherding the manuscript through its final stages. I would also like to express my thanks for the superb editorial assistance I have received from copy editor Tara Tovell, who has laboured over the manuscript and helped turn it into a book.

Fen Osler Hampson

ONE

Introduction: "Speak Me True"

———

"Am I remembered in Erin? I charge you, speak me true! . . . "
—THOMAS D'ARCY MCGEE, Canadian founding father and poet

HIGH ON A RIDGE IN THE SIMI HILLS just north of Los Angeles sits a sprawling Spanish Mission–style structure. Flanked by a rose garden and a replica of the South Lawn of the White House, the building houses the presidential papers of the fortieth president of the United States, Ronald Reagan, and a permanent exhibition chronicling his life. Several hundred thousand visitors pass through the library each year. The highlight of the tour is the Air Force One Pavilion, which contains the gleaming silver, white, and blue Boeing 707 used by President Reagan and six other presidents. Elevated on pedestals almost eight metres high, the plane looks as if it has just taken off and is about to soar through the vast, panelled window on the east side of the pavilion and out into the breathtaking panorama beyond.

On one cool, overcast day in March 2016, even the weather—usually sunny in southern California—seemed to be tipping its hat to the sombre occasion that was unfolding below at the Reagan Library. Nancy Reagan was being laid to rest beside her late husband. Family members, former presidents and first ladies, Hollywood actors, politicians, and leading figures in America's media and business circles gathered under a massive white tent for the funeral. They were there to mourn but also to celebrate the life of America's elegant first lady who had played such a crucial role in her husband's starred career.

Among those paying tribute was Canada's former prime minister, Brian Mulroney, who had been asked by the Reagan family to deliver the opening eulogy. It was his second Reagan funeral. Almost twelve years earlier, he had also delivered one of the three eulogies at Ronald Reagan's funeral in the Washington National Cathedral; the other two were delivered by former British prime minister Margaret Thatcher and former U.S. president George H.W. Bush.

Mulroney began his tribute to Nancy Reagan by recounting a story from another spring day. "In the Spring of 1987," he began, "President Reagan and I were driven into a large hangar at the Ottawa Airport, to await the arrival of Mrs. Reagan and my wife, Mila, prior to departure ceremonies for their return to Washington, following their highly successful State visit to Canada. President Reagan and I were alone except for the security details. When their car drove in a moment later, out stepped Nancy and Mila—looking like a million bucks. As they headed towards us, President Reagan beamed, threw his arm around my shoulder and said with a grin: 'You know, Brian, for two Irishmen we sure married up!'"[1] Mulroney's opening lines drew laughter from the subdued crowd, and even Nancy Reagan's children broke into broad smiles. It was just the kind of icebreaker from another optimistic Irishman that the gathering needed.

Twelve years earlier, Mulroney had recounted the same story in his eulogy to Ronald Reagan. It also evoked laughter. But he also shared more serious comments about Reagan's role as a global leader. In his remarks, Mulroney talked about a president "who inspired his nation and transformed the world."[2] He was a president, Mulroney observed, who "possessed a rare and prized gift called leadership—that ineffable, and sometimes magical quality that sets some men and women apart so that millions will follow them as they conjure up grand visions and invite their countrymen to dream big and exciting dreams." Mulroney touched on Reagan's achievements on the world stage, especially his role in defending the values of the free and democratic world against the threat of communism as well as his contribution to ending the Cold War peacefully.

Mulroney also noted that "Presidents and Prime Ministers every-where regardless of their political stripes or persuasion" often "wonder and worry how history will deal with them." He further remarked on the "insecurity of Thomas d'Arcy McGee, an Irish immigrant to Canada, who became a Father of our Confederation." Mulroney read part of a poem by McGee, in which the immigrant politician reflected poignantly on his homeland:

> Am I remembered in Erin?
> I charge you, speak me true!
> Has my name a sound—a meaning
> In the scenes my boyhood knew?

"Ronald Reagan," he went on say, "will not have to worry about Erin because they remember him well and affectionately there. Indeed, they do: from Erin to Estonia, from Maryland to Madagascar, from Montréal to Monterey. Ronald Reagan does not enter history tentatively—he does so with certitude and panache. At home and on the world stage, his were not the pallid etchings of a timorous politician. They were the bold strokes of a confident and accomplished leader."[3]

Those comments might have also applied to Mulroney himself. Just as Ronald Reagan put his indelible imprint on the world, so too did Canada's eighteenth prime minister. That was one of the reasons why the Reagan family had invited him to speak at the funerals of both the former president and first lady. It was not simply because Brian and Mila Mulroney and the Reagans were good friends. As prime minister, Mulroney led and lifted Canada's voice and influence in world affairs to unprecedented heights. But that influence did not end when Mulroney stepped down as Canada's prime minister. The esteem Reagan had for Mulroney, and the esteem modern Republicans still have for Reagan, have ensured that Mulroney is still relevant in American political circles.

Fast forward to the days after Donald Trump was elected the forty-fifth president of the United States after a tumultuous, bitterly fought

electoral campaign. Trump's election victory rocked America's political establishment to its core and provoked jitters around the world—
including in Ottawa, where Prime Minister Justin Trudeau's Canadian
government had banked on Hillary Clinton, the Democratic contender,
to be the next president. In fact, Trudeau's government was so confident that Clinton would win that they had invited Vice-President Joe
Biden to Ottawa for a post-election state visit, with all the bells and
whistles, to mark what it assumed would be a relatively seamless transition from one Democratic administration to another. Like everyone
else who read the polls before the election, the Trudeau government
was wrong. Ottawa now confronted a president who had run on a protectionist campaign that included tearing up the North American Free
Trade Agreement (NAFTA): a bedrock of Canada's prosperity and the
lifeline to its most important trading partner, the United States.

Fortunately, the government had a significant resource that quickly
came into play, a Canadian with direct experience and an unusual network
of relationships with the new team forming in Washington. Mulroney
knew Trump personally from his frequent business trips to New York, and
two of his sons are friends with Trump's daughter, Ivanka, and her husband, Jared Kushner. Wilbur Ross, Trump's secretary of commerce, is also
one of Mulroney's neighbours at his Palm Beach home in Florida. A few
weeks after Trump's election win, Canada's former prime minister delivered a birthday toast to Ross at his home on American Thanksgiving in the
presence of several other Trump associates. The toast prompted a follow-
up call from Trump himself. Further, Stephen Schwarzman, the CEO of
Blackstone and one of Trump's top economic advisors, was designated
to brief the Canadian cabinet meeting in Calgary shortly after Trump's
inauguration, and Mulroney serves on the Blackstone board. Two other
prominent Trump associates, Rudy Giuliani and Newt Gingrich, also
know Mulroney personally.

In the weeks after Trump's surprise election, Mulroney spoke exten-
sively to several of the prestigious members of the new Washington
power circle, individuals who regard him as a trusted friend and a Canadian

leader who had a close and productive relationship of his own with President Ronald Reagan—still an icon for many in the Republican Party. With each, Mulroney explained the history and underpinnings of the Canada–U.S. Free Trade Agreement (FTA), which led to NAFTA. While probing the new administration's intentions on trade, he underscored both the scope and the mutual benefit of these agreements, as well as the distinct character of more comprehensive relations on security, infrastructure, and the environment.

Whatever was gleaned from conversations Mulroney had with various members of the Trump entourage about attitudes or intentions vis-à-vis Canada was shared privately and discreetly with Canada's prime minister, Justin Trudeau, his principal secretary, Gerald Butts, and the newly minted foreign minister who oversees Canada–U.S. economic relations, Chrystia Freeland. Word soon leaked out from the government that both Mulroney and his former chief of staff, Derek H. Burney, were helping through direct exchanges with the Trump team and with advice during the transition period.

There is no more exacting test for the leadership mettle of any Canadian leader than the way relations with the United States are managed. Personal relationships count, especially in Washington, and Brian Mulroney established a reputation for credible dialogue with U.S. leaders that continues to deliver dividends to this day. The spontaneous exchanges he had with many suddenly prominent Americans early in the Trump era—including Trump himself—recalled the way Mulroney, decades earlier, cultivated a special relationship for Canada in Washington during his time in office. To its credit, the Trudeau government saw Mulroney's unusual access as a key asset, one that extended beyond partisanship to serve the national interest.

As prime minister, Mulroney was determined to act for Canada in a world where, customarily, only the great powers leave a mark. His vision, his discipline, and his personal skills were marshalled selectively but also consistently to ensure that Canada's voice registered where it counted, through negotiation and the deliberate cultivation of close personal links with other world leaders, especially the two presidents of the United States, Reagan and George Herbert Walker Bush, whose presidencies crossed his own tenure in office. Under Mulroney's leadership, there were significant achievements that serve Canadian interests to this day.

As this book shows, Mulroney's achievements included bold initiatives on trade, the environment, and human rights. They turned the tradition and history of his Progressive Conservative Party on their heads and gave distinct emphasis to the adjective "progressive" in the party's name. The pursuit of free trade ran completely counter to the Progressive Conservatives' history. Mulroney's efforts to combat acid rain, repair the ozone layer, and sound the alarm on climate change long before these pursuits became fashionable surprised and satisfied many of the most ardent advocates on the environment, including, notably, the first leader of the Green Party, Elizabeth May. His party followed Mulroney's major policy initiatives in a fiercely loyal manner, even when the polls were sharply adverse.

Mulroney demonstrated most vividly the enormous scope available in Canada's parliamentary system for a leader with a vision and a healthy majority government. He chose to lead rather than to follow public opinion. He was a true master of negotiation and persuasion, but also, as former prime minister William Lyon Mackenzie King might have observed, he sought "consensus if necessary, but not necessarily consensus." The fact that Mulroney's record of achievement in world affairs has not been lauded in Canada is due in large part to the fact that the foundation for his international influence and impact was a close personal relationship with two Republican presidents. Canadians, by political nature and disposition, are generally more receptive to presidents who are Democrats. Mulroney's popularity was not enhanced by some of his domestic initiatives, like the GST (goods and services tax), that did not sit well with Canadians, even though the GST helped eliminate longstanding fiscal deficits and eventually came to be accepted by Canadians after Mulroney left the political scene. Furthermore, it must be said that despite his progressive inclinations, Mulroney was still a

Conservative and not a Liberal, the brand with which Canadians' image of themselves and their place in the world is most comfortable.

The purpose of this book is to set the record straight by assessing the foreign policy legacy of the Mulroney government. There were significant achievements but also some disappointments. More importantly, in today's even more turbulent global landscape, Mulroney's determination to act for Canada and his strong record of achievement offer compelling lessons for the Canadian public and, especially, for Canadian leaders as they struggle to punch above their weight and make their voices heard in a world that is not necessarily waiting for "more Canada." One of the objectives in writing this book is to offer pertinent lessons for Canadian leaders facing global challenges in this new century.

With Mulroney's election in 1984, for the first time in post-war history Canada had a Conservative government about whose accomplishments it is possible to make sensible judgments.[4] The government of John Diefenbaker fell apart almost as soon as it was formed. Diefenbaker and his ministers were frequently at odds with each other, and Diefenbaker was also seen as something of an oddity, especially by President John F. Kennedy, who neither liked nor trusted him. The Conservative government led by Joe Clark was too short-lived to achieve anything of major significance. That was not the case with Brian Mulroney. Not only did Mulroney have a substantial record of achievement domestically and internationally, but he also had a very different kind of relationship with world leaders, including his American counterparts. He also understood better than many of his predecessors that Canada's power and influence derive from its leaders' solid grasp of the nation's vital interests and a purposeful commitment to pursuing those interests and values on the world stage. Mulroney also had other important qualities. In the words of one of his former undersecretaries of state, James H. (Si) Taylor, with whom he worked closely, "he listened, had ideas, and took decisions."[5]

Mulroney changed the tone and not just the substance of Canada's international relations by embarking on a bold, visionary relationship with the United States at great political risk to himself, given latent anti-American moralizing typical in Canada, especially when Republicans are in the White House. Contrary to some images of him, he certainly wasn't expecting popularity to flow, even from within his own party. He did what he concluded best served the national interest. He saw, and continues to see, the relationship between the two nations as vital and being beyond partisanship, which is why he voluntarily chose to help the young government of Prime Minister Justin Trudeau gain its footing with the new Trump administration in Washington.

This book explores how, through Brian Mulroney's leadership, Canada succeeded in advancing its national interests on international trade, the environment, national security, and the global advancement of democracy and human rights. It tells the story of Mulroney's deep relationship with two American presidents and other world leaders like British prime minister Margaret Thatcher, German chancellor Helmut Kohl, and South Africa's charismatic and transformative leader Nelson Mandela. Though much has been written about Mulroney's domestic agenda, his foreign policies have not been subject to the same kind of scrutiny. Mulroney's successful negotiation of the FTA and subsequently NAFTA are signature achievements; however, many Canadians tend to forget that they formed part of a much wider and ambitious foreign policy agenda that included fighting against apartheid in South Africa, advancing a bold new global agenda on the environment, and promoting a new humanitarian vision in Canada's international engagements, all of which, by the end of his tenure, had elevated Canada's standing to that of a major global player and leader on a wide range of substantive global issues.

Perhaps most important of all, Brian Mulroney put to bed that long-standing myth that Canada could not be a respected international player if the country was seen to have too close a relationship with the United States. He showed that a "special relationship" with Washington was in fact a *sine qua non* for Canada to project its interests and achieve global influence. Mulroney spoke truth to power because he was trusted. In sharp contrast to his predecessor, Pierre Trudeau, for Mulroney the path to global influence for Canada began with a principled and trusted dialogue with Washington, one that other world leaders noticed.

As this book argues, there is much to be learned from one of Canada's finest hours on the international stage some three decades ago under Prime Minister Brian Mulroney.

TWO

A Historic Pivot on Trade

"In the U.S., there are those who believe that unilateralism is strength; in Canada, there are those who believe that bilateralism is surrender." [6]
—ALLAN GOTLIEB, Canada's ambassador
to the United States, 1981–89

ON APRIL 6, 2017, Brian Mulroney returned to the cabinet room on Parliament Hill for the first time in more than twenty years. He had been invited, along with his former chief of staff, Derek Burney, to brief the special cabinet committee on Canada–U.S. relations about his direct experience with the negotiation of NAFTA and the extensive nature of his personal links to President Donald Trump and several of his key advisors. It was a homecoming of sorts for the former prime minister, exemplifying a rare spirit of bipartisanship towards Canada's most vital relationship.

Mulroney stressed that a close, personal relationship between the Canadian prime minster and the U.S. president, such as he had with presidents Ronald Reagan and George H.W. Bush, is essential to "access" in Washington, as is the development of close relations with congressional leaders. With access, you get influence. Without it, you are "one of two hundred" in the queue. He acknowledged that Prime Minister Justin Trudeau and his cabinet were off to a good start and had established the proper tone with the new Trump administration. Patience and perseverance were now needed to build and sustain a constructive dialogue, notably on trade.[7]

He also argued that it was necessary for Canada to learn to say no in the face of potentially disruptive American demands on renegotiating NAFTA, and illustrated how Canada had suspended negotiations in 1987 when its primary objective was not being addressed. "No deal is better than a bad deal," Mulroney cautioned. Underlining the advantage of propinquity, he urged the cabinet to take its message about the benefits of the agreement in terms of job creation and economic growth of trade links with Canada right across America. "Remember, too," he added, "the key role of Congress in approving any trade agreement."

Citing examples of his own experience on trade, acid rain, and Arctic sovereignty, Mulroney stated that managing relations with the U.S. was one of two top priorities for any Canadian prime minister—the other being national unity. Success on "big ticket" issues with the U.S. would ultimately determine the legacy of any Canadian prime minister.

THE LONG SHADOWS OF HISTORY

When Mulroney took on free trade as prime minister, it was a bold move. The mere notion was fraught with history in Canada, even before Confederation. In the 1850s, the colonies of Upper and Lower Canada, along with those in the Maritimes, concluded reciprocity trade agreements with the U.S.—a limited form of free trade given the narrow range of tradable goods at the time. A larger percentage of trade then was with Mother Britain. The American Civil War brought an abrupt halt to reciprocal trade agreements, and the post-war mood in Washington was less than enthusiastic about renewing anything similar. Notions of "manifest destiny" or outright assimilation were more in vogue, sentiments that stimulated negotiations that led to Confederation.

After the Civil War, Canada's first prime minister, Sir John A. Macdonald, pressed for reciprocity between the new dominion and the now more muscular U.S., only to be rebuffed on three separate occasions between 1867 and 1874. Macdonald settled on the National Policy as the second-best option, creating a tariff wall to support manufacturing, primarily in

Ontario and Quebec, and establishing U.S. branch plants to serve the Canadian market under the protective tariff cover. Macdonald relied more on the British Empire for export trade, to which both the Maritimes and the West contributed significantly. At the close of the nineteenth century, Prime Minister Sir Wilfrid Laurier saw free trade with the U.S. as a more enlightened approach for all of Canada, but his ambitions were blocked by the 1911 election, which became, in effect, a referendum on free trade. Emotions of nationalism, anti-Americanism, and unbridled Imperial patriotism triumphed over pragmatic, commercial analyses.

The 1930s witnessed an orgy of protectionism, initiated by the infamous Smoot–Hawley tariffs in the U.S.—some in excess of 200 per cent—which plunged the world economy into the Great Depression, a steep downward turn reversed only by the outbreak of World War II.

The 1950s and 1960s were periods of strong population and economic growth for Canada. They also spawned innovations to deepen the economic partnership with the U.S., notably the Auto Pact: a unique sectoral arrangement concluded in 1965 to meet the competing objectives of both countries and to allow the big three automakers—GM, Ford, and Chrysler—to participate more equitably in the rapidly expanding total market of the two countries. By 1980, the Auto Pact was a mainstay of the Ontario economy, directly responsible for more than one hundred thousand jobs and at least as many more in parts and other supply industries. It was a boon for Canada, enabling the nation's plants to be much more efficient and transforming a traditional deficit in automotive trade into a consistent surplus.

In the early 1980s, during cross-Canada consultations on a major trade policy review by the Trudeau government, the then trade and industry minister, Ed Lumley, was told repeatedly and emphatically, "Regardless of what you do on trade policy, your first priority must be to fix relations with the U.S."[8] At that time, relations generally with the U.S. were less than robust. Lumley took the message to heart and became an early and persistent advocate of a more positive trade relationship. This policy review and the success of the Auto Pact prompted at first an exploration of further sectoral trade initiatives—on steel, agricultural equipment, urban transit industries, and informatics. But efforts to find balance within each sector proved either too difficult or too small to justify the expense of political capital by either side. By 1984, Americans and Canadians alike were losing interest and the sectoral initiative was essentially dormant.

CHANGE IN TONE

When Brian Mulroney became prime minister in September 1984, he was aware of the history around free trade. He was also acutely aware of the primordial importance of the United States to Canada's domestic and foreign policy aspirations, and recognized that a positive relationship with U.S. presidents was essential to his major policy aspirations. To achieve this goal, he was determined from the outset to spend more time and effort than any previous Canadian leader on cultivating direct personal links in Washington, announcing his intention to visit Washington as a matter of priority the day after his cabinet was sworn in on September 17, 1984. (He had already met President Reagan during a visit to Washington as leader of the Opposition in June.)

Canada–U.S. relations under his predecessor, Pierre Trudeau, had become cool, if not fractious. The tension extended to several bilateral matters, including trade. The Americans were extremely unhappy with the National Energy Program (NEP), especially its expropriation provisions, and with the foreign investment review procedures, which they saw as infringing on basic economic freedoms. For Canada's part, on any given day, U.S. trade remedy actions made all Canadian exports vulnerable and added more aggravation to bilateral relations. For example, Mulroney's visit to Washington in June 1984 came as Congress was considering a quota on imports of Canadian steel.[9]

As Mulroney recalls, "With the Trudeau government, what surprised me . . . was the ongoing hostility towards America . . . there was enormous hostility coming from him towards the Reagan Administration. Lots of confrontations and [then] began a wave of protectionist measures in the U.S. Congress, which by the time I came around in 1983 going into 1984 . . . was a daily occurrence where Canadian industries were being picked off. And one of the reasons was there was nobody defending them down there. The war of attrition waged by the Canadian government against the Reagan Administration had really cost us."[10] The linchpins of Mulroney's approach were his constructive, personal relationships with presidents Reagan and Bush, supplemented assiduously with systematic meetings and discussions with congressional leaders from both sides of the aisle. He also displayed early on an acute understanding of the unique separation of powers in Washington.

Mulroney's top priority was to use his personal skill to forge a better framework for trade and investment—a key building block in a broader agenda to secure Canada's future prosperity. Free trade, fraught with the emotions of history and exacerbated by the huge power imbalance between the two countries, became the prime litmus test for this objective.

There was certainly scope for a change of tone at the top, which Mulroney was determined to exploit. He knew that it was always easy to get headlines in Canada by taking positions that differed from those of the U.S.—"tweaking the eagle's feathers"—but was less convinced that this tactic helped promote Canadian interests in our most vital market. "Canadians, unlike some members of the Liberal Party, recognize that the Americans—irrespective of the Administration—that the Americans are our friends and allies, and that cordial relations must be maintained at all times," Mulroney told the media in Washington that June after discussing trade with Reagan's commerce secretary, Malcolm Baldridge. "There are three million jobs in Canada that depend on access to American markets, plus another million that we're looking to build in the future."[11]

Reagan never attracted among Canadians the popularity lavished on presidents Kennedy, Clinton, or Obama, whose auras of charm and eloquence transcended any analysis of significant accomplishments in partnership with Canada. Canadians generally seem more inclined to like Democratic rather than Republican presidents, even though the track record of bilateral achievements with Democrats offers little to sustain that predilection. It would be difficult, for example, to point to any notable bilateral achievement vis-à-vis Canada during Barack Obama's eight years as president, yet Obama remained more popular in Canada throughout his presidency than he was in the United States. Perceptions like this in Canada often defy rational analysis but speak clearly to the challenge facing any Canadian leader, especially a Conservative, who charts an ambitious partnership of engagement with the U.S.

As an Irish-Quebecer, Mulroney had little of the smug sense of superiority towards Americans that is prevalent in some political circles in central Canada. Nor did he harbour any of the anti-American, anti-capitalist nostrums of many on the left in Canada.[12] He may have been aware of the political cost of being perceived as getting "too close" to a Republican president, but he decided nonetheless that changing the tone and, as he put it, giving the Reagan administration "the benefit of the doubt" on global issues might prove more favourable to Canadian interests. He also acted on the theory that basic personal courtesies allowed for greater candor and differences of opinion in private more certainly than did telegraphing such differences in public, essentially for domestic consumption.

In a December 1984 address to the Economic Club in New York delivered three months after he took office, Mulroney declared that "Canadians were now mature enough as a nation and confident enough in ourselves to recognize and take pride in an amicable relationship with a neighbour as powerful as the U.S."[13] Nothing expressed his personal sentiments more confidently than this statement.

OPENING THE DOOR TO FREE TRADE

"In times of despair, when strong men turn to drink or religion, Canadians flirt with free trade," political columnist Thomas Walkom wrote.[14] If the mid-1980s wasn't a time of economic despair in Canada, it was certainly close. The 1981–83 recession was followed by a slow recovery. With Mulroney poised to take office in 1984, the unemployment rate was above 11 per cent.[15] Trade with the U.S.—a nation that was recovering faster and had a stronger dollar—was one of the few things keeping Canada afloat. The country was sending nearly 80 per cent of its exports across its southern border. It had had a trade surplus with the U.S. since 1982.[16] Bilateral trade was worth about $120 billion USD, up by one-third from the year before.[17] However, growing protectionism in the U.S. threatened to knock the wind out of Canadian sails.

For free trade advocates, a bold trade initiative was the best possible recourse—offence being the best defence. The primary objective was to spur efficiencies and better productivity in Canada on a level, competitive field in North America, while at the same time checking U.S. protectionism. If Canada expected to be more successful in the global economy and to reap gains from the Uruguay Round of multilateral trade negotiations, which were focused on lowering trade barriers in agriculture and removing restrictions to growing global trade in "services," it had to break out of the constrained "branch plant" method of operation and compete head-on with the U.S. Bilateral free trade provided the framework for that adjustment.

Still, loosening trade restrictions with the U.S. remained a sensitive topic, tapping as it did into a collective national fear about being assimilated by the giant to the south. That fear was typically enough to outweigh economic considerations. "We always paid a higher price for being Canadian," historian J.L. Granatstein told the New York Times in 1985. "People were willing to pay that price because we didn't want to be Americans."[18]

Mulroney had shied away from free trade during the 1983 PC leadership race. As a frontrunner, he had no need for a bold initiative. Two of his adversaries—Michael Wilson and John Crosbie—had been more openly committed. Several subsequent developments changed his political calculus. Mulroney presumably reasoned that if he expected the final choice to be between Joe Clark and himself, he needed to isolate himself from Crosbie with a different position on free trade. Later, and with strong encouragement from Alberta premier Peter Lougheed, a leader he admired, he became a believer, seeing a free trade agreement as potentially beneficial to Canada's economic future and key to his efforts to improve relations with the United States. It must also be said that Mulroney's time (1977–83) as president of the Iron Ore Company, a subsidiary of the Cleveland-based M.A. Hanna Company, gave him direct experience with Canada–U.S. economic relations and a better appreciation of their importance to Canada's economy.

Mulroney stressed the importance of cross-border trade on his first visit to Washington as prime minister in September 1984. "The first task of the new Government is economic renewal— to expand trade, to attract new investment, and to seek out new markets," he said. When asked how he would respond to the nationalists who were warning that Canada's economy would then become too reliant on the U.S., he replied, "I am concerned about the 1.6 million Canadians out of jobs, who are not concerned about nationalism, who are concerned about providing for their families."[19]

This visit, and Mulroney's earlier June trip to Washington as opposition leader, set the stage for the "Shamrock Summit" with Reagan in Quebec City in March 1985. The leaders "pledged to give highest priority to finding mutually acceptable means to reduce and eliminate existing barriers to trade in order to secure and facilitate investment flows." At the summit, Reagan promised Mulroney he would "use all of his energies to pre-empt any move that would put Canada in peril from protectionism." U.S. trade representative William Brock and Canadian international trade minister James Kelleher were given six months to establish "a bilateral mechanism to chart all possible ways to reduce and eliminate existing barriers to trade."[20]

This was the opening salvo in a cautious, carefully orchestrated approach to a comprehensive negotiation. The Americans were smart enough to recognize that the pace would have to be set by Canada, even though they never really grasped what a huge political risk Mulroney was taking domestically. Even using the words "free trade" could have political ramifications in Canada. "This is the old Canadian tradition of being terrified by shibboleths," Mulroney told the press in February 1985. "You throw off a slogan in this country and you scare the hell out of half the people whether it's relevant or not and whether it's true or not. Some people have built careers and empires out of doing that. Free trade is one of them. . . . It conjures up all kinds of scarecrows and myths and problems, and what I think we have to do is try to depoliticize some of it."[21]

Mulroney may have been frustrated with the free trade taboo, but he clearly wasn't willing to fight a battle over semantics. Within ten days of the Shamrock Summit, Kelleher was denying that the Mulroney government had "at any time or any place discussed free trade with the U.S." Mulroney believed that Canada needed secure access to American markets, "but we don't see trying to keep the markets open as free trade," Kelleher told a reporter.[22] A few months later, when a journalist covering a summer meeting of the cabinet priorities and planning committee asked Mulroney if there was any discussion of free trade at the meeting, he replied, "Well, we never discuss free trade." The questioner asked if "enhanced trade" with the U.S. had come up. "Now you've got it," replied Mulroney.[23]

LEAP OF FAITH

In the months that followed the Shamrock Summit, a series of consultations on trade took place across Canada—some chaired by Kelleher, some by a joint House-Senate committee, another set launched by an Ontario parliamentary committee. In addition to all the historical and cultural anxieties, free trade also set off regional tensions. In 1984, a generally unnoticed study for the Ontario Economic Council determined that resource industries such as fishing, agriculture, and forestry—mostly found on Canada's Prairies and coasts—would see their workforces boom by at least 10 per cent under free trade, while manufacturing, machinery, and textiles—based in the industrial heartland and most populous provinces of Ontario and Quebec—would lose 10 per cent or more of their employment.[24] (The prediction was wrong as jobs would grow in virtually all economic sectors.) An Angus Reid survey taken in June 1985 found that 51 per cent of Canadians favoured free trade, compared to 32 per cent opposed. But support varied among the provinces: from 60 per cent in Atlantic Canada and 57 per cent in the West to 45 per cent in Ontario.[25]

The tensions spilled over to the annual premiers' meeting in St. John's, Newfoundland, that August. The ten premiers were supposed to release a communiqué supporting the federal government's free trade negotiations. Alberta's Peter Lougheed argued there was an urgent need to start talks immediately, because with mid-term elections looming the following year, congressional support for free trade could evaporate. Most other premiers agreed with him. But Ontario's new Liberal premier, David Peterson, had come into office that summer after campaigning to protect Ontario's economy, and he refused to support negotiations before the "practical costs" of a deal were known.[26] The communiqué was scrapped.

That summer, both Kelleher's preliminary report to cabinet and the parliamentary committee report cautiously advised that the government pursue talks with the U.S. on finding a path to a more liberal trade policy. Then, on September 5, came the strongest endorsement yet. A Royal Commission on the Canadian economy led by former Liberal finance minister Donald Macdonald urged the government to "take a leap of faith" and contemplate a comprehensive free trade negotiation with the U.S.[27] It called for a gradual approach to free trade, with tariffs being phased out over ten years starting in 1987, with exemptions for the Canadian culture and agriculture sectors.[28] Macdonald and his commissioners (save for one dissenter, union leader Gérard Docquier) emphasized the importance of developing new markets for Canadian goods, and projected that free trade would boost the economy by 3 to 8 per cent while creating jobs and lowering prices on consumer goods.[29]

The Macdonald Commission report was nothing if not comprehensive: it was three years in the making, totalled two thousand pages and weighed seven pounds (just fourteen ounces lighter than Mulroney's youngest son Nicolas, who was delivered the day before it was published).[30] It was also a political masterstroke for Mulroney. Macdonald was a prominent Toronto Liberal once expected to take over the party leadership, and had been a finance minister in Pierre Trudeau's cabinet. When Trudeau established the commission in 1982 and put Macdonald in charge, the Tories slammed the move, and it was assumed they would scrap it as soon as they took power. But instead, as noted by Charles Lynch in the *Ottawa Citizen*, "Somewhere during the three years of hearings, Macdonald says, he was persuaded to abandon Liberal thoughts of nationalism and approach the United States with open arms. Should Mulroney decide to pursue the course of free trade . . . he can do it behind the protective shield of Macdonald's recommendations. And every time the Liberals bleat, he can hit them another blow with the words of the man who once was their Mr. Big."[31]

In addition to securing the endorsement of Macdonald's commission, Mulroney also learned that his toughest provincial critic, Ontario's Peterson, was softening his opposition after a meeting with Kelleher.[32] Western premiers, with the notable exception of Manitoba's NDP leader Howard Pawley, also supported free trade. Robert Bourassa, the premier of Quebec and an economist by training, was also strongly supportive of free trade (though he harboured some residual concerns that too much of an opening of the economy could potentially diminish Canada's independence). Mulroney knew as well that Ronald Reagan had long been a champion of free trade. So, he had in effect a political trifecta. Meanwhile, time was of the essence: there were already more than three hundred protectionist trade bills before Congress.[33]

On September 26, Mulroney announced in the House that he had officially told Reagan that Canada was interested in pursuing free trade talks.[34] The press described the announcement as low-key and vague, so as not to tip Canada's hand to the U.S. before negotiations started, or to worry Canadians that drastic changes were afoot. "Our political sovereignty, our system of social programs, our commitment to fight regional disparities, our unique cultural identity, our special linguistic character— these are the essence of Canada. They are not at issue in these negotiations," Mulroney said.[35]

By moving boldly to grasp free trade with the U.S., Mulroney essentially turned Canadian politics on its head. Since the days of John A. Macdonald's National Policy, the Conservatives had been somewhat protectionist and leery of the U.S., whereas the Liberals since Laurier had generally been free traders and, with the exception of Pierre Trudeau, pro-American. Mulroney reversed the tradition of his party, and by so doing, obliged the Liberals to reverse their traditional stance. More fundamentally, perhaps, he had from the beginning believed that a constructive, "open for business" approach to the U.S. would improve Canada's prospects for economic growth. In time, he saw the free trade initiative as a key part of that objective.

BUILDING A NEGOTIATING TEAM

To further cement the political support for the FTA, Mulroney brought Simon Reisman out of retirement to drive the negotiation. Reisman had been a principal architect of the Auto Pact and had served as deputy minister to former Liberal finance minister John Turner, who was now leader of the Opposition. He had also, as part of his job application, presented Mulroney with a crisp twenty-page analysis of why a free trade deal would serve Canadian interests. Mulroney had first met Reisman while salmon fishing in the rivers of Quebec. Reisman had a been a deputy minister of finance and industry in previous Liberal governments and had retired from the public service in 1975. Mulroney didn't care that Reisman had strong Liberal affiliations. "All I wanted was the very best. I didn't care if the guy was whatever. Simon was clearly the best, I thought. He had done the Auto Pact, he had been there for the beginning of the General Agreement on Tariffs and Trade [GATT] and I knew that he was tough as nails and as smart as they come."[36]

Mulroney knew that Reisman would be perceived in Canada—and in Washington—as a tough negotiator, blunt and outspoken. "Reisman is a bludgeoner, a shouter, a small man of great ego whose salty language blisters the wallpaper of the Rideau Club each noon hour," Allan Fotheringham wrote. "Americans, by their nature, by the nature of their relationship with little Canada, tend to be bullies. The elephant doesn't even know it is stepping on the mouse. The hopes are that they will recognize one of their own: a guy who likes cigars, speaks his mind, swears a lot and loves a fight."[37]

Lester Pearson undoubtedly had Reisman in mind when he observed that "the picture of weak and timid Canadian negotiators being pushed around and brow-beaten by American representatives into settlements that were 'sellouts' is a false and distorted one. It is often painted, however, by Canadians who think that a sure way to get applause and support is to exploit our anxieties and exaggerate our suspicions over U.S. power and politics."[38] Pearson had seen the benefit first hand from the Auto Pact, in which Reisman played a key role.[39]

Reisman assembled a staff of nearly one hundred, plus a new office in Ottawa with a custom-made mahogany and chrome negotiating table.[40] His two top deputies were Gordon Ritchie on Canada–U.S. negotiations and Sylvia Ostry on multilateral trade. A formidable trio! He also travelled to Washington for a preliminary meeting with his American counterpart. Peter Murphy, a U.S. deputy trade representative based in Geneva, was portrayed in the media as a mild-mannered foil to the brash Reisman. Much was also made of his young age: at thirty-seven, he was born the year Reisman attended his first GATT meeting.[41]

Canada's ambassador in Washington, Allan Gotlieb, and an able team of officials at the Canadian embassy that included Léonard Legault, Paul Heinbecker, James Judd, and James Wright, who would all go on to assume major posts in the Canadian government, also played a key role, though some officials in Ottawa felt that Gotlieb was sometimes too ready to make concessions to the Americans. Nevertheless, as Michael Hart, who from 1992 to 1995 served as a senior policy adviser and negotiator in Canada's Department of Foreign Affairs and International Trade, wrote in *Decision at Midnight*, Gotlieb and his team "push[ed] and cajol[ed] often indifferent American officials and legislators and bolster[ed] sometimes flagging Canadian spirits."[42] Gotlieb made speeches to various

American audiences about the importance of free trade. He also helped get powerful senators onside, including bringing "Senator Richard Lugar, the head of the powerful Foreign Relations Committee, on board. At a hearing on Central America Lugar grilled Secretary of State Shultz on why the administration was not putting greater effort into the trade negotiations."[43] One of Gotlieb's biggest challenges after the deal was concluded was to secure the support of Senator Lloyd Bentsen of Texas, the powerful chair of the Senate Finance Committee whom Governor Dukakis chose as his running mate in the 1988 presidential election. Bentsen felt that Canada had got the better of the Americans during the negotiations. Though Bentsen was revered in many quarters, Gotlieb was not a big fan, noting, "Strauss sees him as one of the best minds in Washington. I see him as a protectionist, isolationist, America-centric Texan who has little sympathy for the world beyond U.S. shores. For years he has plugged the 'blame-the-foreigner-line.'"[44]

THE SLAP

Gotlieb and his wife, Sondra, had become one of Washington's most sought-after couples. Their glamorous, celebrity-studded dinner parties attracted the city's "A list." Though Gotlieb had been appointed by Prime Minister Trudeau, Mulroney nonetheless decided to keep him in his post because he was well connected and had come to know President Reagan, George Shultz, Caspar Weinberger, and other key members of Reagan's cabinet and the U.S. Congress.

On March 19, 1986, just before a major dinner was to take place at the embassy residence, where Mulroney and Vice-President George Bush were to be the guests of honour, Sondra Gotlieb lost her temper with her social secretary, Connie Connor, a locally employed member of the embassy staff. The vice-president was late and Mrs. Gotlieb had not been informed that Deputy Treasury Secretary Richard Darman, another high-profile guest, had decided to pull out of the dinner at the last minute, throwing her carefully prearranged seating plan into disarray.

Allan Gotlieb had earlier promised Paul Reichmann of Olympia & York, a wealthy Canadian developer with major real estate holdings in New York and London, that if he attended the dinner he could sit beside Darman. In a tantrum, Sondra Gotlieb, who was under enormous pressure to deliver a successful event, slapped her secretary across the face, sending one of her earrings bouncing across the driveway in front of the residence entrance. Missed by the two hundred vips who were assembled inside a large tent in the garden where the dinner was to be held, the slap was nonetheless witnessed by the Canadian press corps, who were standing outside waiting for Bush to arrive.

The dinner, like all Gotlieb dinners, was a sparkling affair and ran like clockwork once the vice-president arrived. After the speeches and toasts were over and the vice-president, prime minister, and other distinguished guests had thanked their hosts and departed, Allan Gotlieb, who was clearly oblivious to the contretemps that had taken place beforehand between his wife and her social secretary, retired to the living room to do the usual post-mortem of the evening with key members of his staff.[45] He was reportedly very pleased about how well the evening had gone, and nobody wanted, or had the nerve, to upset him by recounting the evening's earlier incident. Gotlieb was just settling down to relax when the telephone rang. It was a call from the Prime Minister's Office in Ottawa. It was close to midnight, but the office had already received media reports, which were burning up the wires, about what the *Washington Post* called "the slap heard 'round the continent."[46] A deeply embarrassed Gotlieb rushed over in the early morning hours to the hotel where the prime minister was staying, to apologize for his wife's behaviour and tender his resignation. Mulroney munificently refused to accept it, and Gotlieb would go on to serve in his post for almost three more years. However, as the *Globe and Mail* recounted later, "Mrs. Gotlieb's expensively built reputation as one of the capital's premier hostesses" was never quite the same after the incident.[47]

THE NEGOTIATIONS

Mulroney's decision to undertake free trade negotiations was accompanied by critics' dire warnings of catastrophic job losses and eventual annexation. This was compounded by the publication of leaked strategy documents, purported to come from a government communications task force, that encouraged the government to publicly downplay the FTA as much as possible. "It is likely that the higher the profile the issue attains, the lower the degree of public approval will be," the documents said.[48] But giving the issue a low profile only allowed critics to dominate the public discussion. As Michael Hart noted, "Quixotic, emotional and exaggerated, the nationalist opposition provided an undertone of varying intensity during the negotiating process rooted in fear of the unknown. Its shrillness reflected a lamentable lack of seriousness."[49] Eventually the low-key strategy was abandoned, with Mulroney and his ministers of external affairs, labour, and trade touting the benefits of free trade in campaign-style stops in critical regions.[50]

Some of the fiercest objections came from within the ranks of public servants in Ottawa, including some trade officials who preferred that Canada focus exclusively on multilateral trade negotiations. Proponents of the FTA contended correctly that the two approaches to trade—bilateral and multilateral—were compatible, not exclusive. The GATT (now the World Trade Organization or WTO) makes explicit provision for free trade agreements that are by their nature preferential but that encompass "substantially all trade" between parties. Moreover, multilateral trade negotiations are essentially clusters of bilateral negotiations rolled together, in which Canada's first priority had always been to secure benefits vis-à-vis the U.S.

The provinces, meanwhile, insisted on having a say in the free trade negotiations, which required another set of discussions throughout the opening months of 1986. There were even skeptics in Mulroney's caucus and cabinet, notably Agriculture Minister John Wise, Fisheries Minister Tom Siddon, Secretary of State Flora MacDonald, and ironically, Trade Minister Pat Carney, who was often among the most negative.[51] Cabinet ministers were seldom unanimous on matters of free trade. On occasion, momentum was sustained in a Lincoln-esque manner. (Votes in Lincoln's cabinet could be ten to one, but the one that carried it was his.)

Mulroney's objective in the free trade negotiations was to seek a comprehensive, traditional free trade agreement that would reduce all tariffs over a specific period of time, with a shared or common regime on trade remedy measures. The ultimate agreement was close to the traditional model, with some exceptions, such as softwood lumber and some supply-managed agriculture sectors. A common trade remedy regime would have been potentially more restrictive on Canada, which is more dependent on trade than the U.S. That is why, in the end, "binding dispute settlement" became the *sine qua non* for Canada instead of a single trade remedy regime. A similar system of adjudicating trade disputes was eventually adopted in the Uruguay Round negotiations, which created the WTO.

But negotiations almost died stillborn in April 1986, days after the two negotiators met in Washington. Canada's plans hinged on Reagan securing "fast-track" bargaining authority, which would allow Congress to vote yes or no to a completed international agreement but not make any changes to it. The Senate Finance Committee—led by Senator Robert Packwood of Oregon, a state with grievances about Canadian lumber imports—caught the Canadians off guard by threatening to block fast-track bargaining.[52] It took intense Canadian lobbying, and an eleventh-hour request from Reagan, to postpone the committee vote by a week in order to secure the votes needed to keep fast-tracking alive.

When the committee met again on April 23, it featured a rancorous chorus of complaints extending well beyond the notion of free trade with Canada. One Republican senator voted to disapprove because of the lack of action against "slave labour" in the Soviet Union. The vote ended in a ten-to-ten tie—not the majority needed to block fast-tracking. "This took all of the muscle and all of the ingenuity and a lot of clout by the president of the United States to get that vote today," Mulroney said afterwards. He also warned: "The road ahead will not be easy."[53]

That much was true. Given the huge power imbalance at play, it was inevitable that the Canadian team had to plan better and have complete confidence from the top.[54] Unfortunately, their U.S. counterparts were at the outset deficient on both counts. While Canada mobilized a top-flight negotiating team, with Reisman reporting via a cabinet committee directly to the prime minister, the American Murphy was a second-tier trade official who was hobbled by a lack of political oversight and the customary turf battles among competing U.S. departments. Murphy had no direct link to the White House and little authority to do much more than collect the individual grievances (or "scalps" as they were labelled by the Canadian team)—a laundry list of irritants on which individual departments or agencies sought redress.

Adding insult to injury, in September 1986, with no warning, the U.S. slapped a 35 per cent tariff on imports of Canadian shakes and shingles—precisely the kind of punitive "trade remedy" action that the negotiations were intended to thwart. This prompted Mulroney to exclaim that "actions like this make it extremely difficult for anyone, including Canadians, to be friends with Americans."[55] A firm letter of protest to the president followed. Shortly afterwards, a "managed trade" agreement on a dispute over softwood lumber was concluded, one that further chilled the ardour of many Canadian free trade advocates. Neither action was conducive to a positive atmosphere at the negotiating table. Frustration and bad blood mounted on both sides.

Progress was made on the basic tariff reductions for an agreement—because Canadian tariffs were on average twice that of the U.S., these reductions had to be phased in over a period of years and structured in a fashion to offset the opening imbalance. Meanwhile, concerns about exempting Canadian culture from the negotiations proved to be more about posture than effect. Canada publicly removed "cultural industries" from the agenda. The U.S., meanwhile, took the position that what Canada called "culture," they regarded as "business."[56] In the end, they reserved their GATT rights to challenge actions taken in the name of culture that they saw as discriminatory to business interests, such as restrictions on U.S. magazines entering Canada. But by 1987, there were still no breakthroughs on the hard issues: primarily for Canada, binding dispute settlement, and for the U.S., a relaxation of investment review procedures. The two delegations often talked past one another, leaving any real movement to the very last moment.

Reagan spoke to Canada's Parliament in April 1987. He lavished praise on the prime minister for his vision and boldness on trade and declared that the bilateral negotiations were an example to the rest of the world. "To those who would hunker down behind barriers to fight a destructive and self-defeating round of trade battles, Canada and the United States will show the positive way," he said.[57] During the leaders' private session, Mulroney pressed Canadian concerns about the lack of progress and about U.S. protectionist actions that undermined the negotiating efforts. But there was no discernible impact at the negotiating table during the summer, and talks began to drift aimlessly.

The fundamental problem was that the priority level of free trade was vastly different in both capitals. Free trade had become an all-consuming issue in Canada, debated intensively, heatedly, and in highly partisan terms. (When the Conservative government passed the legislation needed to pave the way for a free trade agreement on August 31, 1988, it did so over the din of protesters chanting from a visitors' gallery and opposition MPs singing the national anthem while unfurling a giant Canadian flag.[58]) In Washington, it barely raised a ripple. Despite Reagan's known support for the concept, there was no political champion in Washington, no one capable of delivering for the president. Polls in the summer of 1987 began to reflect growing pessimism in Canada about the prospect. Fifty-eight per cent of Canadians did not think that the prime minister "could represent their interests in the negotiation" because he was too pro-American, up from 45 per cent in January 1986.

Under the terms of the fast-track negotiations, a deal had to be reached by October 4, 1987. With the deadline looming, Mulroney began to lower expectations. On September 14, he said there was "precious little to show on the negotiating front." Five days later, he dispatched his chief of staff, Derek Burney, and Finance Minister Michael Wilson, to meet Treasury

Secretary James Baker in Washington to outline the basic elements needed by Canada. Baker essentially urged the negotiators to "clear out the underbrush" but made no personal commitment. On September 23, with no discernible progress on the key outstanding issues, Mulroney directed the Canadian team to walk away from the negotiations. Reisman made the public announcement: "Because the U.S. is not responding to elements fundamental to Canada's position," he stated, "I have therefore suspended the negotiations."[59]

Alarm bells rang out in Washington and Ottawa. Some in Washington saw it simply as a bluff or negotiating ploy. But when Chief of Staff Howard Baker urged that the negotiators get back to work, he was told bluntly that, in the absence of concrete movement by the U.S., there would be no point—and no purpose, either. New trade remedy proposals from Washington were considered politely, but rejected. Binding dispute settlement became essential for restarting the process.

Finally, James Baker was put in charge in Washington. Burney was handed the negotiating task at the political level in Ottawa. In many negotiations, leaders will put their direct personal representatives in charge to break a deadlock that stands in the way of a deal. After a frantic two-day session in Washington, the basic elements of an agreement were cobbled together on a term sheet. However, the key issue for Canada—binding dispute settlement—remained outstanding, along with the American demand for increases in the thresholds for foreign investment reviews by Canada.

The discussions were not without theatrics on the Canadian side. When the Americans pressed for longer periods of intellectual property protection, Burney exploded. He asked pointedly whether the Americans had any appreciation at all of the political difficulty his prime minister faced in trying to get further changes to a new regime that had itself been rejected three times by our Liberal-controlled Senate before finally passing. With a flourish, he then added, "If it is not good enough, you can delete the entire chapter."[60] He threw the chapter on the desk and stomped out. As a result, there is no chapter on intellectual property in the FTA, but it was resuscitated in NAFTA.

At about 9 p.m., three hours before the expiration of the fast-track authority from Congress, Baker phoned the prime minister to report that talks were deadlocked over the dispute settlement issue. Mulroney said he wanted to talk to the president immediately. He asked Baker how it was possible for the United States to conclude a nuclear arms reduction agreement with its Cold War adversary, the Soviet Union, and at the same time fail to summon the will to conclude a trade agreement with its Canadian ally and neighbour. Baker asked for "20 minutes more." Shortly before 10 p.m., he burst into the ante room to his office, where the Canadian team of eight were assembled. He flung a piece of paper on the table and declared, "All right, there is your goddamn Dispute Settlement Mechanism. Now can I send the report to Congress?" Burney quickly reviewed the paper with his inner team, signalled agreement to Baker, and promptly telephoned the prime minister to report the sudden breakthrough. During the interval following his call to Ottawa, Baker had secured support from the powerful chair of the House Ways and Means Committee , Dan Rostenkowski, which enabled him to override his law-yers' concerns about an intrusion into U.S. sovereignty (because the U.S. would now be bound to the decision of a tribunal comprised of represen-tatives from both countries).[61] The ultimate trade-offs were concessions from the U.S. on binding dispute settlement, and increases by Canada on investment review thresholds. It was, according to Baker's memoir, a "near run thing . . . the agreement almost didn't happen. Negotiations were protracted, painful and more than once on the verge of complete collapse,"[62] but it was "one of the two most important economic achieve-ments of the Reagan Administration."[63] The other was tax reform.

The overriding directive from Mulroney to Canada's negotiators had been firm. The deal had to be "significantly better" for Canada than the status quo. He cautioned persistently that "no deal was better than a bad deal."[64] Mulroney was disciplined and determined in guiding the nego-tiations, never flinching even when the objective seemed unattainable. His earlier experience as a labour negotiator (Mulroney helped negotiate a settlement for workers with the closing of the Schefferville mine in

Quebec) was fundamental. For those around him, his cool emotion in absorbing negative reports and his unstinting resolve to get a deal that would be good for Canada emboldened them to try harder. He was fond of quoting the British statesman Lord Thomas Macaulay, who in 1824 observed, "Free trade, one of the greatest blessings which a government can confer on a people, is in almost every country unpopular"—a maxim as true today as it was then. The negotiations succeeded in the end because of the personal directives of the president and the prime minister. Political will from the top ultimately galvanized both sides. Baker and Burney were determined to deliver an agreement that met their leaders' wishes, not a "deal for the sake of a deal" but a deal that would be mutually beneficial—both economically and politically.

For Canada, the FTA was that and then some. It is unquestionably the pinnacle of achievement in the bilateral relationship and, easily, the most significant element in the Mulroney government's foreign policy legacy. There were obviously economic gains for the U.S., too, but for the Americans, the strategic advantage of the FTA was that it prompted progress on the Uruguay Round of multilateral negotiations, especially on the part of the recalcitrant Europeans. These negotiations were concluded six years after the FTA, but both Canada and the U.S. were in a better position to take advantage of broader trade liberalization because of the adjustments already being made to their own bilateral agreement.

ELECTION 1988

Still ahead was a riveting election in Canada—one of very few fought almost exclusively on a single issue. Free trade became a lightning rod, with the opposition parties vowing to scrap the FTA if they took power. All the bogeys of anti-Americanism were stimulated. Even John Turner, who ran as a Bay Street–friendly Liberal in 1984, released a populist, "anti-business" platform. A typical excerpt: "The Mulroney trade agreement sells out Canada's sovereign control over its own economic, social, cultural and regional policies. It turns Canada into a colony of the United States."[65]

Mulroney's approach, deploying analyses and endorsements from economists and business leaders, proved less effective in rebutting the opposition's vigorous emotional attacks. The polls swung sharply against the PC Party, which started the campaign at 43 per cent in the polls but slumped to 34 per cent. The top campaign advisers recommended that Mulroney call for a referendum on the free trade agreement. He rejected the advice out of hand, saying that such a call would be the antithesis of leadership. Instead he took ownership of the deal, brandishing it at each campaign event with forceful, personal passion and pride that matched the opposition's emotional impact.

At one rally in Victoria, B.C., Mulroney urged hecklers in the audience to let him conclude his speech, promising to answer at the end and before the TV cameras any questions they had about what was in the agreement. During that later discussion, when one heckler lamented that the FTA would "destroy our social programs," Mulroney asked him to show exactly where the agreement said that. The heckler demurred, saying, "Well, it may not say that but that is what it will do."

"That, sir, is the problem with your question," Mulroney replied. "It is not based on anything in the agreement."[66] He dismissed the small group without further comment.

Seven of Canada's ten premiers were on Mulroney's side, including notably Don Getty of Alberta and Robert Bourassa of Quebec. Howard Pawley of Manitoba and Joe Ghiz of P.E.I. were firmly opposed. David Peterson of Ontario was queasy for reasons he could not fully explain, but, after all, he and Ontario already enjoyed the benefits of the Auto Pact. Mulroney was at his best in sessions with the premiers—unfailingly patient and careful never to embarrass or isolate one of the critics while mustering support from allies selectively, not overwhelmingly. The business community—led by Tom d'Aquino, David Culver, Guy Saint-Pierre, Ted Newall, and others—participated vigorously in the campaign as never before.

The national debate proved cathartic and the tide began to turn in Mulroney's favour. The last few weeks of the 1988 election campaign were very tense as the government fought its way back in the polls. In the final week of the campaign, the PCS gained about 1 per cent per day in polls in the Toronto area. The party gained a crucial advantage when Mr. Justice Emmett Hall spoke out, denying that free trade would end public health care. The fear of losing Canada's potential economic advantage ultimately struck a chord with voters. In the end, Mulroney's party captured 43 per cent of the vote—the first back-to-back majority wins for a Conservative prime minister in a hundred years.

The two major parties had reversed their customary positions on free trade, with the Liberals now being opposed and the Conservatives in favour. Most of the Liberal opponents eventually became champions of the result, perhaps its finest compliment.

But it was an unusually bold risk, an act of political courage at the time, and the results confirmed the fundamental validity of the economic theory. By becoming more efficient and more competitive within North America, Canada would also be better positioned to compete in global markets.

ECONOMIC (AND PSYCHOLOGICAL) RESULTS

The proof is in the pudding. A North American recession in 1990–91 and a severe monetary policy from the Bank of Canada initially chilled much of the ardour for and benefits from the FTA, but in time the lowering of tariff barriers substantially bolstered investment, production, and trade. As Philip Cross has observed, free trade "proved to be a boon to our economy, without the cuts to social programs, mass diversions of water exports and the ultimate assimilation that its shrill opponents imagined."[67]

Trade volumes between Canada and the United States more than tripled in the first twenty years of the FTA—from $235 billion in 1989 to $743 billion in 2008—becoming the largest two-way exchange between any two countries in the world, helping to create millions of high-value jobs in both countries, and bringing investments and other economic benefits to both sides of the border. Industries that were supposed to be "paved over" as a result of free trade, like the wine-making in Niagara and the Okanagan, are flourishing with better quality, more variety, and higher-priced, widely acclaimed products. Peerless Clothing, Inc. of Montreal has become the largest manufacturer of men's suits in the world. Quite apart from the fact that Canada won several early disputes once the panels were created, the dispute settlement mechanism served over time to check or constrain egregious trade remedy actions—which was, of course, part of its original intent.

By demonstrating convincingly that Canada could compete on a level playing field in North America, the FTA had a psychological impact as well, redressing historical anxieties about identity, ability, and sovereignty. It helped make Canada more confident not just in managing relations with the U.S. but also in charting a more outward-turning and more determined sense of space globally.

After more than a quarter century of free trade, a whole generation of Canadians has become accustomed to the benefits and more open to the prospects of broader trade liberalization—NAFTA, CETA (the Canada–European Union Comprehensive Economic and Trade Agreement), and the TPP (Trans-Pacific Partnership) being the most notable examples. Each of these agreements represents an enduring part of the Mulroney legacy.

After a lengthy implementation process in Canada's Parliament and the U.S. Congress, free trade came into effect on January 1, 1989. When he signed the agreement formally that day, Mulroney stated, "A hundred years from now, what will be remembered was that it was done and the naysayers will be forgotten."[68]

NAFTA

Mexico quickly took note of the FTA's success and, after several learning sessions with Canadian negotiators, the administration of President Carlos Salinas urged U.S. president George H.W. Bush in early 1990 to contemplate a separate free trade agreement with them. Bush, who had lived in Texas for much of his professional career, was attracted to the idea, but neither he nor Salinas thought through the implications of a U.S.–Mexico agreement for Canada. Brian Mulroney did. Canada had secured a competitive advantage in the FTA, particularly for investors who were attracted to a larger and more open North American market, and Mulroney did not want anyone diluting it. Nor did he want Canada to become a single spoke in the American "hub-and-spoke" approach to hemispheric trade. Canada's objectives in the NAFTA negotiations were primarily defensive, just as they would subsequently be in the TPP negotiations. Canada did not have a huge economic stake in the Mexican market, but it could not afford to be left out.

Mulroney was determined that Canada would be at the table. Some in his own cabinet were less keen, suffering undoubtedly from "free trade fatigue" by that time, with the memory of the bruising 1988 election still fresh. The Americans were wary that Canadian negotiators might re-open matters from the FTA and simply hinder their negotiation with Mexico. And the Mexicans saw no advantage in having Canada share the negotiating task.

The U.S.–Mexico talks started in June 1990. Mulroney used all his personal skill and charm to persuade Bush and Salinas that Canada had to be included. He was an avid student of American politics. At a dinner in the new Canadian embassy in Washington, he knew each of the more than fifty top-tier American guests personally. He even introduced some of them to the president. "Brian," asked a perplexed Bush, "how is it that you know all these people?" Despite stout resistance from several agencies in both the U.S. and Mexican governments, Mulroney succeeded in securing for Canada a seat at the table. He and Burney, now ambassador to Washington, strenuously lobbied James Baker, now secretary of state, and the undersecretary of state for economic and agricultural affairs, Robert Zoellick, to override objections from other U.S. agencies.[69]

The NAFTA negotiations were successfully concluded in 1992, and Canada ratified the agreement long before the U.S. Congress. Despite the initial concern from the U.S. side that Canada would delay matters, it wasn't the Canadians doing the foot-dragging. NAFTA refined some parts of the FTA, such as rules of origin for automobiles, made the dispute settlement process a permanent feature, and expanded the scope to include intellectual property protection (a chapter jettisoned at the last minute in the FTA negotiations due to U.S. intransigence) and a provision to adjudicate investment provisions.

The NAFTA negotiations were much less frenetic for Canada and more systematic than those for the FTA, because they were not conducted under a heavy media spotlight and were relatively free from the national-ist bombast that had engulfed the earlier free trade conversation. The economic adjustment in Canada was much less significant after the FTA began to take effect. Instead, most of the rancor erupted after the fact and in the U.S., where it continues to reverberate to this day.

NAFTA's labour and environmental side deals were successfully negoti-ated under Kim Campbell's short-lived Conservative government. They basically amounted to requiring NAFTA's three parties to enforce legisla-tion already on their books. In the 1993 election, both the Liberals and the NDP campaigned against NAFTA, but once elected, the new Liberal government of Jean Chrétien quietly ratified the agreement.

LESSONS

The 2016 U.S. election campaign raised the anti-NAFTA, anti-trade agree-ment crescendo to new heights, ignoring the benefits of free trade but finding it a convenient scapegoat for all that ails the U.S. economy. "America First" rhetoric is just a fancy dress for protectionism, and as Robert Zoellick astutely observed in the *Wall Street Journal*, "President Hoover achieved the trade surplus that Trump demands but also an unemploy-ment rate of 25 percent and the Great Depression."[70]

Economic change, good and bad, is generated by innovation, techno-logical advances, competition, and changing customer tastes, not simply by trade arrangements alone. Again, to quote Zoellick, "The task of government is to help people adjust to change, not pretend that change can be prevented. Policy makers should advance ideas to get people back into jobs, assist with their relocation, supplement earned incomes, cut taxes on wages and make useful training and skills upgrades part of ongoing support for economic security."[71]

Despite the fact that the numbers from NAFTA and other trade agreements are positive[72] and that dislocations in the global economy stem from much more than trade agreements, it would be difficult to imagine anything like the Canada–U.S. free trade deal or NAFTA being approved by the U.S. Congress in the current political environment. Both deals were made possible by bold, persistent political leadership and a unique chemistry between those at the top. That nothing of similar scope has been achieved in the years since then is further proof of the agreements' significance. The basic lesson to be derived is that careful nurturing of personal relationships at the top is pivotal to results for initiatives that combine vision with political courage. As Jeffrey L. Chidester observed about the key bilateral issues during Reagan's presidency, "Personal diplomacy was the only way to break bureaucratic inertia on (these) issues."[73]

As importantly, this historic pivot in trade policy shattered many of the free trade bogeys in Canada, boosted national self-confidence, and left Canadian companies more competitive in North America and beyond, allowing them to attract increased investments, create supply chain efficiencies, and generate higher-paying jobs. The deals also served as a catalyst for broader trade liberalization initiatives in the Western Hemisphere and beyond. Together with the Uruguay Round in 1994—the last successful multilateral trade effort—the two North American agreements provided a solid foundation for trade expansion and economic growth.

Nothing tested the mettle of Mulroney's political leadership more than the up-and-down hurly-burly of the free trade negotiations with the U.S. and the ensuing, highly charged election in Canada. Nothing has had a more lasting impact on the national psyche and Canada's economy than the success of that negotiation. Enshrined and refined further under NAFTA, it stands as the centrepiece of Mulroney's legacy as prime minister. These achievements resonate eloquently to this day, offering a blueprint for his successors to emulate. As the prospect of renegotiating

NAFTA rises to the surface, there are many lessons to be learned from Mulroney's time in office. The most important is that no deal is preferable to a bad deal. That was the basic principle that guided Canada in its first free trade negotiation. We need to know when and how to say no. Mutual self-interest is the most sobering tonic of all in any trade negotiation. Canada will need to determine shrewdly what it will and will not renegotiate and how to define a success that serves Canadian interests.

THREE

Tears Are Not Enough: Famine in Ethiopia

———————

"It is a high-pitched, eerie howl that slices through the night,
gathering strength until it lingers and echoes over the mile-high
valley—thousands of voices united in prayerful pleas for
mercy and forgiveness, voices that mourn the dead and beg
the privilege of living another wretched day."
—DAVID LAMB, *Los Angeles Times*

O NE OF THE FIRST CRISES that the Mulroney government confronted early in its first term was the famine in Ethiopia. This was neither the first nor the last time that starvation on a massive scale would strike in the Horn of Africa. In the fall–winter of 2016–17, the world ignored another humanitarian catastrophe of epic proportions unfolding on the African subcontinent. Warm waters in the Pacific Ocean, otherwise known as El Niño, were wreaking havoc on global weather patterns. The worst effects were being felt in the Horn, where millions faced widespread famine and drought. "With their escape route to the United States endangered by the orders of President Donald Trump, the people of Somalia now face a new threat: a looming famine that could bring starvation to millions," the *Globe and Mail's* Geoffrey York warned.[74] He also pointed out that there had been another famine six years earlier that had killed over a quarter of a million Somalis in a country that had seen little peace over the years or any semblance of functional government.

But it was not just in Somalia that temperatures spiked and seasonal rains never fell. Virtually all the countries on the eastern and southern side of the continent, including Ethiopia, Kenya, Mozambique, Zimbabwe, and South Africa, were suffering from record-breaking temperatures that were killing crops, cattle, and people. In all, the lives of thirty-six million people in eastern and southern Africa were at risk. The woefully under-funded United Nations (UN) refugee and relief agencies were struggling to meet the needs of those who were starving and displaced by this crisis. In Ethiopia alone, the United Nations International Children's Emergency Fund (UNICEF) had to feed two million children and deliver food aid to another ten million people.

Once again, drought and widespread famine threatened to set back a continent that had experienced widespread growth and development over the past two decades—a boom that was largely fuelled by rising commodity prices and generous infusions of foreign direct investment, particularly from China. That boom was also coming to a crashing end as worldwide demand for commodities, including oil and gas, fell, including in many of the emerging market economies that were the destination for African exports.

It's an all-too-familiar story. Some thirty years earlier, a similar crisis had unfolded in the same part of the world. As the late David Lamb of the *Los Angeles Times*—who was perhaps best known for his reportage of the Vietnam war but who also covered the Ethiopian famine—wrote,

> ALAMATA, Ethiopia—In the last moments of the icy, windy night, when all the valley is as still as death and the foreboding darkness seems eternal, the wailing begins, softly at first like the distant chant of ghosts.
>
> It is a high-pitched, eerie howl that slices through the night, gathering strength until it lingers and echoes over the mile-high valley— thousands of voices united in prayerful pleas for mercy and forgive-ness, voices that mourn the dead and beg the privilege of living another wretched day.
>
> When the half-light of dawn reaches over the stone-face mountains that surround the valley, the wailing passes, giving way to the husky

coughs of waking children. As far as the eye can see, in a scene resembling a medieval battlefield, stretch the legions of peasants— barefooted and wrapped in rags, a vast civilian army, conquered by famine, that now waits for its daily rations of porridge.

The word has spread quickly. There is food here. There are doctors. Sometimes there are blankets. And from their mud homes deep in the mountains, crossing parched earth that once bore bountiful harvests of grain, trudging past corpses and carcasses, finally, after many days, settling on this hillside where the morning is heavy with the smell of sickness, they have come, first by the hundreds, then by the thousands.[75]

A volatile mix of environmental and political conditions contributed to the great Ethiopian famine of 1984, including twenty years of civil war, Cold War politics, and drought. That famine came a little more than ten years after an earlier famine led to the creation of the World Food Council in 1973.[76] The world had eventually responded, if half-heartedly, to the earlier crisis in Ethiopia, but only after word of it leaked out. As David Lamb further noted, "Haile Selassie was then 81 years old and partly senile, and not wanting to admit his inability to care for his people, he tried to keep the famine a secret from the world. In 1974, dissident army officers distributed photographs of the emperor tossing scraps of fresh meat to his two Great Danes. Within months, he was overthrown, destined for eventual burial in an unmarked grave."[77]

After Emperor Haile Selassie was deposed and a new Marxist regime seized power, many key donors, including Canada, the U.S., and the U.K., suspended humanitarian and development aid to Ethiopia. In 1980, Canada decided to resume some of its assistance programs. However, the United States chose not to, and by then British aid was being channelled through the European Economic Community (EEC).[78]

There were many problems with the delivery of Canadian aid. Food, medicine, and other supplies had to go through the Red Sea to the port of Assab, which was hundreds of kilometres away from the relief centres where it was disbursed to the local populace. What few roads existed were either impassible or extremely treacherous, passing through rocky mountains in the Ethiopian highlands. The relief centres themselves were also widely dispersed across Ethiopia's vast territory—more than two hundred in all according to the government at the time.[79] Compounding the problem was the fact that the northern region of the country was under the control of anti-government rebels. In many rebel-held areas, the Ethiopian government simply refused to allow humanitarian relief workers to deliver their precious consignment of food and medicine. It was not long before an increasingly jaundiced public heard reports of Canadian grain rotting in warehouses or sitting in sacks that had been split open by looters on the wharfs where they had been unceremoniously dumped. Worst still, there were even reports that 10 per cent of food and aid shipments were being stolen by criminal gangs out of warehouses in the Port of Montreal before they could even get loaded onto the ships.

As the humanitarian crisis deepened, the UN Food and Agriculture Organization (UNFAO) issued a worldwide alert.[80] Other dire warnings followed: "In March 1984, the Ethiopian Relief Commission said 6.4 million Ethiopians were in imminent danger of starvation and emergency food supplies were needed immediately." In response, Canada decided to ramp up its wheat shipments to Ethiopia, but most Western donors simply chose to ignore the warnings even as alarming reports that hundreds of thousands of people were dying because they didn't have food or water began to reach Addis Ababa, Ethiopia's capital.[81] By early November, those estimates were running into the millions, although a later report by Africa Watch cautioned that any figures issued by the Ethiopian government were notoriously unreliable.[82]

While much of the media coverage focused on drought and the civil war as the main causes of the famine, the government itself was a major contributor to the crisis and the destruction of the country's agriculture and food distribution systems. Crops in rebel-held areas were burned to the ground by government troops. Local markets were bombed into oblivion, along with victims who had the misfortune to be in harm's way. The government also began to forcibly remove people from rebel-held areas, or restrict their movement, in its relentless military campaign to root out the rebels and gain territorial control. Much of the country's fragile agricultural infrastructure was destroyed beyond repair.[83] In the period 1983–85, estimates put the death toll at almost half a million, not including those who died during their forcible "resettlement."[84]

THE CBC FACTOR

News reports about Ethiopia's unfolding crisis were patchy and usually relegated to the back pages of Western newspapers. Ethiopia's Marxist government had all but shut out foreign journalists. However, as the famine worsened and the situation became increasingly dire, the government allowed a team of BBC reporters into the country in late October. Their stories aired later that month.[85] The CBC also sent a TV reporting team to the country for three weeks. "As we grimly moved from one refugee camp to another, we kept running into exhausted Canadian doctors and nurses who were horrified at the growing death toll and appalled that the world didn't seem to know. They kept pleading with us to get the message out," journalist Tony Burman, who was a producer on the story, wrote some thirty years later.[86] To get his footage out, he had to smuggle the videotapes past the border guards by taping them onto his back, and then transport them to Nairobi, Kenya, where they were flown back to Canada. This was the pre–satellite phone era for journalists.

A four-minute video by reporter Brian Stewart, which aired on the CBC television network November 1, 1984, set off what can only be described as a political tsunami. News anchor Peter Mansbridge introduced it as a story of "almost unbelievable horror of people without food, without hope." The report began in Tigray province, showing people dead or dying in the streets, skeletal children, and a suffering child who viewers were told died several hours after the footage was taken. As reported by Stewart, many adults there were "losing the will to live," according to one of his relief worker interviewees, Sister Jean Harris. In the town of

Korem, footage showed the appalling suffering at relief camps where one hundred people were dying every day—up from twenty a day just three months earlier. The camps had enough food for about twenty thousand people, but ten times that many were seeking help, Stewart reported. Thousands of people had to sleep outdoors in the freezing mountain air, with only thin rag blankets for warmth. Pneumonia was rampant. After showing piles of corpses and wailing mourners, Stewart warned that the problem was about to get much worse: "That's the most frightening thing of all here: the fact that this might not be the height of a catastrophe but the beginning of an even greater one."[87]

The public was shocked. Canada's newly appointed ambassador to the UN, Stephen Lewis, described his own family's reaction to the broadcast the following week in his first speech at the UN: "'I cannot remember in my entire adult life such scenes of such unendurable human desolation,' he said. 'It was heartbreaking. There is no doubt in my mind that Canadians sat and wept as we did and would wish to respond with compassion, generosity, fervour.'"[88] Lewis's appointment to the UN had come as a surprise to many, given his background as a former Ontario NDP leader and his reputation for being outspoken and highly partisan. But Mulroney, emboldened by a recommendation from Premier Bill Davis of Ontario, had chosen to cross partisan lines because he wanted someone who had exactly those qualities and would shake things up in New York.

The political response to the CBC story was instantaneous, as Stewart wrote twenty-five years later:

> That following morning, Lewis remembers, his first phone call came
> from an emotional Mulroney asking what the UN was doing about
> the disaster. When Lewis replied it was doing nothing, there was a
> pause and then a quick let's-do-it commitment by the prime minister
> that would launch both men onto the world stage. In the absence
> of action elsewhere, Mulroney told Lewis that Canada was going
> to lead a worldwide rescue mission in Ethiopia and he immediately
> dispatched his new ambassador to New York to stir up the General

Assembly. Within days, in his maiden address, Lewis galvanized the General Assembly into taking action on African famine, demanding nothing less than "a Herculean effort on the part of all member nations." Days later, the UN and Red Cross launched what was at the time the greatest single humanitarian relief effort in history, to save an estimated seven million facing starvation in Ethiopia, along with a further 22 million others across the continent.[89]

The speech that Lewis delivered to the General Assembly was an impassioned wake-up call that caught the world's attention. But it was not the speech that had been crafted for him by officials in the Department of External Affairs, who wanted him to deliver something far more anodyne about the problems of agriculture in Ethiopia. Lewis spent much of the night completely redrafting his remarks, which did not sit well in Ottawa. It would not be the first or the last time Lewis would shake things up at External Affairs headquarters.[90]

External Affairs Minister Joe Clark, who was attending the funeral of Indira Gandhi in India, was instructed by the prime minister to get on the ground fast and find out what was happening. Arriving in Addis Ababa on November 4, Clark was the first senior Western official to visit Ethiopia.[91] As Brian Stewart—who had just returned from northern Ethiopia and was therefore able to cover Clark's visit—recollects,

I saw his arrival as one of the defining moments in the darkest
early days. His presence there gave a needed shot in the arm to
foreign embassies and humanitarian groups that had been until then
deeply depressed by the lack of outside world interest to that point.
Something about Clark's bouncy and confident manner as he went
to meetings of foreign groups in Addis seemed to suggest that help-
had-arrived and more would be coming. I could sense a mood change
almost immediately. . . . Clark had heard of our footage that had just
played in Canada, of course, but had not seen any of it due to his
travels. He asked if we could show him the report and raw footage of

the famine we'd manage to get, including scenes still too horrifying to include in broadcasting at that time. Tony Burman and I arranged that night for a very private screening for Clark and his staff in a very crowded hotel room we used for editing. We filmed the moment without objection from his officials. The Minister and his people were shaken by the images, there were more tears and his genuine response shown in a subsequent item became a powerful reminder to viewers that this was disaster on an unprecedented scale and proof that Canadian leadership was not about to turn away. I always felt a lot of respect for Clark for allowing that—it took some courage as most politicians would have refused to display the fact on TV that they didn't actually get to the actual famine, but he insisted on getting as full a picture as he could and did not hide anything."[92]

Lewis also observed from New York that a visit from the foreign minister would signal to African leaders and the Canadian public just how seriously the Canadian government was taking the crisis: "It seems to me to be a pretty dramatic demonstration that the Government response to Ethiopia is a serious business."[93] He was, of course, right about that.

One reporter who accompanied Clark wrote, "The famine has been going on for a year, reported in increasingly alarmed language by the United Nations Food and Agricultural Organization. Yet only in the past fortnight has the international community, in particularly the wealthy West, indicated the same measure of alarm as the FAO." When asked why it had taken so long for the Canadian government to react, Clark had one a one-word response: "Television." When pressed further by his questioner about the reasons for the delay—Did this mean that governments did not act until something appeared on television?—Clark replied, "The people of High River [Clark's home town in Alberta] don't read FAO reports, but they do watch television." "Governments," he said, "particularly democratic governments, are affected by public priorities."[94]

Clark did not visit the famine-struck areas of the country because it was simply too dangerous for him to do so, but he did meet with Ethiopian leader Mengistu Haile Mariam and invited him to come to Canada to serve as "Ethiopia's bridge to the West." Mengistu agreed, although the visit never took place and he was deposed in a rebel coup in 1991.[95] Before he left Ethiopia, Clark told a press conference, "I can recommend with confidence that Canadians should contribute."[96]

CANADA'S RESPONSE

In 1984, Canada was already the world's top donor of food to Ethiopia, delivering between one-quarter and one-third of all global food aid to the country, as an official with the Canadian International Development Agency (CIDA) told the Globe and Mail.[97] Earlier in 1984, before the Conservatives were elected, Liberal agriculture minister Eugene Whelan increased Canada's food aid to Ethiopia by 50 per cent.[98] The new budget was $25 million in food aid for Ethiopia, plus $4.3 million in medicine, transport, and other aid, and $9.2 million for a rural water project.[99]

In the ensuing weeks, Clark and Prime Minister Mulroney tried to drum up international support for Ethiopia. Together, they "worked the phones around the clock and were appalled to find that there seemed a common Western front to do as little as possible about the famine— driven, it seemed, by fellow conservatives Ronald Reagan in the U.S. and Margaret Thatcher in Britain."[100] Both Thatcher and Reagan were virulent anti-communists and wanted to have nothing to do with Ethiopia's Marxist government, notwithstanding the dire circumstances of millions of Ethiopians who were starving to death.

Undaunted, Mulroney and Clark both believed that humanitarian concerns should trump Cold War ideological rivalries and that it was important to engage Ethiopia's government and assist them with the crisis. Clark named David MacDonald Canada's emergency coordinator of aid to Africa. MacDonald was a former United Church minister from Prince Edward Island who had been the communications minister in Clark's cabinet.[101] MacDonald was technically on a contract with CIDA but was put in charge of spending the government's relief funds, with

"a wide mandate to cut red tape, crack heads in Government departments, sort out the relationship with the non-government agencies and
concentrate more on speed than formalities."[102]

On November 6 at the UN, during a special debate on the famine,
Lewis spoke forcefully in support of an African economic development
plan designed to address the crisis in Ethiopia and other African countries: "It stamps with approval the urgent need for coordination; and
it argues, with irrefutable cogency, the case for a substantial increase in
bilateral and multilateral funding."[103] He spoke of his emotional reaction to seeing images of starving Ethiopians. He said the plan wouldn't be
enough to solve everything on its own, but could "act as a remarkable
catalyst to collective action."[104] The Canadian Press reported that "Several
African delegates praised Lewis' speech." One of them, Ambassador Bassy
Camara of Guinea, said it was "one of the most encouraging" he had
heard in the assembly debate "because he (Lewis) had spoken about the
real problem; the real tragedy the African people are experiencing."[105]
Lewis's pleadings, however, fell on deaf ears when it came to the United
States. Its ambassador, Jeane Kirkpatrick, who was everything Lewis was
not—crusty, cold, arrogant, and dismissive—brushed aside his pleas by
suggesting that Ethiopia's problems were best left to be dealt with by the
private sector.[106]

That same day, Ethiopian relief spokesman Major Dawit Wolde-
Giorgis met with Clark, who was now back in Ottawa, and Deputy
Prime Minister Erik Nielsen. The government announced it was offering
a "commitment in principle" for more aid, although it did not at that
point spell out how much it would provide or how it would be delivered.
Still, Wolde-Giorgis said he was "deeply encouraged."[107] Clark hinted at
the direction Canadian relief would take by saying, "Our job, it seems to
me, is to set in place some mechanism that will make effective the desire
of individual Canadians to help the millions of starving people." He also
asked the provinces to step up to the plate.[108]

But barely a week later, there were concerns that Canada would back
away from its Ethiopian aid commitments. Finance Minister Michael

Wilson, who was in the process of sharpening his fiscal pencils, announced a $180 million cut to CIDA's budget for 1985–86,[109] and backed away from the government's earlier announcement that it planned to raise foreign aid spending to 0.7 per cent of GDP by 1990, saying instead that it would be reached in 1995.[110] In an editorial, the *Globe and Mail* called it "an unfortunate retreat from a worthy commitment," and described Wilson as a finance minister "who plays to Bay Street rather than Addis Ababa."[111]

However, on November 16, Clark announced in the House of Commons that the government would contribute an extra $7.5 million in aid to Ethiopia: $3.5 million for humanitarian relief to be delivered by NGOs, and $4 million to send 10,000–15,000 tonnes of cereal to Ethiopia. Some of that would be delivered through non-governmental channels to reach rebel-controlled areas such as Eritrea.[112] Fourteen NGOs banded together under the name African Emergency Aid to handle the aid funding.[113] Clark also announced a $50 million special fund for African aid.[114] Notably, $15 million of the African aid fund was set aside to match individual Canadians' donations dollar for dollar.[115] The plan would also restore $13 million of the proposed cut to CIDA, as well as the $28 million that been cut from CIDA's budget by the Liberal government of John Turner.[116] On December 7, MacDonald announced that Canada was organizing an emergency airlift to Ethiopia in time for Christmas. Air Canada provided five DC-8 planes, each carrying about 44 tonnes of supplies, food, medical equipment, and doctors.[117] They also distributed 30,000 blankets from UNICEF.[118] In early December, Colin Rainsbury of UNICEF Canada told the *Globe and Mail* that he saw Canadian wheat being delivered throughout Ethiopia: "There seemed to be Canadian grain all over the place in red plastic bags."[119] No more rotting sacks in Ethiopia's ports.

The response from the Canadian public was so overwhelming that in February 1985, the government doubled the amount for matching donations from $15 million to $30 million. Then, in April 1985, it added another $25 million for recovery.[120] MacDonald tabled his report on African famine in the House of Commons on March 26, 1986. He praised the outpouring of aid from Canadian individuals, governments, and organizations, saying it had saved millions of lives. Most of the aid reached people in need, despite some "minor losses." He said the government's focus over the next decade should be to encourage "self-sufficiency in food production," to boost trade with African countries, and to help with their debt. He also emphasized that famine remained an ongoing crisis: "The famine . . . will not disappear simply by the provision of food aid. Africa is in the midst of a crisis which must be addressed on an ongoing basis over the next few decades if the present course of decline is to be turned in the direction of development and hope."[121]

PUBLIC REACTION

Five weeks after Brian Stewart's story about the Ethiopian famine aired on CBC, Canadian agencies had taken in about $11 million for African relief efforts, with $9.7 million of that directed to Ethiopian refugee camps.[122] By the end of January, the public had donated $30 million—twice what the government had set aside for matching funds.[123] When MacDonald filed his final report in March 1986, he found that Canadian individuals, organizations, and governments had contributed $170 million, and that two out of three Canadian families had donated in some way.[124] The response was described as unprecedented and newspapers reported on the unique contributions of all sizes:

"For example, a campaign organized by one woman to have mothers donate their November family allowance cheques has inundated one Ottawa-based relief agency."[125]

". . . one Winnipeg agency receives about $8,000 a day and Montreal's Fondation Jules et Paul-Émile Léger has hundreds of cash-filled envelopes unopened."[126]

"The technician called to fix a computer in Mr. MacDonald's office made his connections and left behind 'a very large cheque.' Students in the fine arts faculty at York University raised $4,000 by organizing an art and bake sale. An ad hoc organization in Hamilton is determined to raise a dollar for each of the 414,000 residents of Hamilton-Wentworth. A gentleman adventurer discovered a forgotten formula for a special food supplement in a Toronto laboratory and flew it to Addis Ababa. A Prince Edward Island potato farmer resorted to tremendous political pressure to have his crop shipped to Africa. In the words of Mr. MacDonald: 'There's something really gripping people out there. . . . There doesn't seem to be any part of society that hasn't got turned on.'"[127]

In his first Christmas address, Prime Minister Mulroney praised Canadians for their generosity and willingness to contribute to famine relief, and said their overwhelming response "illustrates the best instincts and benevolence of Canadians."[128]

In February 1985, Canada's musicians got on board, with a charity single called "Tears Are Not Enough." The song was written and produced by David Foster, who helped organize the project along with music manager Bruce Allen.[129] It followed the model of the British song "Do They Know It's Christmas?" and the American "We Are the World." About fifty musicians gathered at Manta Sound studios in Toronto to record the single as a group called the Northern Lights, which included Bryan Adams, Tom Cochrane, Bruce Cockburn, Burton Cummings, Corey Hart, Geddy Lee, Gordon Lightfoot, Joni Mitchell, Anne Murray, Oscar Peterson, and Neil Young. (As one news story put it, "If an earthquake had opened up the ground yesterday on Adelaide Street East in Toronto, the loss to the Canadian music industry would have been incalculable."[130])

"Tears Are Not Enough" went triple-platinum, rose to number one on the singles chart, and raised $3.2 million for famine relief.[131] This was a first in terms of the amount of money that was raised. The 1985 Juno Awards honoured the song with a special Juno for the Canadian people, to recognize their support for the fundraising anthem. Mulroney accepted the award on behalf of the Canadian people at the November 1985 ceremony at the Harbour Castle hotel in Toronto.[132]

CONTROVERSIES

Inevitably, there were conflicting reports about whether the aid was being effectively distributed to those in need and not siphoned off into black markets. In December 1984, George Galloway, the head of the British NGO War on Want (and a future British MP with a reputation for stirring up controversy) told the Canadian Press that Canadian grain was being used in a commercial biscuit bakery and sold on the black market. "'None of the food aid is reaching those territories that are outside of the Government's control,' he said, 'despite the fact that 60 to 80 per cent of those most at risk in the famine are living in those areas. We think that the donors in Canada, and the United States and Britain, and Europe . . . whose wave of generosity has been so productive, are unaware and, if they were aware, would be extremely angry that politics is being played with food in this way.'" He had previously reported seeing skim milk powder from Canada, the U.S., and West Germany being sold in Sudan.[133] An External Affairs spokesperson denied reports of such diversions or misuse from Canadian NGOs or the UN World Food Program, which was monitoring the Ethiopian Relief and Rehabilitation Commission's food aid.[134] The UN later set up a relief monitoring unit to make sure aid was reaching the relief centres.[135]

The CBC also reported in January that Ethiopian officials were withholding aid to Eritrea and Tigray, the rebel-controlled northern provinces that were the hardest hit by famine. It also claimed government forces were destroying crops in the provinces, shooting at famine refugees, and undertaking a forced resettlement campaign. Liberal MP Brian Tobin called for an independent investigation into the claims, but External Relations Minister Monique Vézina dismissed his request and said aid efforts would continue. "We knew very well that helping Ethiopia was helping a country where a civil war was under way," she told the Commons on January 23.[136]

Another claim made by the CBC report was that the Ethiopian government was forcibly relocating people from the northern territories where the famine had struck hardest and rebels were in control. Those reports were of course not new for those in the know. The head of the Ethiopian government's Relief Coordinating Committee, Berhanu Bayih, told a 1984 donor meeting that resettlement was "the only alternative to ensure the continued survival of those people."[137] Meanwhile, the government's ten-year economic plan called for 62 per cent of the country's arable land to be converted to collective farms, compared to 8 per cent at the time.[138]

MacDonald's final report, which called for Ottawa to continue funding the resettlement program, was controversial, especially since the program had been resoundingly condemned by the United States and human rights NGOs for human rights violations. MacDonald and UN officials defended it on the grounds that it was an unfortunate necessity.[139] In February 1988, it was reported that the Canadian government had contributed at least $1.5 million to the Ethiopian government for resettlement over the next three years. Officials "stressed that the support should not be seen as an endorsement of the resettlement program." Rather, they described it as assistance that had been "approved to try to ease the plight of thousands of people who have already been moved from their homes in the drought-ravaged north to more fertile areas in the west and southwest."[140] Africa Watch reported in 1991 that the resettlement program had killed at least fifty thousand people.[141]

POST-CRISIS RESPONSE

In June 1986, Stephen Lewis helped negotiate a UN recovery plan for Africa. The five-year, $112 billion plan was directed at "agricultural development, drought relief, education and training." Mulroney praised Lewis for his role in the "exceptional initiative."[142] In September 1986, MacDonald was named Canada's ambassador to Ethiopia in order to allow him to continue his work in the country. He told the Canadian Press, "It's an indication of the government's determination to follow up on the unparalleled Canadian interest and response to the famine—not only in Ethiopia but in other affected parts of Africa. . . . I think the challenge to us now is to make the same kind of difference on the whole recovery aspect and rehabilitation. And I think there is a willingness and a real determination to do so."[143] However, by late 1989, Ethiopia was again facing a massive drought. African countries complained that the developed world's attention and aid donations had shifted away from them and towards the newly liberated countries of Eastern Europe with the fall of communism.[144] There was indeed real truth to those concerns. Canada had cut its budget for food aid by $66 million from 1988 figures.[145]

Further cuts were supposed to come in the government's 1990 budget, but they did not materialize thanks to "Canadian overseas development groups, who succeeded in convincing the Mulroney government that further deep cuts in foreign aid spending would be catastrophic both for the Third World and for Canada's international reputation."[146] NGO officials credited Clark for the reprieve. Ottawa was rife with rumours that he had threatened to resign from cabinet if the foreign aid budget was slashed any further.[147] That November, though, the OECD's development assistance committee criticized the "significant decline in Canadian aid . . . given Canada's proud record in drawing attention to the global importance of development issues and its concern for alleviating poverty."[148]

Looking back on the Canadian response to the famine twenty-five years later, Brian Stewart called it "the time when the better parts of [Mulroney's] nature roared through and he set in motion a chain of events that resulted in one of the greatest mobilizations of global empathy and humanitarian relief in the latter part of the 20th century." He also wrote that the main players in the Canadian relief effort "agree that Mulroney was the key figure in the campaign, totally committed and in charge."[149] Said Stewart, "Lewis confessed to me later that he had his doubts about Mulroney but was surprised to find him deeply interested in developing nations, a passion that began in his late teens at St. Francis Xavier University, where he drew direct inspiration from the Coady Institute, which had pioneered student projects to help Africa. Lewis believes Mulroney knew more about and cared more for Africa than any Canadian leader before or since." Stewart went on to say, paraphrasing Lewis, that,

"It was clear he had a particular feeling about the continent . . . and there was that underdog feeling of Mulroney's where you want to come to the aid of the beleaguered. It was a fascinating dimension of the man, which is not widely appreciated by Canadians."[150]

Lewis also spoke directly about Canada's famine response in a 1986 interview: "I was very concerned about the response to famine in Africa, not merely in the raising of money but in the way it would be apportioned—long term, what we do around the survival of that continent—and I have to say, again, particularly with aid coordinator David MacDonald doing the job he did out of Ottawa, with his extraordinary team, and with what we have said and done at the United Nations, Canada is seen among the western countries, along with the Nordics and Australia-New Zealand, as the most forthcoming, the most flexible, the most determined to find solutions . . . ."[151]

But when all is said and done, this is one crisis where Canada truly made a difference. Years later, Brian Stewart, reflecting on the Canadian contribution, had this to say: "I went back to Ethiopia several times to cover more of the famine relief in 1985 and '86 and as I watched convoy after convoy of trucks bringing in Canadian food aid and medicine, and airdrops of Canadian food bags into the hardest hit and most remote parts of the famine zone I often wondered what was the direct effect of Canada official and volunteer relief. I eventually came to believe at least 700,000 saved lives were directly related to Canada as we made up more than 10 percent of supplies—and that's before counting other foreign relief Mulroney shamed other leaders into giving. The International Red Cross later estimated total world aid saved something like 6 million from risk of death (one million were lost). I never confirmed a full figure, and it is likely impossible to do, but have no doubt Mulroney's actions helped saved a huge portion of those, along with what he could of western honor."[152]

LESSONS

There are some important lessons here about humanitarian emergency response for Canada when it chooses to take the lead. First, as Mulroney did with the then UN ambassador, Stephen Lewis, it is important to galvanize the international community through the UN, which is the world's first emergency responder. That response typically should begin with a call from the prime minister to Canada's ambassador to the UN, instructing him or her to get on top of the problem and create a sense of urgency in a body that is not prone to move quickly on the need to act.

Second, instead of leaving the problem in the hands of foreign affairs bureaucrats in Ottawa, the prime minister should appoint a special emergency coordinator to oversee Canadian humanitarian aid and disaster-relief efforts, just as Mulroney did when he appointed David MacDonald to do that job. Such an individual should have a direct reporting line to the prime minister to break bureaucratic log-jams and inertia. This individual should be assisted by an advisory body of representatives of non-governmental organizations that have an on-the-ground presence in those regions where the crisis is most acute. There is no substitute for bringing groups with real local knowledge about what needs to be done into the trusted councils of decision making and creating a strategic focal point to mobilize the bureaucracy.

Third, it is important to get senior cabinet officials out into the field so that they can see the problem first-hand and mobilize public opinion, as the then foreign affairs minister, Joe Clark, did when he went to Ethiopia in 1984.

Fourth, in world of sovereign nations, you can't always choose the ideology of your local partners if your goal is to help the people of a country. That may mean making concessions in order to deliver humanitarian and development assistance, as David Macdonald was forced to do with Ethiopia's controversial resettlement program.

Finally, perhaps the most important lesson is that Canada must lead with tangible deeds—put its own skin into the game instead of making empty pious rhetorical pronouncements. That is clearly the best, perhaps the only, way to show the world that Canada is indeed a global leader.

FOUR

A Light in the Window:
Ending Apartheid in South Africa

"One recalls the momentous time of our transition and remembers the
people involved both within and outside South Africa. As prime minister
of Canada and within the Commonwealth, you provided strong and
principled leadership in the battle against apartheid."
—NELSON MANDELA, former president of South Africa

NELSON MANDELA IS ONE OF THE TOWERING FIGURES of the
twentieth century, a man who stands larger than life—and with
good reason—as a symbol of freedom, human rights, dignity,
and national unity not just in his own country but around the globe. It
was no surprise, therefore, that on his death Canada assembled a full
court press of the country's serving and former prime ministers to attend
his state funeral and mourn his passing alongside other world leaders.

But the symbolism of four of Canada's leaders of different political
stripes finding themselves on the same plane flying to South Africa for
Mandela's state funeral on December 10, 2013, was not lost on some
members of the Canadian media. As Terry Pedwell of the Canadian Press
wryly observed, "Even after his death, Nelson Mandela has done what no
one else seemingly could—bring Canada's past-and-present political leadership together, in one space, for a single cause—if only for a few hours.
Prime Minister Stephen Harper and three of his predecessors—Jean
Chrétien, Brian Mulroney and Kim Campbell—sat in close quarters as

they winged their way to South Africa late Sunday in the elaborate front cabin of a government Airbus." Pedwell went on to point out that it was "not just any aircraft" the leaders were flying on. "The leaders were headed to pay their respects to Mandela comfortably seated in what Chrétien once non-affectionately dubbed the 'Taj Mahal,' a reference to the front stateroom with which the plane was retrofitted when Mulroney bought a fleet of the jetliners during his time in office. Now, however, the animosity of the past was gone, at least on the surface. 'I'm not a grubby politician anymore,' Mulroney said with a smile as he spoke of the significance of being in such close proximity with his former rivals. 'I'm a statesman now,' he laughed."[153]

Of those on Canadian Air Force 001 that day, Mulroney had played the biggest role in helping to end apartheid in South Africa and working to secure Mandela's release from the fifty-six-foot-square cell on Robben Island where he had spent twenty-seven years of his life. Why had Mulroney been an anti-apartheid crusader? His own views and personal commitment to ending apartheid had been indelibly shaped as a young man by the efforts of another Canadian prime minister on March 17, 1961.

On that day, John Diefenbaker, Canada's thirteenth prime minister, from 1957 to 1963, was welcomed home by a large crowd of well-wishers after flying overnight from the United Kingdom. He was coming home in triumph, having led the efforts that saw apartheid South Africa withdraw from the Commonwealth due to its racist internal policies. Diefenbaker's instinctual opposition to apartheid, driven in part by his life-long championing of the disenfranchised in Canada—Japanese Canadians, prisoners, and others he represented as a defence lawyer before achieving his dream of becoming prime minister—came from his gut. As a result, in taking up the cause of black South Africans he had no hesitation in splitting with, and angering, the prime ministers of traditional Canadian allies such as Britain, New Zealand, and Australia.

The *Ottawa Journal* of the day described the scene at Uplands Air Force Base in Ottawa that greeted Diefenbaker when he and his wife, Olive, stepped onto Canadian soil after exiting their RCAF plane that historic day.

"Prime Minister Diefenbaker came home today to that kind of full-dress red carpet welcome the Capital usually reserves for its most distinguished heads-of-state visitors from abroad," the *Journal's* Richard Jackson reported. "It was such a welcome as the Prime Minister has often accorded others but until this morning never himself had received at home."[154] Jackson continued, making special mention of the young people who joined in the excitement of welcoming their nation's prime minister home. "The Young Conservatives took a 50-car cavalcade to the airport and were waiting, lined up on either side of the red carpet with their signs and placards 'Welcome Home' and 'A Job Well done' when the Prime Minister and Mrs. Diefenbaker came into the hanger," Jackson wrote.

Among those cheering the loudest was a young law student from Baie-Comeau, Quebec, who was three days shy of his twenty-second birthday. His name was Martin Brian Mulroney. He never forgot the moment and the time his earliest political hero, Diefenbaker, fought apartheid. And there can be no question that Mulroney's own anti-apartheid sentiments were heartfelt and genuine. As Stephen Lewis recounts, in the very first conversation he had with Mulroney about the conditions of his UN ambassadorial appointment in October 1984, Mulroney made it clear that his top foreign priority was to work to end apartheid in South Africa.[155]

"I remember," Prime Minister Mulroney said, speaking twenty-nine years later in introducing the newly freed Nelson Mandela to Canada's Parliament in June 1990, "with pride, the stand taken by Canada's prime minister, John Diefenbaker, at the Commonwealth Conference of 1961, which resulted in South Africa's withdrawal from that body. Prime Minister Diefenbaker brought the Commonwealth to declare unequivocally that racial discrimination was totally contrary to its fundamental principles and that, if South Africa did not change, Mr. Diefenbaker said then South Africa must leave. He did so against some considerable opposition, but with the strong conviction and the certain knowledge that it was right. Mr. Diefenbaker's action marked the beginning of international pressure on the apartheid regime."[156]

Mulroney then heaped praised on another man who had also been among the crowd of youth cheering on Diefenbaker at Uplands that morning in 1961. "If I may be allowed a strictly Canadian note," Mulroney told Mandela and the Commons, "Outside South Africa itself there are few international leaders, in my judgement, who have made a more sustained and a more effective commitment to fundamental and beneficial change in that country in recent years than the present Secretary of State for External Affairs of the Government of Canada, the Right Honourable Joe Clark."[157]

That day in 1990 was truly a special moment for both Clark and Mulroney. And Clark, Mulroney's deputy in Canada's battles against apartheid between 1984 and 1993 (as well as having been his rival twice for leadership of the Progressive Conservative Party of Canada) also never forgot the path Diefenbaker had modelled for them both. Writing in his 2013 book about foreign policy, *How We Lead: Canada in a Century of Change*, Clark too invoked that day at Uplands. "In the 1990s a former senior advisor to Pierre Trudeau asked me why a Progressive Conservative government had been much more emphatic than Trudeau's Liberal government in making the struggle against apartheid a Canadian cause. . . . Mr. Diefenbaker had promised while in London that there would be 'a light in the window' for South Africa to return to the Commonwealth when apartheid was gone. . . . When our government was elected in 1984, opposing apartheid was part of our 'family' legacy."[158]

MOVING QUICKLY ON SOUTH AFRICA

Upon forming his government in September 1984, Mulroney wasted little time signalling to a reluctant bureaucracy at the Pearson Building that taking up the cause of majority South Africans was a definite political priority. As Mulroney recalls, "I said to the Cabinet, I thought about it, and then I am going to put Mandela and the Apartheid situation on the top of our foreign policy agenda. And we are going to raise this at the G7 every time there is a meeting. At the Commonwealth. At La Francophonie.

And eventually, a year later—I think it was a couple of years later at the OAS, although when we joined the OAS this thing was in the process of being resolved in South Africa. But we had quite a range of options. And I did that. So we started to work on this very seriously."[159]

But it would prove to a be a difficult row to hoe, not least because there was strong, internal bureaucratic opposition in External Affairs (as Canada's foreign ministry was then called) to isolating South Africa and employing sanctions against the regime. More than once, the views and rhetoric of Canada's prime minister ploughed ahead of the actions of his own senior officials and the Canadian business community, prompting Linda Freeman, one of the most careful observers of Canada's policies towards South Africa during the Trudeau and Mulroney years, to title her important book on the subject *The Ambiguous Champion*. "In the Trudeau years," Freeman writes, "the approach to South Africa was established early, reconsidered briefly, and then reaffirmed as an item of faith. The system of apartheid could be called detestable, worthy now (as it had not been in the 1950s) of denunciation in the appropriate international fora. Yet official support for full economic and diplomatic relations never wavered. Even contraventions of the UN arms embargo were led by a wink and a nod. . . . The pretense was opposition to apartheid; the reality was business as usual."[160]

The contrast between Trudeau's and Mulroney's policies towards South Africa could not have been more striking. Trudeau supported full relations with South Africa. Though no fan of apartheid, Trudeau was not about to upset the apple cart either in the Commonwealth or other international forums by beating the anti-apartheid drum. In contrast, there was clearly no moral ambiguity in Mulroney's own position towards the apartheid regime. Says Freeman, "in his first two years in power, Mulroney did more on South Africa than Trudeau had in his entire fifteen. . . . Indeed, it is a considerable irony that it was a neo-conservative Tory prime minister who ultimately challenged the nostrums of 'Whig' policy on southern Africa. On the sacrosanct issue of promoting a free exchange of capital and goods, Mulroney imposed concrete economic sanctions. On the issue of dialogue and keeping a light in the window for white South African regimes, Mulroney stated that this community had had more than enough time to come to their senses. On the question of violence, Mulroney stated that, while his government could not condone violence, it understood the reasons why political movements like the ANC took up arms. On the Cold War Alliance with white South Africa, Mulroney argued that the region and a future non-racial government in South Africa would be lost to the West unless it gave the black majority more support."[161]

Carleton University's Africanist scholar Chris Brown came to a similar conclusion in 1990 about the anti-apartheid policies that were staked out by the Mulroney government. Brown was particularly struck by the key leadership role played by the prime minister himself, especially in the 1985–87 period, when Canadians, in Brown's words "recoiled in horror from the nightly scenes of repression in South Africa on their television screens." He gives full credit to Mulroney for taking "the lead in establishing an activist stance on South Africa" and in "one area where Canada could make a difference." Further, Brown noted, "The extent of Canada's commitment was such that, if no change occurred in South Africa, Canada was willing to impose mandatory sanctions and cut all diplomatic ties. This bold proclamation henceforth became the measure of Canada's sincerity on apartheid."[162]

As Brown observed, Mulroney took his campaign against apartheid into the Commonwealth arena and wasted little time in introducing, shortly after taking office, a whole series of new measures, some of which were largely symbolic and some of which had real teeth, against the regime. They included, for example, a strengthened code of conduct for Canadian firms that were doing business in South Africa, a tightened arms embargo, abrogation of a double-taxation agreement that Canada had with South Africa, a voluntary ban on the sale of Krugerrands, a ban on loans to South Africa's public and private sectors, a voluntary ban on the sale of oil products, and an embargo on direct air links. Mulroney was also instrumental in creating an eminent persons group from the

Commonwealth whose goal was to persuade the South Africa regime to move to majority rule. With the collapse of that mission, because the South Africa regime refused to budge, Canada implemented further sanctions, which included ending the Canadian government's procurement of South African products, a voluntary ban on tourist promotion, and a ban on imports of agricultural goods and other commodities such as special steel alloys and wood products.[163]

A BUREAUCRATIC TUG OF WAR

Mulroney's point man on the South Africa file in the UN was also encouraged to use his bully pulpit at the UN to rally others to the anti-apartheid cause. In his 2007 memoirs, Mulroney noted that he had "stunned" the foreign affairs establishment by appointing former Ontario NDP leader Stephen Lewis, no fan of conservatives and the son of famed federal NDP leader David Lewis, as his UN ambassador.

Later, Mulroney also revealed in his memoirs Lewis's view of the bureaucratic reality he faced. "He [Lewis] is shocked at what he sees at the Department," Mulroney advisor Charley McMillan wrote to his prime minister after a discussion with Canada's rookie ambassador to the UN. "In-fighting, woefully weak analysis, no information exchange across departmental boundaries. . . . On several political issues—Nicaragua, South Africa, SDI, UNESCO . . . he feels analytical work is weak and indeed misleading. . . . And perhaps with good reason." Early in his tenure, Lewis endorsed a UN resolution "to end trade, military, and nuclear collaboration and nuclear collaboration with South Africa and to support liberation movements" only to discover that the Department of External Affairs had simultaneously issued a statement in Ottawa supporting dialogue with South Africa.[164]

The Department of External Affairs was, in Linda Freeman's unforgettable words, "a Hotbed of Cold Feet." There was little inclination on the part of Ottawa's senior bureaucrats to put human rights on a foreign policy pedestal. In the case of South Africa, officials also worried that Canada would find itself offside vis-à-vis its principal allies, Britain and the United States. Mulroney's increasingly strident challenge to Margaret Thatcher and U.S. president Ronald Reagan to take stronger action against South Africa sent real jitters through the bureaucracy. "The resistance to change," explains Freeman, "'grooved thinking' . . . in a commitment to the older policy of 'balance' and a real discomfort with economic sanctions; they touched a strong ideological nerve in the context of the government's commitment to free trade and open economic relations. In the early years of the Mulroney administration, officials in the Department of External Affairs continued to argue for constructive engagement, insisting that investment in South Africa did not support apartheid."[165]

The one notable exception was Roy McMurtry, who was appointed by Mulroney to serve as Canada's high commissioner to the United Kingdom (1985–88). Previously, McMurtry had served as attorney general and solicitor general in Premier Bill Davis's Conservative government in Ontario. (After his appointment in London, McMurtry would be appointed associate chief justice on Ontario, later to be elevated to chief justice.) McMurtry had to deal with Thatcher on a regular basis as Canada's envoy to the U.K. Carrying Canada's message to Downing Street and the Commonwealth was not easy, but McMurtry did so admirably and effectively.

LOCKING HORNS WITH MARGARET THATCHER

Although the bureaucratic tug of war continued behind the scenes, Mulroney pushed forward. Stephen Lewis marshalled his unmatched eloquence—both in public and in private at the UN—as Canada upped the political ante in joining the world's voices calling for an end to apartheid. A first round of Canadian sanctions levied against South Africa's government—mild, admittedly, but some with bite all the same—were announced by Clark at a cabinet meeting in July of 1985 in Mulroney's hometown of Baie-Comeau. At a minimum, it is hard to argue that Canada had not changed its tone.

The timing of this announcement was significant because the eighteenth prime minister was just weeks away from his maiden Commonwealth Heads of Government Meeting (CHOGM), scheduled to take place in Nassau in October. It was there, in the normally peaceful Caribbean, that Mulroney—like Diefenbaker before him in facing apartheid—faced his greatest Commonwealth obstacle on the file: the United Kingdom's prime minister. But while Diefenbaker had to deal with the gentle patrician that was Harold Macmillan, Mulroney had Margaret Thatcher, the Iron Lady, to contend with.

It is important to recall that by the time Commonwealth leaders met at Nassau in 1985, Thatcher had been prime minister for six years. Supremely self-confident and with her success in the Falklands War already a historical fact, she had little time for political "rookies" on the world summit scene, especially a young Canadian prime minister who was a neophyte. That view included her take on the new Canadian prime minister and his new Commonwealth supporters who were now calling on her to give her blessing to sanctions against South Africa. Decades later, in fact, in 2007, Thatcher revealed her views about leadership and experience to a visiting Canadian over tea at the House of Lords. "I recently met your new prime minister, Mr. Harper," she said. "He's awfully young and inexperienced."

"Well," the Canadian replied, "he's older than Mr. Mulroney was when he became prime minister."

"Yes, you have a point there," she answered.

"And Prime Minister Harper is much older than Joe Clark was when he became prime minister."

At this Thatcher laughed. "Yes," she said grinning, "and we all know what happened to him."[166]

In his 2015 study *Margaret Thatcher, the Authorized Biography: Volume Two: Everything She Wants*, British writer Charles Moore described his subject's attitude towards Commonwealth sanctions going into the Nassau meeting. "[The meeting] toxically combined all the things she disliked with the subject of South African sanctions," Moore wrote, "She opposed the idea of a Commonwealth contact group for South Africa and, of course, resisted economic sanctions: 'she had heard it all before,' she told the Canadian prime minister Brian Mulroney on the first evening at Lyford Cay when he argued for new measures. Sanctions 'would only damage industry which was in the lead in breaking down apartheid.' Mulroney . . . tried to win Mrs. Thatcher over by telling her how a British initiative over South Africa would make Commonwealth members 'all stand in line and salute.' Mrs. Thatcher was not tempted, believing, on the contrary, that the Commonwealth liked to treat Britain as a target, not a guiding star."[167]

In a footnote, Moore offers further explanation of his subject's attitudes and her private views of them. "One fact," he wrote, "that may have swayed Mrs. Thatcher towards high-handedness was her irritation at the pretensions of Commonwealth leaders less experienced than she. She regarded India's Rajiv Gandhi in particular as 'posturing and shallow' and believed that 'He and Mulroney were obviously keen to cut a figure at the meeting, but did not really have the experience for their self-appointed role.'" These comments on Thatcher's position, Moore reports, were made by her senior advisor Charles Powell.[168]

Still, the Commonwealth did not split completely, and Mulroney, joined by Rajiv Gandhi of India, Bob Hawke of Australia, and others, soldiered on. Right after the Nassau meeting, Mulroney made his debut address before the UN General Assembly in New York City. Sources confirm that in the original speech Mulroney was supposed to deliver, Department of External Affairs officials had carefully removed any reference to the use of sanctions against South Africa.[169] As Mulroney and Lewis sat outside the General Assembly Hall moments before he was to deliver his speech, they discussed whether Mulroney should reinsert the reference to sanctions. And, so he did. Mulroney's speech to the Assembly was electrifying. Delegates rose to their feet. They were stunned and exhilarated.

In a word, the speech transfixed not just the delegates in the General Assembly who had never heard a major Western leader speak so passionately against apartheid, but also many Canadians, even those who were still suspicious of Mulroney and his government's true commitment to the anti-apartheid cause. "My government has said to Canadians that if there are not fundamental changes in South Africa, we are prepared to invoke total sanctions against that country and its repressive regime," Mulroney declared. "If there is no progress in the dismantling of apartheid, our relations with South Africa may have to be severed completely. Our purpose is not to punish or to penalize, but to hasten peaceful change. We do not aim at conflict but at reconciliation—within South Africa and between South Africa and its neighbours. The way of dialogue starts with the repudiation of apartheid. It ends with the full and equal participation of all South Africans in the governing of their country. It leads towards peace. If it is not accepted, the course of sanctions will surely be further pursued. Canada is ready, if there are no fundamental changes in South Africa, to invoke total sanctions against that country and its repressive regime. More than that, if there is no progress in the dismantling of apartheid, relations with South Africa may have to be severed absolutely."[170]

It is doubtful that any other Canadian prime minister, up to Justin Trudeau and including Lester B. Pearson, has made such a clear and risky address to the UN and put Canada's reputation on the line before the world. In the Mulroney papers at Library and Archives Canada is found a letter in response to this address, sent to the prime minister by Liberal MP Brian Tobin, no political friend of Mulroney's during this period. It is worth repeating today. "As a Canadian, I am proud of the efforts you made on this nation's behalf to preserve the Commonwealth and to combat institutional racism in South Africa," Tobin wrote. "Your UN speech was superb."[171]

However, the sparks with Thatcher would fly, and more than once. At one meeting that took place between Mulroney and Thatcher at Mirabel airport—after she attended Expo 1986 in Vancouver in advance of the meeting of six Commonwealth countries in London that was scheduled for August 1, 1986—the two locked horns. Si Taylor, who was undersecretary of state for external affairs at the time, recalled, "with Thatcher you had to be polite, but if she wanted to savage you there were no holds barred." Mulroney, he said, "was rather old-fashioned from this point of view and was brought up to be polite. I think he found it hard to deal with her. At this meeting, she ranted on for about half to three-quarters-of-an-hour. She scorched him up and down and sideways. It was just because he opposed her policies on South Africa. She thought the whole of idea of sanctions was utterly misguided and she expressed herself in ferocious terms. I think he had difficulty responding. The contrast at the time was with people like Bob Hawke, Australian Prime Minister, who treated Thatcher as if they were having a fight on the wharf. And used language that was just as abusive. Mulroney could not bring himself to do that."[172] The conversation,as Mulroney himself recalled, ended abruptly:

> Mulroney: "You will do a disservice [with your position] to the U.K.,
>   placing it on the wrong side of history. I am putting
>   Canada on the right side of history."
> Thatcher: "We will see what history says about that."
> Mulroney: "You can bet on that."[173]

Taylor himself believed that Thatcher "got away with murder on that occasion." In fact, according to his recollection, "she was so violent her officials were a little bit alarmed by the effect of all of this. A couple of months later we went to London, we were received at Downing Street and again there was a private meeting. The first thing she said, to give her credit, was 'Brian, I understand the last time we met I treated you rather rudely' and she apologized." And, according to Taylor, "in the end she was affectionate towards him and he towards her. They eventually got on."[174]

On another occasion, Thatcher attended a private lunch at 24 Sussex Drive before the G7 summit in 1988. The ostensible purpose of the meeting was to talk about submarines because the Canadian government was about to embark on a major acquisition. The government's June 1987 White Paper on defence, *Challenge and Commitment: A Defence Policy for*

Canada, had included an announcement that the government would buy ten to twelve nuclear-powered attack submarines to defend Canadian sovereignty in the Arctic, including the territorial waters in the Northwest Passage. Canada was looking at French and British submarines because the Americans were opposed to transferring nuclear propulsion technology to Canada for both security and safety reasons. Those attending the lunch assumed that Thatcher would make a real pitch for the U.K. version. As Derek Burney, Mulroney's chief of staff at the time, recalled, "We went through the whole lunch and she never raised it. We talked about everything, including South Africa. Then just as she was about to leave, having said her goodbyes, she wheeled around and said, 'Now Brian, I understand you are about to buy some boats. You don't want the French because they are awfully noisy you know. She then turned on her heels and out the door she went!"[175]

The Mulroney government, politically at least, kept up the pressure, with the prime minister becoming, in 1987, the first G7 leader to visit the front-line African states that bordered South Africa. Canada also lobbied incessantly to have condemnation of South African apartheid made a regular feature of G7 pronouncements. But it was at the annual CHOGM, which had in recent years been tepid, rather anodyne gatherings with lots of photo ops, that the real battle about how to deal with South Africa's apartheid regime was fought. If the pot had come to a slow boil in Nassau, and bubbled some more in the private meeting between the two leaders at Mirabel airport in 1986, it boiled over at the 1987 summit in Vancouver, where Thatcher and the rest of the Commonwealth broke ranks. Not only did Thatcher refuse to implement the sanctions package that had been crafted earlier at Nassau, but she lambasted Canada for being a poor role model for others when it came to curbing trade with South Africa (there was more than a grain of truth to her assertion Canada was a poor role model). Her tone was vitriolic, and again she pulled no punches in dressing down the Canadian prime minister privately and publicly.

However, Mulroney fought back just as hard. In the presence of all the leaders at the Vancouver meeting, he went after Thatcher. He pointedly reversed the apartheid equation and asked Thatcher what her response would be if she was dealing with a country with a population of twenty-five million whites that was ruled by four million blacks. There were gasps around the room. Commonwealth secretary-general Shridath "Sonny" Ramphal was literally beside himself and astounded by the determination of Mulroney to confront Thatcher in the presence of everyone.[176]

In a bid to defuse tensions and move things forward, Canada proposed the creation of a Commonwealth Committee of Foreign Ministers on South Africa (CCFMSA), whose role would be to coordinate actions among Commonwealth countries against South Africa. Britain refused to join the group, leaving Canada, in the form of its foreign minister, Joe Clark, to chair it. But the group was not terribly effective, beyond issuing several studies on how sanctions could be strengthened, because Britain refused to change its stance of opposing any kind of sanctions. Nevertheless, as David Black, an Africanist scholar at Dalhousie University points out, "Clark and his officials attempted to use the meetings to focus more attention on 'reaching into South Africa to aid the victims and opponents of apartheid to promote dialogue, and counteract South African censorship and propaganda."[177]

CANADA'S PERFORMANCE ON SANCTIONS

Although the Mulroney government (and Joe Clark especially) went out of its way to curry favour with local NGOs and local church groups who were on a moral crusade against the apartheid regime, they soon found themselves coming under a blistering attack for Canada's less than stellar performance on sanctions. The Canadian Council of Churches, for example, openly criticized the government for is "lax" policy on South Africa, urging comprehensive sanctions. Stung by the criticism, the government pushed the CCFMSA to impose financial sanctions on South Africa by prohibiting any further loans. Even that proved too big a pill for the committee to swallow, and a diluted debt-rescheduling plan to was put forward requiring South Africa to accelerate its loan repayments schedules and pay a higher rate of interest on its $8 billion worth of loans that were coming up for renewal just before the 1989 CHOGM in Kuala Lumpur.

As Chris Brown further observes, "the Canadian government found itself subject to a string of embarrassments in 1989 as it struggled to live up to the inflated expectations created by Mulroney's UN speech." The first of these was a release of trade statistics just prior to the CCFMSA in Kuala Lumpur, which "showed a 68 percent increase in [Canada's] imports from South Africa and a 44 percent rise in exports to South Africa over 1987," because little was being done by External Affairs bureaucrats to curb trade and investment between the two countries. (However, these figures appeared large because of currency fluctuations between the two countries.) Matters were only made worse when the Bank of Nova Scotia announced, "a $600 million loan to Minorco, an off-shore subsidiary of the giant South African conglomerate, Anglo-American." A red-faced Joe Clark lamely explained that the loan did not violate the letter "of Canada's voluntary ban on private sector loans to South Africa, and was therefore acceptable."[178]

On the matter of South Africa's loans, there was more bad news. Thatcher had worked quietly behind the scenes with the banking community in the City of London to ensure that South Africa would secure its new loans on highly favourable terms. The announcement of this arrangement came just as Commonwealth leaders were assembling in Kuala Lumpur. Mulroney and those leaders who wanted tougher sanctions had been outfoxed by the wily and increasingly tetchy British prime minister. The whole matter exploded into full public view at the summit's conclusion: "Thatcher released her own declaration on sanctions . . . contradicting many key points of the agreed Commonwealth statement which she herself had signed. Mulroney denounced Thatcher for undermining Commonwealth cooperation while Thatcher found it 'astounding and appalling' that Mulroney would suggest that she should not explain her position publicly." The Canadian media wasn't charitable to either politician: "If Thatcher had 'willfully put herself on the wrong side of morality and history,' Mulroney's grandiose claims were 'pompous, self-serving and hypocritical.'"[179]

In the end, though, Canada was on the right side of history and Thatcher was not. The walls of apartheid came tumbling down barely a year later, beginning with President de Klerk's announcement in February 1990 of a series of political reforms that allowed the African National Congress (ANC) to be recognized as a legitimate political party, and of his decision to end the state of emergency and, most importantly, to release Nelson Mandela and other black leaders from prison.

THE ROLE OF SANCTIONS IN ENDING APARTHEID

Much has been written about the role of economic sanctions, as well as other political efforts to isolate South Africa's apartheid regime, in bringing about political change in South Africa.[180] This body of scholarship is relevant to the question as to whether Canada's own efforts to tighten sanctions and quarantine the regime, which were part of this broader effort, had any discernable impact or whether, when all is said and done, their effect was nil. Alexander Laverty characterizes this debate as follows: "Nelson Mandela, the first president in post-apartheid South Africa, believes the results from the anti-apartheid movement, sanctions, were effective. On the side that believes the anti-apartheid movement had no discernable impact on the dismantling of apartheid is the former South African President, F.W. de Klerk. When announcing the end of apartheid in his 1990 address to Parliament, de Klerk mentions the conflict and violence that had pervaded South Africa as his considerations for the ending of apartheid. With the end of Communism in Europe, de Klerk felt that that the removal of the African National Congress from the banned organization list was now reasonable, as they would no longer have any financial support from Moscow to continue their fight against the apartheid government. Eventually a negotiated peace was agreed upon and the first elections for all South Africans took place in 1994, resulting in an electoral victory for the ANC. De Klerk continued to deny the importance of sanctions in his acceptance of the Nobel Prize for Peace in 1993 in Oslo."[181]

However, after carefully reviewing the extensive literature on sanctions, Laverty concludes that Mandela was likely right: "The view championed by Nelson Mandela has a significant amount of empirical and scholarly evidence that would support his view that the international anti-apartheid movement against the National Party–led South African government was successful. Despite the campaign against apartheid not always meeting the requirements . . . for successful sanctions, the political and overall isolation felt by South Africans, which was manufactured by the global anti-apartheid campaign, made up for the lapses in economic sanctions."[182] He goes on to note that "Eventually the 'total onslaught' that the government and white society felt they were under, beginning in the 1960s, encompassed the riots caused by students within the country and the ANC's fight from exile. The international sanction movement against the South African government was the final push that brought the National Party to near bankruptcy and brought them to the negotiating table with the ANC. While each factor of 'total onslaught' played a role, the global anti-apartheid movement was a significant dynamic in causing the turning the tide against the white-minority government and eventually bringing to power a true democracy on the southern tip of the African continent."[183] In this respect, Canada's strident voice in the halls of the UN and around the table at the annual CHOGMs were seemingly more important than the half-hearted and incomplete economic measures that we took against the regime.

NON-GOVERNMENTAL ORGANIZATIONS AND THEIR IMPACT

At this point, it is also worth pausing in our consideration of Mulroney's work against apartheid to pay tribute to the many non-governmental actors in Canada who also marshalled their efforts and groups in the cause. While the Trudeau government, including officials in External Affairs, had felt constrained—by other priorities and by often justified fears of Canada taking the lead on an issue where its interests were conflicted, many Canadians were not so inclined. The Mulroney government's political actions opposing apartheid would not have been feasible without the ground-breaking efforts of thousands of Canadians, such as members of the United Church and its leadership.

Writing in *How We Lead*, Joe Clark makes this fact clear. "In the campaign against apartheid in South Africa," Clark wrote, "our government's indispensable partners were NGOs, including prominently the Canadian Labour Congress—not simply its then-president Shirley Carr and her senior associates, but rank-and-file members of across Canada. They had knowledge, authority and networks—through the Congress of South African Trade Unions (COSATU)—which Canada's excellent officials could not replicate."[184] In the same chapter, Clark mentions the overall sense of empowerment Canadians felt and demonstrated during this era on issues of developing world assistance. "In 1984–85, there was an . . . outpouring of citizen and NGO engagement when Canadians responded to the crisis of famine in Ethiopia," Clark noted. "CBC correspondent Brian Stewart, whose reports from Ethiopia galvanized Canadians, wrote: 'By December (1984) an astonishing two-thirds of Canadians were contributing money or supplies to African famine relief. In the end, this country supplied over ten per cent of all the international aid that flowed to Ethiopia and was probably responsible for saving more than 700,000 lives.'"[185]

And so it was that in early 1990 Nelson Mandela walked out of a South African prison. The next day, he spoke by phone with Mulroney in Ottawa. The former prisoner quickly agreed—with apartheid regime South African security agents listening in—to visit Canada and address Canada's Parliament not least because he had heard of Mulroney's vigorous efforts to end apartheid while listening to the BBC in his prison cell.

In June 1990, Mandela, soon to be the duly elected president of South Africa after non-racial elections, did just that, saying, "I would . . . like to pay special tribute to the prime minister of this country, Brian Mulroney, who has continued along the path charted by Prime Minister Diefenbaker, who acted against apartheid because he knew that no person of conscience could stand aside as a crime against humanity was being committed. Our people and organization (the African National Congress) respect you and admire you as a friend. We have been greatly strengthened by your personal involvement in the struggle against apartheid with the UN, the Commonwealth, the Group of 7 and the Francophone Summits. We are certain that you will, together with the rest of the Canadian people, stay the course with us, not only as we battle on to end the apartheid system, but also as we work to build a happy, peaceful, and prosperous future for all the people of the South and southern Africa."[186]

The rest of the story is well known. Mandela was soon elected the first president of his nation to be sent to South Africa's highest office after a non-racial election. Despite obvious tensions in his society after generations of mistrust and institutionalized racism, his success in ensuring racial peace in the transition out of apartheid will be studied by all peoples for generations to come. Again, Joe Clark in *How We Lead* gives us a description of Mandela's magic and an illustrative reason why Canada's prime minister was right to gamble so much on our nation's behalf for this man from South Africa. Clark recalled Mandela's remarks in Zambia in 1990 to ANC exiles from their nearby homeland. "He spoke briefly," Clark remembers, "expressing his profound thanks, and then took a question from an ANC veteran about how to deal with the Afrikaner leaders who had created apartheid and imprisoned him for twenty-seven years. Mr. Mandela's answer was: 'We have to understand how difficult all this is for them.' I have never, before or since—heard such generosity, which was profoundly genuine and a signal and instruction of the way to put the future ahead of the past."[187]

Some Canadian academics, however, are not so sure Mulroney and Canada deserve the high marks they usually receive for their work on the South African apartheid battle. David Black argues that "Overall, Canada's Commonwealth diplomacy with regard to South Africa was pivotal to the organization's overall effort, but that effort was ultimately limited in effects and effectiveness. Moreover, Ottawa's effort was always carefully orchestrated with several other sources of Commonwealth leadership, notably Australia, India, Zambia, Zimbabwe, and the Commonwealth Secretariat. Clearly, Canada did not 'prevail upon' the rest of the organization to adopt sanctions against South Africa . . . rather, it was catching up with other Commonwealth members, in particular the Australian Labor Party government of Bob Hawke." But as Black concedes, the Mulroney government also recognized that staking the "middle ground" was no longer a tenable option if the Commonwealth was going to survive politically: "In the past, Canada had frequently acted to hold the Commonwealth together by attempting (with considerable success) to bridge the differences between Britain and the organization's 'Third World' majority. In this case, however, it was clear that the Commonwealth could be preserved as a credible organization only if it were to take a collective position in support of sanctions—even if this meant isolating Britain. Thus, in keeping with Canada's traditional role, its diplomacy was aimed partly at Commonwealth survival in the new southern African conjuncture."[188]

In *The Ambiguous Champion*, Linda Freeman asks questions worth considering even now: "While pro-government South Africans regarded Canada as an enemy, anti-apartheid forces [were] compelled to reappraise their conviction that only the communist world and the Nordic countries cared about their plight," she writes. "In the view of one black South African journalist, Canada's anti-apartheid action had made it 'the conscience of the major Western governments.'" She goes on to state that "A succession of African leaders bolstered this perception. . . . Such are the events which have built the common wisdom about the Canadian government's role in the struggle against apartheid. Yet . . . even for the Mulroney period, the general view is simplistic and distorted, . . . Canadian policy was limited, and the claims made for it excessive. The Canadian state, no less than other Western states, was faced with hard and soft options in its approach to the regime in South Africa and with competing internal and international pressures. As in much of the West, its record is complex, ambiguous, and contradictory."[189] This description certainly applies to Canada's less-than-stellar performance on sanctions, which became the litmus test for just about everything else the government did or said.

Others, however, who were there, disagree with Freeman's assessment. Stephen Lewis, who subsequently forged a special personal relationship with Mandela during the course of his work to combat AIDS in Africa, reports that Mandela was unequivocal in his belief that Mulroney was fundamental to his release, and that he said so on more than one occasion. "On the tenth anniversary of our democracy," Mandela wrote in a personal letter to Mulroney, "one recalls the momentous time of our transition and remembers the people involved both within and outside South Africa. As prime minister of Canada [and within the] Commonwealth, you provided strong and principled leadership in the battle against apartheid. This was not a popular position in all quarters, but South Africans today acknowledge the importance of your contribution to our eventual liberation and success."[190] That letter has a point of pride in Mulroney's private post-politics office today.

LESSONS

Canada's relations with South Africa's apartheid regime are a textbook case of the internal conflict that sometimes arises between so-called "values" and "interests" in Canadian diplomacy. Both have their political, public, and bureaucratic champions. When allowed to run free, such champions usually fight themselves to a draw and result in a policy through which Canada plants itself firmly on the fence.

Mulroney believed that the policy of previous governments was wrong and that Canada could no longer sit on the fence. This was a case where Canada had to lead with its values and principles, even if it meant locking horns with Margaret Thatcher. But he encountered strong headwinds from officials in External Affairs who continued to view the world in various shades of grey, especially on the matter of economic sanctions and how deeply they should be applied and enforced.

If there was a fault to the policies of the Mulroney government, it really lay in their implementation and his government's inability to align itself completely with the prime minister's lofty rhetoric through tangible enforcement. This left Mulroney politically exposed when he took on Thatcher at the 1991 Commonwealth Heads of Government Meeting in Harare—not the sort of position any leader wants to be in when he or she adopts the moral high ground. And it was not just Thatcher who seized on Canada's double standard, but also Mulroney's domestic critics in the media and NGO community. If you set a high bar for yourself, you have to jump over it.

Successful policy implementation also requires standard bearers in the bureaucracy who won't second guess their political masters. Mulroney had those standard bearers on other files like free trade and the famine in Ethiopia, and they had a direct line to the Prime Minister's Office. Mulroney's principal standard bearer on South Africa was Stephen Lewis, his envoy to the UN. But Lewis only fielded a small battalion of diplomats in New York, and he ultimately took instruction from External Affairs headquarters, not the other way around.

It is also readily apparent that decision makers and their critics alike often don't know how their policies and positions are playing on the ground until well after the fact. As Mandela languished in prison, he took genuine comfort in the fact that key leaders in the Commonwealth, spurred by Canada and Australia, were finally breaking political ranks with Britain, the key backer of the apartheid regime. So too did his followers. Many white South Africans also increasingly came to understand that they were a pariah in the international community and that things had to change. Being banned from international sporting events also helped drive that point home.

Mulroney was often criticized for being too strident and too public in his criticisms of Thatcher, even though she gave as good as she got. But the deeper political symbolism of his remarks was not lost on much of South Africa's black community and its leaders, who went out of their way to acknowledge Mulroney's and Canada's role in bringing an end to apartheid. Mandela's letter to Mulroney said it all.

FIVE

Lessons from the Spittoon: Engaging Asia

"It does not matter if a cat is black or white as long as it catches mice."
—DENG XIAOPING, former paramount leader
of the People's Republic of China

CANADA IS FONDER OF ASSERTING ITS CREDENTIALS as a Pacific country than of doing something to justify the attribute.[191] Brian Mulroney, however, chose to spend a good deal of time and effort cultivating personal relations with key leaders in the Asia-Pacific region, notably in China and Japan, two countries that have an abundance of confrontational history as rivals for primacy in Asia. Attitudes of superiority and inferiority have created a clash between cultures that revere respect and recognition. The common denominator or glue for each is nationalism, imbued with pride. As arch rivals, they are also acutely sensitive to slights, intentional or otherwise, a truth underpinned vividly by their legendary descriptions—"The Middle Kingdom" and "The Land of the Rising Sun." Since the latter half of the twentieth century, China and Japan have also represented sharply different political systems.

These days each nation is, for different reasons, preoccupied with relations with the United States. China, now the largest global economy in terms of purchasing power, offers increasing potential for friction with the U.S. and Japan on trade and security. Japan, whose economic growth has stagnated for two decades, is caught between the need to expand its commercial ties with China and the fear of risking its security guarantees from the U.S. Japan is also obliged to adjust to the uncomfortable fact that China is now unquestionably the dominant power in Asia.

For Canada's government, the priority in Asia is still both China and Japan, but whereas Japan is seen essentially as an ally and a fellow G7 member that shares democratic values, China presents a much more complex package. There is optimism about the prospect of greater economic opportunity that is mixed with reservations, if not concerns, about China's territorial—some might say imperial—ambitions. The chronically dismal human rights record of China's totalitarian political system undermines public support in Canada for closer engagement with that country. Japan is seen in essentially benign terms despite the events of World War II, while China arouses some distinct allergies, not the least being its impact these days on housing prices in Vancouver and Toronto spawned by suddenly wealthy Chinese magnates—a problem that provincial governments have dealt with through the imposition of a special tax directed at foreign buyers.

With Japan, the perennial challenge for Canada is to divert attention in Tokyo away from Washington sufficiently so that the advantages of closer relations with Canada are seen to be attractive in themselves. In short, Canada today, as in Mulroney's time, strives to be taken seriously by Japan as a North American entity in its own right. With China, the task is trickier. There is a need to strike a delicate balance between the economic opportunities (which many Canadians see as lopsided in China's favour) and legitimate concerns about China's human rights behaviour and the threat its great power ambitions may bring to global stability.

During Brian Mulroney's term in office, Japan was very much in the ascendancy. Predictions were even made that its economy, not China's, would soon overtake that of the U.S. (Shintaro Ishihara's *The Japan That Can Say No* was a popular book at the time, as was Harvard scholar Ezra Vogel's bestseller, *Japan as Number One*.)[192] The fruits of Deng Xiaoping's reforms were fast taking root, but China was not yet seen as a threat—economically or in security terms—or as a major global power and rival to the U.S. for predominance in the Asia-Pacific region. Mulroney chose to emphasize his strong suit, interpersonal skills, to maximum effect with his counterparts in each capital—Beijing and Tokyo. He witnessed first-hand both the advantages and the complications of relations with each nation. His intense interest in all things political attracted him to the two distinct political cultures, as well as to the major Chinese and Japanese personalities of the day, but his determination to seek advantage for Canadian interests—primarily but not exclusively economic—was the rudder for his approach. However, the overwhelming priority he gave to major engagements with the U.S. meant that his focus on Asia was more sporadic than intensive.

CHINA

By the mid-1980s, China was beginning to move beyond the ravages of the Cultural Revolution, the "Great Leap Forward," and other manifestations of Chairman Mao Tse-tung's rule that had confined the once great civilization to the global backwater. The initial breakthrough for Canada—formal recognition of China—had been a major achievement by Pierre Trudeau in 1970. But, because of persistent internal disarray in China under Chairman Mao, little more than symbolism had improved in the bilateral relationship before the rise to power of Deng Xiaoping in 1978. Trudeau had first visited in 1960, and in 1968 he co-wrote a starry-eyed book, *Two Innocents in Red China*, which flatly and falsely rejected reports of famine in the nation at that time. He was not the only one duped, but over twenty-two million people there died of starvation in 1960 alone.[193]

Deng dramatically and virtually single-handedly opened China to the world, adapting basic capitalist or market-based reforms to the economy, particularly in China's coastal region, while maintaining firm political control under the ruling Communist Party structure. Deng's son, Deng Pufang had been treated at the Ottawa Civic Hospital in 1980 for injuries suffered during the 1966–76 Cultural Revolution when he was pushed out a window by Mao's fanatical Red Guards. He received no medical treatment until after Mao's death in 1976. Although he remained incapacitated following his treatment in Ottawa, Deng Pufang's life had been saved, and that provided an indelible personal connection for his father with Canada.

A key result of the reforms introduced by Deng was the dramatic expansion of China's steel production. This stimulated strong demand for iron ore from countries like Canada and Australia. Mulroney had visited China as a businessman when he was head of the Iron Ore Company and was keen as prime minister to promote deeper relations with the People's Republic. He went to Beijing in May 1986, a visit that came on the heels of the G7 Summit in Tokyo and also included a stop in South Korea.

Mulroney brought with him Alvin Hamilton, who, as a minister in the Diefenbaker government, had negotiated the first major wheat deal with China. Hamilton and Mulroney's ties went back a long way. When Mulroney was still a student, he had served as Hamilton's private secretary during the 1962 election campaign. This proved to be his introduction to western Canada and an upfront encounter with electoral politics. The future prime minister quickly shifted matters in favour of his candidate, volunteering to provide candid, first-hand accounts of the campaign, with some embellishment, to a leading Regina radio station, CKRM, in which he recounted mostly fictitious campaign stops from Ontario to New Brunswick in a manner that earned him a job offer, "if this law business doesn't work out."[194]

When he met with China's leader, Deng Xiaoping, the prime minister told him that Canada sought to emulate the mutually beneficial arrangement on wheat on a broader scope for trade. Deng readily agreed. The Chinese veneration of Canadians like Hamilton and Dr. Norman Bethune—a hero in the eyes of many of Mao's entourage, including Deng—was a distinct advantage.

Mulroney got direct insight into Deng's thinking during his private meeting. When asked by Mulroney what his greatest challenge was at that time, Deng's one-word reply, "Envy," aptly summarized the transformation underway and the challenges posed for China. While utilizing sporadically, but with pinpoint accuracy, the spittoon positioned between him and the prime minister, Deng explained to the assembled group, "Before, no-one in China had much of anything." Waving his hand for emphasis, he added. "Now, she has a refrigerator, but they do not. He has a TV; others do not, but everyone wants what others are getting."[195] Deng was literally moving a nation of one billion people through one hundred years of economic development in a single decade. His was an extraordinary achievement.

The aura of Mao was still evident in 1986, but the dynamism inculcated by Deng and the new Chinese leadership was producing tangible benefits for millions of people, notably improvements to the quality of life. Economic success stemming from more open market forces was also creating serious political challenges as well as much discomfort for diehard ideologues in the ruling party, for whom the slogans and doctrines of Chairman Mao still held sway. Not surprising, given that those among them who managed to survive the upheaval of the Cultural Revolution had enjoyed a better quality of life than most under Chairman Mao. (Deng, along with many fellow reformers had spent time in the early 1970s being re-educated on farms or in even less salubrious circumstances.) Deng was clearly taking his cue on economic policy from the stunning success of China's neighbours—namely Taiwan, Japan, and Korea—and harnessing the power of China's huge and industrious labour force to reach unprecedented levels of production, beginning a process that would thirty years hence have China on top of the world in terms of economic performance. One of his guiding adages was, "It does not matter if a cat is black or white as long as it catches mice."[196]

Turning to security concerns, and aware of the tense relations prevailing then between Beijing and Moscow, Mulroney asked Deng how many Soviet troops were situated along the border with China. Deng suggested that it was "more than one million." Mulroney then explained that, conversely, there were no American soldiers straddling the border with Canada. His point was that the U.S. posed no threat either to Canada or, for that matter, to China. "You can," he added, "do business with Canada and the U.S., without being concerned about our strategic intent." Deng also told Mulroney he was dubious that Gorbachev's approach to reform would work in the Soviet Union: "His mistake has been to begin political reforms before the economic reforms, so there is nothing to sustain them and nothing to keep him in office as a result."[197] His prognostication proved accurate. Gorbachev was gone five years later, whereas in China, economic reforms took root and the leadership remained in place long after Deng's death in 1997. Progressive political reform, however, has been piecemeal at best in China, primarily because internal unity is still the most serious challenge confronting the nation. The staying power of the regime is the uppermost concern, especially under President Xi Jinping who is consolidating his political control and cracking down on corruption.

Mulroney's discussions with Premier Zhao Ziyang focused more on foreign policy issues. Zhao had many questions about the personalities and the political system in Washington, and distinct concerns about the intentions of the Soviet Union. He also offered advice that he hoped Mulroney would transmit to Washington, and especially to President Reagan, about Chinese sensitivities regarding Congressional overtures to Taiwan and about the need for a "more even-handed" approach to the Middle East.[198] Mulroney explained that neither the U.S. nor Canada would ever contemplate actions in the Middle East that would diminish support for Israel. As for Taiwan, he advised that the U.S. administration should not be held responsible for comments made by individual Congressmen. Those were, in effect, examples of American democracy and their unique system of separating executive and legislative powers.

The most fundamental impression Mulroney gained from the first visit was that the reforms instituted by Deng were real, were catapulting China's economy forward, and in the process were generating genuine opportunities for Canadian exporters. Given the two nations' different political systems, there were, to be sure, fundamental concerns about human rights that could not be ignored, but direct personal dialogue between leaders worked as efficiently for Brian Mulroney in Beijing as it did in other capitals he visited. It proved to be the most essential ingredient for any constructive engagement.

Mulroney tasked his officials to develop a strategy of engagement with China that would "seize opportunities created by [China's] modernization drive" and "position [Canada] for the year 2000 when China will be a major world power with a GNP approaching $1 trillion." The strategy was outlined on March 16, 1987, in a secret memorandum to cabinet entitled *A Canadian Strategy for China*. It included *inter alia* recommendations to develop "a coordinated drive to promote Canadian trade objectives in China"; "to convene periodic meetings of leading business, academic and other China specialists to ensure that Canada's strategy towards China is based on a national consensus"; to create "ad hoc federal, provincial, private sector working committees . . . under the authority of the interdepartmental China Working Group to prepare action plans where Canadian capabilities match sectoral Chinese economic priorities"; and "to pursue co-financing arrangements with international financial institutions to lever greater procurement opportunities for Canadian companies." The *Strategy* also directed the secretary of state for external affairs and the minister of international trade "to approve a negotiating strategy for China's entry into the GATT [General Agreement on Tariffs and Trade] to bring greater discipline to Chinese trading practices" and ramp up academic, cultural, sports, and media exchanges while simplifying visa requirements to allow for such exchanges.[199] The plan was subsequently approved by cabinet.[200]

If charm was the watchword for Mulroney's initial visit to China, the Tiananmen protests in 1989 provoked an immediate and blunt response, underscoring the prime minister's profound personal concern for basic human rights. Students had begun massing in Tiananmen Square in late April 1989, ostensibly to mourn the death of Hu Yaobang, who was considered a genuine reformer. The demonstrators called specifically for political reforms, more democratic freedoms, and a crackdown on corruption. Coming on the eve of Gorbachev's visit—the first by a Soviet leader in more than three decades—the student protests posed a potential embarrassment or loss of face for the Chinese leadership. Deng Xiaoping labelled the students "counter-revolutionaries." This prompted sharp divisions at the top in Beijing, culminating ultimately in the ouster of General Secretary Zhao Ziyang, who had also been seen as a "reformer," and the rise of a real hard-liner, Li Peng.

Attempts at mediation with the students failed and, in early June, martial law was declared and People's Liberation Army (PLA) troops from outside Beijing were summoned. The armed soldiers shot their way into the square and violently cleared the area. Hundreds of students were killed and arrested. Some were executed. As much of what happened was aired on television, the Western world reacted with shock. Along with other Western countries, Canada strongly condemned the brutal crackdown on student demonstrations, imposed sanctions on business, cancelled all ministerial contact with China, and suspended aid contributions.[201] Special measures were also taken to assist Chinese students in Canada. Canada's foreign minister, Joe Clark, was the first Western foreign minister to denounce the "indiscriminate use of force against unarmed students and citizens" following the massacre in Tiananmen Square on June 4.[202]

In developing its "package of policies" against the Chinese, the government sought to make it abundantly clear "that the Canada–China relationship is on a fundamentally new footing" and that Canada was not accepting "China's international call for 'business as usual.'"[203] At the same time, the government did not want to jeopardize either programs that would be of direct benefit to the people of China or people-to-people contacts between our two countries. Regular updates on the evolving situation were delivered to the cabinet by Joe Clark, the secretary of state for external affairs. At one meeting on June 15, 1989, Clark noted that "after discussions with the Minister of Communications, he had made the decision to find a substitute for the film *The First Emperor*, which was to be shown as part of the opening ceremony for the new Museum of Civilization. It was felt that it would be too sensitive and controversial to show the film." At the same meeting, "it was noted that Radio Canada was to commence its Mandarin broadcasts into China on June 20, 1989, ten months ahead of schedule" in a "worthy attempt to transmit factual reports into the country" notwithstanding the fact that there was a high probability that such broadcasts would be blocked by Chinese authorities.[204]

The Chinese bitterly resented foreign "interference" in their internal affairs. They were focused on security and stability, not democratic freedoms, and this mindset presented what would become a perennial challenge for Western powers: how to balance fundamental concerns about human rights in China with long-term interests and aspirations. It is never easy to square that circle. Not only was the Chinese government action denounced in concrete terms, but Canada's prime minister also ordered an immediate opening for refugees to Canada, some fifty thousand, primarily from Hong Kong, earning for him and for Canada the undying gratitude of Li Ka-shing, a major Hong Kong business magnate and investor.

At the Houston G7 summit in July 1990, the Japanese attempted to have the sanctions against China dropped. Their relations with China were fraught with much history and were much more complex than those of other G7 states. The normalization process on relations with China were protracted and were, for Japan, a greater priority than concerns about human rights. Under the prime minister's instructions, the Canadian Sherpa (Derek Burney) was instrumental in holding the line with communiqué language reflecting a slight compromise: "We acknowledge some of the recent developments in China, but believe that the prospects for closer cooperation will be enhanced by renewed political and economic reform, particularly in the field of human rights."[205] However, Japan observed the undertakings more symbolically than in practice.

Over time, the sanctions were eased by all in the G7, and a degree of normalcy in relations with China was re-established. Mulroney was the first G7 leader to receive Premier Zhu Rongji, in 1993, a gesture that established another vital and enduring link with the newer breed of Chinese leaders. (Zhu's daughter eventually came to Canada to work at a major bank.) Zhu was from Shanghai—the home base of the economic reform group within the Chinese leadership. He, more than anyone else, emulated closely the policy direction and reforms of Deng Xiaoping.

In all his dealings with China, Mulroney followed a delicate balancing act between constructive engagement to advance Canadian economic interests when the environment was cordial, and assertions of concern when necessary to underscore fundamental differences regarding human rights. It is a pattern for effective diplomacy with China that resonates to this day, and one in which the tone at the top is the most critical ingredient.

JAPAN

Japan was also central to Mulroney's approach to Asia, for both foreign policy and domestic reasons. But there was a distinct personal dimension as well. Since his time as Opposition leader, Mulroney had been concerned about what he regarded as the unlawful internment of Japanese Canadians during World War II. On Pierre Trudeau's last day in Parliament, June 29, 1984, Mulroney urged him to "right an historic wrong" and render a formal apology. Trudeau rebuffed the overture, declaring that "it is not the purpose of government to right the past. It cannot rewrite history."[206]

Later, however, in September 1988, as prime minister, Mulroney presented a formal parliamentary apology to Japanese Canadians and established a $300 million restitution fund. He had been motivated by a poignant gesture made earlier by Bill Kempling, a fellow Conservative, MP for Burlington, and a WWII veteran who had literally walked out of Burma after serving on raiding parties behind enemy lines. In a moving ceremony in Parliament, Kempling returned the battle flag and some personal effects of a deceased Japanese soldier to the soldier's family.

Mulroney was not unmindful of the disgraceful way Canadian POWs had been treated by the Japanese in the Asia-Pacific theatre, notably those who had been stationed in Hong Kong. In 1991, Japan's Prime

Minister Kaifu had acknowledged in Singapore "sensitivity" to the suffering caused there by Japanese forces during the war. When Mulroney urged him to extend that acknowledgement to the Canadians who had suffered following the battle in Hong Kong, Kaifu readily agreed and confirmed publicly that Japan's actions had brought "unbearable suffering in Asia and the Pacific during the war on people . . . including Canadians who had served there."[207] It is never possible to right or rewrite history, or to know exactly where to draw the line for sins of the past, but acknowledging actions that violate basic principles of law or humanity, especially with some degree of reciprocity, can help alleviate the stain of each.

Mulroney's first visit to Japan was in May 1986, to attend the G7 summit hosted in Tokyo. During the official bilateral visit that followed, he became the first Canadian prime minister invited to address the Japanese Diet (parliament). He urged Japan to do more "in securing macro-economic coordination among Developed countries, in expanding the global trading system—the G 7 Summit in Tokyo had welcomed the launch of the Uruguay Round of Trade negotiations— and in promoting more equitable development in the Third World."[208]

Specifically, on trade, Mulroney noted that Canadians were "especially concerned to ensure greater stability and fairness in world agricultural markets," a statement nuanced presumably to balance Canada's devotion to supply management for dairy and poultry production with Japan's fierce protection of its rice farmers. Because there had been terrorist demonstrations at the summit, Mulroney also gave special emphasis in his speech to the threat of terrorism. This was long before 9/11 or the rise of ISIS, but his remarks resonate powerfully today: "In their indiscriminate slaughter of the innocent, terrorists demonstrate their disdain for common decency; violence and anarchy are their only accomplishments. They murder the innocent to terrorize the living. They make a mockery of the institutions and conventions so carefully nurtured to promote and protect individual liberty. The struggle against terrorism is a battle in the defence of our most fundamental values, a struggle to preserve world order and civilized conduct among peoples—a battle where there can be no neutrals."[209]

Mulroney stressed the need for *"nemawashi"*—the Japanese practice of cultivating or nurturing the root—as the basis for "an enhanced bilateral relationship" or "real partnership."[210] He made a conscious effort to cultivate close personal ties, especially at G7 sessions, with Yasuhiro Nakasone, Japan's prime minister from 1982 to 1987, an unusually lengthy term for a Japanese prime minister. The connection did not reach the level of the "Yasu–Ron" relationship that Japan prominently celebrated, but Mulroney's own close relationship with Reagan obviously helped.

During a subsequent visit to Japan in May 1991, Mulroney both publicly and privately endorsed Japan's claim for a permanent seat on the UN Security Council, a bold policy stance subsequently revoked by the Chrétien government. He also opened Canada's new embassy in Tokyo, designed by the Canadian architect Raymond Moriyama. Recognizing the growing importance of trade in the bilateral relationship (Japan ranked number two among Canada's export markets), Mulroney confirmed as well that five new trade offices would be established in Japan. (In the wake of Japan's two lost decades since that time, and with Japan's economy barely treading water, all five were subsequently closed in favour of openings in the much more rapidly growing China, a clear sign of the major shift occurring in Asia.) During the same Asian trip, Mulroney also spent five days in Hong Kong, sending a clear signal to Beijing—following Tiananmen—that human rights were a real concern for the G7. He was also determined to enhance both the immigration and investment potential of the island, which was then still under British rule.

Mulroney was both proud and fiercely protective of Canada's status in the G7. When, at the Tokyo summit in 1986, the Europeans, including Margaret Thatcher, tried to exclude Canada and Italy from the economic discussions, Mulroney fought back vigorously, saying in effect that there was little a G5 could do or coordinate that would be less effective under the G7 umbrella. "Canada is not asking for any favours," he added. "We're here as a major powerful nation that should be in the G7 as a matter of course, on our merits."[211] President Reagan ultimately resolved the debate, declaring firmly, "I don't want to be part of any club that doesn't include Canada."[212] That ended the discussion and the challenge to Canada's G7 status.

The Americans were themselves of two minds about the value of annual summitry. For one thing, they thought that too many Europeans were involved given the occasional addition of representatives from both the European Commission and the European Council, which granted Europe six representatives in attendance out of nine in total. At the Houston summit in July 1990, the Americans even suggested that the summits should occur every two years instead of annually. Following that summit and the attempted coup in Moscow against Gorbachev, President Bush (as the G7 host of the moment) invited Prime Minister Mulroney urgently to Kennebunkport to join him in a remarkable global teleconference with each of the other G7 leaders to try to develop a common response.

After the conversation both leaders had with Japan's Prime Minister Kaifu, and with the American aversion to summitry in mind, Mulroney asked whether the president ever considered just how important G7 membership was to a country like Japan, noting that it was the only international gathering that recognized or was commensurate with Japan's stature as the then number two global economy. Bush acknowledged that he had not really thought about that, but this exchange, along with the challenge emerging in Moscow, put the issue of displacing annual summitry to rest. It was clear from the president's own memoir, *A World Transformed*, co-written with Brent Scowcroft, that the point about Japan had registered. There, Bush lamented "the lack of courtesy" given the Japanese prime minister by G7 leaders other than John Major and Brian Mulroney.[213] He worried that this was "not only hurtful but could also be counterproductive for the G7." "Incidentally," he added, "the Japanese put great stock in G7 meetings, viewing them as perhaps the most important forum in which they participate."[214]

Conversely, as pressure mounted within the G7 to include the Soviet Union formally in the G7, the strongest resistance came from Japan—much to the consternation of German chancellor Helmut Kohl. The Japanese may simply have been concerned about "too many Europeans" as well, but their dispute over the Northern Territories seized by the Russians in the final week of World War II is a perennial thorn in that bilateral relationship and undoubtedly influenced their preferences. Gorbachev made a dramatic entry into the G7 summit in London in 1991—an appearance that Mulroney declared constituted "the end of the Cold War." This led eventually, albeit temporarily, to Russia becoming a full member of the G8. Later, following the invasion of Ukraine in 2014, Russia was expelled from the summit group. Canada was in the vanguard of those prompting the expulsion.

Yasuhiro Nakasone (prime minister from 1982 to 1987) and Junichiro Koizumi (prime minister from 2001 to 2006) were exceptions to what was otherwise an almost annual turnover of Japanese prime ministers, a practice that clearly limited Japan's effectiveness in G7 and global diplomacy more generally and contrasted sharply with the much more consistent political leadership in Beijing. It also clearly worked to Japan's disadvantage in managing its most sensitive bilateral relationship. Tokyo was persistently obliged to react rather than act on delicate disputes with China over island territories as well on commercial and security issues.

LESSONS

Much has changed in China and Japan since Mulroney's tenure. China has moved inexorably to great power status while Japan's economy has stagnated, thereby reducing its global significance. The bilateral trade volumes alone are revealing. In 1993, Canada's bilateral trade with China was $4.8 billion. By 2015, it rose to $85 billion as China became Canada's number two trading partner. Japan had been number two in 1993, when trade volumes reached $18 billion. But by 2015, bilateral trade with Japan rose only marginally, to $24 billion, and Japan slipped to number four behind the U.S., China, and Britain.

The striking contrast with Australia—Canada's natural competitor in the region for trade and investment—is also revealing. Buoyed by formal trade agreements with both Asian powers, Australia's exports to China reached $155 billion in 2015, up from roughly $4 billion in 1993. Even if Canada were to meet the objective of doubling trade by 2025, to $170 billion, we would be only slightly above where Australia was in 2015. Similarly, with Japan, Australia's trade reached $64 billion in 2015, almost triple that of Canada and up strongly from $27 billion in 1993. Investment flows reflect a similarly sluggish pattern for Canada versus Australia. Investment was roughly in balance between Australia and China for a total of $144 billion in 2015, whereas with Canada the total was $32 billion. In the case of Japan, investments with Australia totalled $292 billion in 2015. For Canada, the total was a mere $30 billion.[215]

What these numbers clearly reflect is that Australia has a distinct strategy and is less complacent about expanding trade and investment with China and Japan. One reason is geographic proximity. Australia does not have the luxury of being next door to the U.S. market, an advantage that has certainly served Canada well but that has also bred a degree of complacency in Canada, less zeal to tackle markets outside the comfort of the North American cocoon.

China today presents a hard mix of opportunities and concerns for countries like Canada that strive to strike a responsible balance between the two, but there is no consistent strategy underpinning our objectives. Team Canada junkets popularized by the Chrétien government had some momentary impact but not much in the way of follow through. The Harper government was ambivalent about closer relations with China and left few footprints. The current Liberal government has signalled a readiness to engage in a formal economic partnership, but the overtures are a bit tentative, in part because public opinion in Canada is sharply divided, with more negative than positive sentiments about a deeper partnership. The lack of serious engagement to date means that Canada has fallen sharply behind competitors in getting privileged access to the burgeoning Chinese market.

Japan's "lost decades" have not only reduced its potential for global influence but also altered its relative position in Asia vis-à-vis China and seemingly its interest in countries like Canada, which is seen essentially as a somewhat benign appendage of the United States. Japan is preoccupied with the U.S. even more now, given the security threats posed by China and North Korea. It was focused almost exclusively on ratifying the TPP even after the election of Donald Trump and his withdrawal from what had been agreed to. Repeated attempts by Canada to breathe life into the Economic Partnership Agreement (EPA), or essentially free trade talks, fell on deaf ears in Tokyo. The nation's obsession with Washington is paramount as Japan is now intent on negotiating a bilateral agreement with the U.S. Negotiations with Canada languish on the back burner. Getting any traction at all on bilateral relations is a persistent but unrequited challenge for Canada, especially after Canada declined to sign an agreement-in-principle on an updated TPP.

The Asia Pacific Foundation gave a more charitable description, saying in 2004 that Canada's relations with Japan were "comfortable but not dynamic."[216] The fact that Japan's foreign minister has visited Canada once in the past twenty years is indicative of the comfortable rut into which relations have fallen. Neglect is the most corrosive diplomatic disease.

There are some building blocks in place with Japan that offer examples to emulate. Manulife is the largest Canadian investor in Japan and the first Canadian life insurance company to launch a joint venture in Japan, one that has expanded to 100 offices served by 2,500 agents. CAE, a Canadian firm that is the world's largest purveyor of flight simulators and training, has a flight training joint venture with Japan Airlines and is the global leader in flight training, offering service in more than 30 countries globally. Two Japanese auto companies—Toyota and Honda—established highly successful assembly plants in Ontario, something that neither their

German nor their Korean counterparts—each of which enjoy strong sales in Canada—have seen fit to match. Canadian negotiators sought specifically to safeguard the position of the Japanese assembly plants in the free trade negotiations with the U.S.[217]

Both Japan and China have targeted investments in Canada's resource base, yet both share concerns about the seeming inability of governments in Canada to gain approval for infrastructure, namely pipelines, that would enable shipments/exports beyond North America. Canada's concerns about the competitive nature of Chinese state-owned enterprises (SOEs) have placed additional constraints on further investments.

Quite apart from the direct merits for Canada of more structured economic partnerships with Japan and China, there would be distinct strategic benefits from enhanced leverage or less dependence on the predominant U.S. market. By way of example, because the U.S. is Canada's only market for oil exports, we are obliged to sell our oil at a 30 per cent discount. One pipeline to tidewater would help eliminate this discount.

On a personal basis, relations at the top with both Japan and China during Brian Mulroney's tenure were cordial, with the significant exception of the clash over events in Tiananmen Square. Lacking were formal bilateral agreements that would have provided sinews and structure to galvanize action on major policy fronts, notably trade. All three countries were preoccupied with safeguarding and advancing their more pivotal relations at the time with the U.S.

Canada still has a long way to go to demonstrate convincingly that it is a genuine Pacific power with interests and capacities that extend beyond commercial matters. The approach taken by Brian Mulroney in tackling real substance on economic, environmental, and territorial issues with the U.S. offers a bold blueprint for any leader attempting to respond to the challenge of what is becoming Asia's, if not China's, century. For one thing, in a democracy, political capital is intended to be spent, and there are times when public opinion needs to be led, not followed. What is needed is vision and the political courage to pursue objectives that will deliver dividends.

If Canada wants to be treated as an Asia-Pacific power and something more than a North American attic of the United States, we need leadership, a focused strategy, and organizational zeal from the top, emulating what Brian Mulroney did to enhance relations with the U.S. It will not happen by osmosis or by sporadic visits that feature more symbolism than substance, but by emphasizing vision, persistent commitment, and pragmatic negotiations driven from the top. Given the relative power imbalance in place and the fact that other players like Australia have already moved far ahead of us, the initiative will inevitably rest primarily with Canada.

SIX

No More Dithering:

La Francophonie and the OAS

"Vive le Canada!"

—LAURENT FABIUS, former prime minister of France

IT WAS A HARD-FOUGHT CAMPAIGN. In the end, Canada won. But only after its candidate to head an organization that represents the French-speaking nations of the world had been subjected to a marathon round of job interviews with key leaders in Asia, Europe, and Africa, and four other candidates decided to drop out of the race. On November 29, 2014, Michaëlle Jean, Canada's former governor general, was elected secretary-general of La Francophonie. She had all the right qualifications, being a francophone, Haitian born, a superb communicator, and a former vice-regal representative of the Queen. She also comes from a country that is the second-largest contributor to the organization, after France.

Dial back to thirty years earlier. It was unthinkable then that Canada would join such an organization, let alone lead it. Although Canada was a member of the British Commonwealth from its inception, membership in a similar body for the French-speaking world was quite another matter. There were fears that membership would further stoke the fires of Quebec nationalism because Quebec felt it was owed a separate seat at the table. Prime Minister Pierre Elliott Trudeau, a staunch defender of federalism, was loath to allow Quebec (let alone any of the other provinces) to join an international institution, even if it meant that Canada had to stay out. His view, which was shared by senior officials in the Department of External Affairs, was that Ottawa had sole, exclusive jurisdiction when it came to representing Canada on the world stage.

All that changed after Brian Mulroney became prime minister of Canada. Under Mulroney, the nation took its own seat in La Francophonie, alongside Quebec and New Brunswick. Under his leadership, Canada also became a full-fledged member of the Organization of American States after years of dithering about whether it should take a permanent seat. Both decisions were controversial, especially in the ranks of the External Affairs bureaucracy. Today, membership in these organizations seems a natural part of the country's DNA, so much so that it makes one wonder what all the fuss was about. Why did Mulroney end years of equivocation by having Canada join both organizations? That is the story we take up in this chapter.

LA FRANCOPHONIE

At the outset, it is important to understand that La Francophonie only came into existence after Canada agreed to join the organization alongside Quebec and New Brunswick. That is because the French government under President François Mitterrand, who had developed a close friendship with the Canadian prime minister, was reluctant to create a forum for heads of government of French-speaking nations without Canada's presence.

The idea of a French commonwealth was not new. In the early 1960s, the president of the former French colony Senegal, Léopold Sédar Senghor, had pitched the idea of such a grouping to France's leaders.[218] Surprisingly, there was little pickup. The French government preferred to manage its relations with its former colonies on a direct, bilateral basis—taking a "hub-and-spoke" approach—because it was afraid the creation of a formal entity would dilute, not enhance, France's global influence. That was the certainly the view of French president Charles de Gaulle, who poured gasoline on the fires of Quebec separatism with his infamous "Vive le Québec libre!" rallying cry to an ecstatic crowd from the balcony of Montreal's old City Hall. At the multilateral level, France's trade and aid relations with its former colonies were also being managed through the European Community, which meant there was little appetite to add another layer of complexity to French diplomacy.[219]

When the French government invited officials from Quebec to attend a conference of educational ministers from French-speaking countries in 1968, all hell broke loose, as the invitation had not been cleared with Ottawa in advance. Quebec took the view that educational and cultural matters fell within its constitutional purview, even in the international realm. Ottawa was not only piqued that it hadn't been invited to the meeting, but it also took the position was it was solely responsible for representing Canada at such international gatherings. Quebec went to the conference anyway. Federal–provincial tensions were eased somewhat by Ottawa agreeing that Quebec could take part in the meeting as a "participating government" but not as a national entity.[220]

In the 1980s, France changed its position on creating a heads of government forum where the leaders of the French-speaking world could occasionally meet. France's new socialist president, François Mitterrand, felt it was time to do things differently. The French economy was not in great shape. Bilateral ties, especially with francophone Africa, were proving to be expensive. Mitterrand also believed that a multilateral forum would be a less costly and ultimately more effective way to promote French interests and cultural values internationally. But he also understood Canadian sensitivities on the matter and made it clear that France would only agree to establish such an entity if Canada could join after it worked out its own internal federal–provincial differences.[221]

Mitterrand also wanted to reset relations between France and Canada, which had been frosty since de Gaulle's diplomatic faux pas. He recognized that with the election in 1984 of Canada's new prime minister, Brian Mulroney, there was an opportunity to do so. As Lise Bissonnette, writer-in-chief for *Le Devoir* who later went on to become a columnist for the *Globe and Mail*, reported, "Only when the newly elected Brian Mulroney agreed to Quebec's presence at the summit did Mr. Mitterrand give the green light to the 40-country meeting. . . . The 'normal' but unusual relationship between France and Quebec is not suffering from the end of the Canada–France cold war. Since the federalist Robert Bourassa came to power in December, 1985, no fewer than 13 provincial Cabinet ministers have gone to France for official visits, and eight French ministers have travelled to Quebec City. The Premier of Quebec and the Prime Minister of France still meet yearly, to oversee countless 'accords' and 'ententes' signed over the past two decades in matters of culture, education, language, and more and more in economic fields, such as communications, energy, industrial research and high technology."[222]

On November 7, 1984, French prime minister Laurent Fabius arrived in Ottawa for an official visit at the invitation of the new Conservative government. As Mulroney recalls, "He [Fabius] was young (only thirty-seven), brilliant, and very close to President François Mitterrand, who wanted stronger ties with Canada and, if possible, a resolution of the thorny triangular question involving Paris, Quebec, and Ottawa."[223] At the state dinner held in his honour on his first night in Ottawa, Fabius made it clear where his government stood on the question of Canadian unity. "Vive le Canada!" he declared to thunderous applause.

Fabius's speech had been carefully crafted by the Quai d'Orsay well in advance of his trip. The message was clear and unambiguous: no more Gaullist chicanery to undermine Canadian unity. France wanted to see Canada stay together as one country. In return, Mulroney sent the message back to Mitterrand through Fabius that he too wanted better and close relations with France. He also signalled that he would break the internal political log-jam with Quebec so that Canada could join a French commonwealth and help bring such an entity into existence. As Mulroney wrote, "Pierre Trudeau's confrontational approach to federal–provincial relations—and Canada–Quebec–France relations in particular—had held up the creation of a French-speaking commonwealth of nations (what was later to become La Francophonie) for too long. That evening [over dinner] I made my views known. 'Six million of us,' I said, 'are immensely privileged to share with you the treasures of your language, and to live in the French culture. . . . We are not talking about simple nostalgia and folklore. Rather, we are talking about vital commitment and collective roots.'"[224]

Mulroney also made it clear that he believed it was "completely normal" for Quebec to aspire to have cultural relations with France, "as long as these relations respect federal institutions and involve subjects that do not conflict with federal jurisdiction." As *Globe and Mail* journalist Graham Fraser wrote, that speech "began the process of compromise and conciliation that made the first Francophone Summit possible."[225]

A year later, Canada, Quebec, and New Brunswick took their seats at the very first Sommet de la Francophonie, as it was formally called, in Paris. They did so after thrashing out an agreement that allowed the provinces to participate in international gatherings provided the issue(s) fell within their jurisdiction. Quebec's premier at the time, Pierre-Marc Johnson, was supportive of the arrangement, as were key leaders in the Parti Québécois, like Claude Morin.[226] But not everybody was happy. There were grumblings in the Department of External Affairs from officials who thought Trudeau had got it right—no provincial representation at international gatherings. Many federal Liberals were also unhappy with the new precedent that was being set in federal–provincial relations.

There was nothing down market about the first summit of French leaders. The meeting was held at the magnificent Palais de Versailles just outside Paris, evoking the grandeur and opulence of an earlier era when France was Europe's leading power. The Canadian prime minister was given a privileged platform at the summit (and was even invited to stay on afterwards for an official two-day state visit). In his prepared remarks, Mulroney spoke eloquently about the importance of the occasion, which had assembled the leaders of forty-one French-speaking countries and governments under one roof. "We cannot fail to recognize that we are," said Mulroney, "at this moment, participating in a historic event. There are very few examples in the history of international relations, or indeed anywhere in history, of an occasion where so many heads of state and government have come together in order to knit between their peoples the bonds of friendship which are already symbolized by today's meeting. . . . Canada comes before you, knowing that it can contribute a youthful, modern approach to La Francophonie, but one which is also imbued with pragmatism and tolerance. It is also proud of the reconciliation which it is achieving within its own borders."[227]

In his speech, Mulroney also stressed the importance of strengthening economic cooperation with developing countries, a recurring theme that he also pushed at the G7 summit of world leaders. He also talked about the need to fight apartheid in South Africa and pressed delegates to pass a resolution calling on the South African government to abolish its racially discriminatory laws, free all political prisoners, and lift the ban on the African National Congress.

But not everything ran smoothly at the summit. The Quebec premier, Robert Bourassa, went public about his views on international development assistance, weighing into the summit conversation in contravention to Quebec's prior agreement with Ottawa not to discuss areas of federal responsibility. Mulroney was furious: "I gave him [Bourassa] the cold shoulder during the rest of the summit. 'This is the kind of thing Trudeau predicted you would do,' I told him later in a frosty telephone conversation, when he called to apologize. 'This is why he wouldn't agree to summit, because he was afraid of people like you. There will never be another Francophonie Summit unless you give me ironclad guarantees.' As I told the press, 'You can only blindside me once.' A contrite Bourassa assured me there had been an 'error in communications,' and that no such lapse would ever happen again. In the twenty years since, it's been smooth sailing for Canada's involvement in the organization."[228]

All eyes were on the second summit of La Francophonie, which was held in Quebec City eighteen months later. Many expected that there would be more fireworks between Ottawa and Quebec City. Mulroney wisely tasked his ambassador to France, Lucien Bouchard, a former separatist supporter whom he had earlier courted to join the federalist ranks, to serve as president of the organizing committee and handle arrangements for the summit. Bouchard did so skillfully. In his interviews with the press before the summit, however, Bouchard acknowledged that he had to walk a very fine line. As the *Globe and Mail*'s Bertrand Marotte reported, "If he touts the international benefits Canada will derive from playing host to the three-day affair, he says he risks angering Quebec. But if he talks of Quebec playing a bigger role on the international scene, of 'affirming itself as a francophone community,' the rest of Canada bristles. 'We're stuck between the two. In the end, it's probably better not to say anything and just act. That's what we're doing.'"[229]

Because the summit was held in Quebec City, Mulroney invited Quebec premier Robert Bourassa to serve as co-chair of the gathering. It was an astute political move. Whatever differences there were between Ottawa and Quebec City in the run-up to the meeting, they were not allowed to erupt into the open and spoil the occasion. Mulroney went out of his way to acknowledge the "important role Quebec is playing at [the] confer-ence." When it was over, Bourassa called the summit a "diplomatic tri-umph for Quebec." Lucien Bouchard also assured reporters that "there are no conflicts between Quebec and Ottawa at the summit, contrary to some press reports."[230] For his part, "Mr. Mulroney praised Quebec Premier Robert Bourassa for 'showing great leadership' in helping bring the summit to fruition. The Quebec Government, he said, played a 'principal role' as host alongside Canada."[231] Mulroney also received a letter from Bouchard, who praised the prime minister for his initiative on the franco-phone summit, viewing it as a "catalyst for the global process that could lead to the formal adhesion of Quebec to a renewed Canada."[232]

The summit covered a wide range of issues, but Mulroney was keen to eschew the usual vacuous, tepid communiqués that typically mark such gatherings of world leaders and to focus instead on concrete results. One of the summit's achievements was the creation of an international television consortium of French television channels, the global network TV5, and the Institut de l'Energie to promote academic training, scien-tific research, and information dissemination on energy-related topics in francophone countries. The summit also passed a resolution calling for the end of apartheid in South Africa and for official recognition of the ANC. One of the most significant gestures was Mulroney's announcement that the Canadian government would erase the debt of participating African countries to help them with their economic development. Years later, Mulroney would recall that it was he who first proposed African debt forgiveness at the G7. Mitterrand wanted to do it but told Mulroney that "'[Jacques] Chirac is now my Prime Minister and he disagrees with me.'" "When we wrote it off," Mulroney said, "we were the first industrialized country to do so. All the other G7 countries were against it."[233]

Surprisingly, the only sour note after the summit was sounded by the "spiritual father of La Francophonie," Léopold Sédar Senghor, who was "pleased to see his dream come true" but nevertheless expressed "reservations about the priorities that [had] emerged at . . . [the summit]." In particular, he was worried that "La Francophonie . . . [was trying] too hard to emulate the Commonwealth with an economic and technical approach." He also said "there should be less infatuation with the glamor of computers, high-technology and communications, in favor of a more humble approach stressing two things: the development of self-sufficiency in agriculture and the spread of French language and culture through teaching."[234]

However, by the time of the third summit of La Francophonie, held in 1989 in Dakar, Senegal, whatever lingering frictions there were between Ottawa and Quebec City had all but disappeared. As Lise Bissonnette wrote, "The members of the troublesome Quebec–Canada–France triangle have forgone their usual bickering this year, while preparing for the first francophone summit in a developing country. Satisfied with the political benefits earned from the pompous, much publicized 1986 and 1987 meetings in Paris and Quebec City, France and 'Canada–Quebec' have agreed 'consolidation' is in order."[235] The summit agenda had also evolved to address broader political and economic issues alongside the more immediate concerns of developing countries. As Philippe Therrien explains, "The summit meetings are now divided into two parts: the first half of the meeting is devoted to discussions on the international political and economic situation and the second half to development co-operation. This format has confirmed the centrality of North–South issues while bolstering the influence and political cohesion of the francophone community."[236]

Mulroney believed that Canada's decision to join La Francophonie "meant a great deal to Mitterrand personally but also a great deal for Canada because Trudeau's position had been you can't trust Quebec on the international scene and so we are going to keep them out. As a result, this extinguished any possible intimate relationship. I remember Si Taylor (who was then Undersecretary of State for External Affairs) in the car one day [as] we were leaving a private lunch with Mitterrand, saying, 'when I served in Paris it was like serving in Siberia. We were totally excluded from the French circle of influence. Now,' he said, 'the President shows up at the Embassy for lunch.' So, we . . . really strengthened our relationship with the French and, of course, it gave us an impressive opening into French Africa. And we covered the other side with the Commonwealth."[237]

On December 6, 2016, the thirtieth anniversary of the first summit of La Francophonie at Versailles, the French government honoured Brian Mulroney for his role in creating the organization by conferring its highest civilian honour on him, making him a Commander of the Legion of Honour and the first Canadian prime minister to receive France's highest award. In the speech he delivered after being inducted into the Legion by Nicolas Chapuis, France's ambassador to Canada, Mulroney joked about the irony of a descendant of Irish immigrants receiving an honour that had been created by Napoleon Bonaparte to ensure the loyalty of French citizens to the emperor. But that was not the only irony about the evening. Canada's serving prime minister, Justin Trudeau, also joined the celebration as a mark of his own respect for and friendship with the former prime minister. He did not try to upstage Mulroney, but instead stood quietly by his side during his induction. The irony was that the prime minister's father, Pierre Elliott Trudeau, had strongly opposed giving Quebec or any of the other provinces a seat in La Francophonie. The elder Trudeau had also openly fought against Mulroney's Meech Lake proposals to revise the Canadian constitution. Time clearly heals some political wounds. It was a first-class act all around.

ORGANIZATION OF AMERICAN STATES

The annual parade of world leaders to the gathering of the UN General Assembly in the fall is always something of a spectacle, not least because of the ensuing gridlock in the streets of New York caused by fleets of black limousines transporting their VIP cargo down to Turtle Bay, where the modernist buildings of the UN overlook the East River. But the term "spectacle" was given an entirely new meaning when, on September 27, 1991, Haiti's newly, democratically elected leader, Jean-Bertrand Aristide, showed up at the General Assembly for his inaugural debut. The then UN secretary-general, Pérez de Cuéllar, reflecting on the scene that day, simply shook his head and said he had never in his life seen such a circus.[238]

Canada's foreign minister at the time, Barbara McDougall, who succeeded Joe Clark in that portfolio, was just ahead of Aristide in the roster of speakers. In her recollection of the events that day, Aristide "was the only head of government in the history of the United Nations to have a gallery." And what a gallery it was! "The public seats above the assembly were packed with Haitians who laughed and cheered and egged their leader on." McDougall further observes that "Aristide gave a lengthy and fiery political speech in French, English, and the Creole that confounded even the long-suffering UN interpreters, reinforcing the enthusiasm of his followers." The secretary-general was less generous in his assessment of the speech, calling it "totally incomprehensible." Nevertheless, "It was a remarkable experience to witness such an event," wrote McDougall, not least "because it demonstrated both how important Aristide was to the Haitian people, and how vocal the Haitian diaspora could be."[239]

A few months later, Aristide would be deposed as Haiti's leader in a bloodless coup led by the Haitian military. McDougall, in turn, would find herself deep in the midst of talks with Haiti's military in a bid to restore democracy. Those negotiations were directed by a group of foreign ministers of the Organization of American States (OAS), an organization that Canada had only finally decided to join barely a year earlier. It was a file that required a lot of heavy diplomatic lifting, not just in Port-au-Prince but also in Washington, where some of the real problems lay. Whereas the Department of State was keen to see democracy restored to Haiti—notwithstanding Aristide's reputation for being an erratic leader who was already displaying some alarming demagogic tendencies—officials in the Pentagon preferred to deal with the Haitian military and were likely providing "behind-the-scenes encouragement" to them. As McDougall further observes, "Although difficult to confirm, such a stance helps to explain why the military in such an impoverished country was able to sustain itself for so long in the face of damning world opinion . . . ."[240]

Eventually, Aristide was restored as Haiti's democratic leader. But it would take international pressure on Washington to focus on the crisis and use the threat of U.S. military intervention to get the coup leaders to stand down. Much of that diplomatic pressure was led by Canada's prime minister, Brian Mulroney, who worked the phones with the U.S. president George H.W. Bush. As McDougall notes, "Haiti was of genuine concern to the prime minister and his frequent exhortations, like water on stone, had their impact on President Bush. This was highly useful, given what seemed to be an inexplicable confusion in the U.S. position."[241]

Membership in the OAS had its price, and there was no escaping the commitments that came with it, which Canada clearly took seriously after joining the organization. But membership was a long time coming. As the Canadian diplomat John Graham—who served as Canada's ambassador in a number of Latin American nations and was the founding director of the Unit for the Promotion of Democracy in the OAS—caustically observed, "Canada joined the OAS in January 1990 after a half century of dithering."[242] Peter McKenna, a close observer of Canada–Latin America relations in the last century, was equally withering in his own assessment: "Canada's involvement in Inter-American affairs, particularly for the years 1910–1968, can best be characterized as irregular or inconsistent. Successive Canadian governments had blown hot and cold over the question of drawing closer to the hemisphere's principal political institutions—namely the Organization of American States (oas) and its predecessor, the Pan-American Union (pau). This seemingly 'on-again, off-again' disposition towards greater involvement in the inter-American system has engendered a panoply of confusing and contradictory signals—domestically as well as internationally."[243]

And hot and cold it was—though it wasn't just Canada's leaders or diplomats who poured cold water on the idea of membership. In 1942, the pau extended an invitation to Canada to join a special conference on defence that was scheduled to be held in Rio de Janeiro. But the invitation was vetoed by U.S. president Franklin Delano Roosevelt, who worried that Canada was too pro-British and far too removed in spirit and purpose from the Americas. Roosevelt was right. Canadian prime minister William Lyon Mackenzie King took a "cautious and go-slow" approach towards the possibility of membership in the pau, notwithstanding the entreaties of some countries with whom we now enjoy close relations, such as Mexico and Chile, and the fact that trade was also growing, especially during World War II, when we were shut out of European markets.[244]

At the end of the war, U.S. senator Arthur Vandenberg, the esteemed head of the Senate Foreign Relations Committee, publicly welcomed the prospect of greater Canadian involvement in the Western Hemisphere and expressed his hope "that the time may soon come when our continental fellowship will be geographically and spiritually complete through the association with us on some appropriate basis of the great and splendid Dominion of Canada." He went on to argue that "By every rule of righteousness she is eligible. . . . By every rule of reason we should wish her here. I would welcome the final and total New World unity which will be nobly dramatized when the twenty-second chair is filled and our continental brotherhood is complete from the Arctic Circle to Cape Horn."[245] Nevertheless, Canadians remained cool to the idea, preferring to devote the bulk of their diplomatic energies and attentions to the new UN, NATO, and the Commonwealth.[246]

With the founding in 1948 of the OAS—the first regional organization to come into existence, though others would soon follow—Canada made it clear that it did not wish to receive a formal invitation to join the organization, although many countries in the region welcomed the idea of having Canada as a counterweight to the United States. The general sense in Ottawa was that the OAS would provide little benefit to Canada and that the diplomatic effort was not commensurate with the result.[247]

When Conservative leader John Diefenbaker came to office in June 1957, both of his foreign ministers—Sidney Smith, who served briefly in office, and Howard Green, who succeeded Smith after his sudden, untimely death—were receptive to the idea of greater engagement with Latin America, including potential membership in the OAS. Green even went so far as to raise the issue when he appeared before a parliamentary committee. However, Canadian public opinion was divided. Some groups, like the United Church of Canada, were opposed because they worried about U.S. dominance in the organization, whereas labour and student groups were generally supportive. The idea even had some support among the opposition parties. But the prime minister himself was undecided, and when President John F. Kennedy, during his May 1961 visit to Ottawa, had the temerity to suggest greater Canadian involvement in the affairs of the hemisphere—a suggestion that took his Canadian hosts by complete surprise—Diefenbaker, who had taken an instant dislike to the young, charismatic American leader, was quick to rebuff the idea.

When the tables were turned and the Liberals took the reins of power in 1963 under Lester B. Pearson, little changed in Canadian inclinations towards greater regional involvement. For a brief, fleeting moment, there was a flicker of interest. Canada's secretary of state for external affairs, Paul Martin, declared in 1964 that "Canadian membership in the OAS is part of the ultimate destiny of Canada as a country of this hemisphere." However, the U.S.-led military intervention in the Dominican Republic in 1965 quelled whatever remaining inclination there might have been. The last thing Canadians wanted was to become embroiled in the turbulent politics of the region or be forced to choose sides between the interests of their powerful American neighbour and the countries of the region. It was far better, certainly in the eyes of their leaders, to remain aloof from a region where Canada had few vital interests and the public was generally indifferent towards engagement, including taking on OAS membership. As Heath MacQuarrie, a Canadian scholar and a Progressive Conservative politician who served in both the House of Commons and the Senate, explained, "Some Canadians are of the opinion that involvement in what they might call Latin-American disturbances (e.g., in Cuba and the Dominican Republic) would limit their effectiveness. Better, they believe, to keep out of these eruptions which, so long as they are not OAS members, do not concern them. . . . Some Canadians have [also] expressed fear that they might be placed in the position of having to disagree with the United States or, if they agreed, would be accused of acting as mere advocates for the U.S. point of view."[248]

The policy did not change much under Pierre Trudeau, who won the leadership of the Liberal Party and the federal election of June 1968. Prior to his election victory, the well-travelled and worldly Trudeau had signalled his interest in deepening Canadian ties with Latin America. The region was therefore one of the subjects of his government's foreign policy review in 1970. The review, however, did not recommend that Canada join the OAS. Instead, it called for "closer" relations with "individual Latin American countries and . . . elected inter-American institutions" so that it could acquire a deeper knowledge and understanding of the region when the day came that it might become "a full member of the OAS."[249] Canada did apply to be a member of the Pan-American Health Organization, and was admitted in 1971. Canada also applied to become a permanent observer of the OAS and a full member of the Inter-American Development Bank in 1972, applications that were also approved by the members of the organization. Notwithstanding Trudeau's official visits to Cuba, Mexico, and Venezuela, and his budding, close personal friendship with Cuba's leader, Fidel Castro, when the issue of Canadian membership in the organization came up for discussion, he demurred by saying that Canada was not in a hurry to join.[250] For Conservative leader Joe Clark and Liberal leader John Turner, both of whom served briefly as prime minister, membership in the OAS was not a priority either.

In the early days of his tenure, much of Mulroney's engagement with Latin America landed on the proverbial cutting room floor. As York University Latin American scholar Edgar Dosman writes, "In 1986–7, budget cuts closed the resident consul general's office in Rio de Janeiro, the embassy in Ecuador, and the permanent mission to the OAS in Washington (the permanent observer now operated out of Ottawa). The Canadian Association—Latin America and the Caribbean had collapsed in disgrace in 1985; the Canadian Association for Latin American and Caribbean Studies (CALACS), its academic counterpart, had barely survived a financial scandal and was only just alive. . . . With neither leadership nor co-ordination, a general pattern of competitive fragmentation emerged as each agency went its own way. CIDA (which benefited from the preoccupation with Central America and announced an additional $100 million in assistance to that area in 1988) and the IDRC seemed to be working without any overall foreign policy direction or framework."[251]

Nevertheless, there were good working relations with a number of key Latin American countries and the volume of trade with the region was growing, amounting to some $2.2 billion, with high value added to many of those products.[252] In the ranks of External Affairs, some key officials were keen to put Latin America back on the map. As Dosman notes, "Both the new assistant deputy minister for Latin American and Caribbean affairs, Louise Fréchette, and Richard V. Gorham, the department's 'roving ambassador' for the region and Canada's permanent observer at the OAS . . . proposed the drafting of a new policy document entitled 'A Long-Term Strategy for Latin America.' The issue, as presented to cabinet, was simply stated: 'Whether and how to give higher priority to Canada's relations with Latin America, including whether to join the OAS.'"[253]

During his campaign for the leadership of the PC Party, Brian Mulroney made it clear that "Canada should fully engage throughout the Americas." "We should join the OAS and take a position of responsibility in our hemisphere," he wrote in his campaign newspaper *Let's Win Together*."[254] Joe Clark, Mulroney's foreign minister, was also supportive of the idea of expanding the breadth of Canada's international engagements. As Mulroney recounted later, "I had spent a lot of time in Latin America because, as President of the Iron Ore Company of Canada I was also a Director of Hanna Mining in Cleveland, some of the Board meetings were held in Brazil. . . . So, because of the trips to Brazil and elsewhere in Latin America, I became quite familiar with [the region] before I came to Ottawa. . . . I wondered from time to time why I didn't go to this country or that country, you know in the time I was in office. Well, our agenda was so driven by East–West in those days— Soviet Union, U.S. and South Africa—that we missed a lot of places but when I got there it became apparent to me that we had chosen to amputate any influence, possible influence, or really friendships with the entire continent."

Mulroney goes on to recount, "I remember a meeting with the high officials of the Department of External Affairs, including Mr. de Montigny Marchand the Deputy at the time, and I said to them, why is it that we are not a member of the OAS, because if we aren't a member we can't have any influence down there, we can't build an alliance, and so on. And the answer that came back was that the previous government, referring to [Trudeau], took the position the OAS was completely dominated by the Americans and that because of that there was no role for us to play. So, I remember saying, well there is some truth in that, in which case I think we should probably resign from NATO and the G7, and probably the United Nations because of the influence the Americans had. Meanwhile, we are depriving ourselves of any influence whatsoever. Someone said, I forget who it was, maybe Paul Heinbecker at that time, said well there was a paper being prepared by Foreign Affairs. I said I don't need any paper. Join! Join the OAS right now."[255]

Brian Mulroney and President Ronald Reagan at the Shamrock Summit, Quebec City, March 1985

British Prime Minister Margaret Thatcher and Brian Mulroney in private conversation at the 40th Session of the United Nations General Assembly in New York, October 1985

Brian Mulroney with Prime Minister Yasuhiro Nakasone of Japan, at the 12th G7 Summit in Tokyo, May 1986

Brian Mulroney with Chinese leader Deng Xiaoping in Beijing, May 1986

Brian Mulroney meets with the leaders of the Front Line States, January 1987. From left to right: President Kenneth Kaunda (Zambia); Mulroney; President Robert Mugabe (Zimbabwe); and Quett Masire (Botswana)

Welcoming French President François Mitterrand to the Francophonie Summit in Quebec City, September 1987. From left to right: Robert Bourassa, Mila Mulroney, Brian Mulroney, and François Mitterrand

Conferring with Indian Prime Minister Rajiv Gandhi at the 1987
Commonwealth Heads of Government Meeting in Vancouver,
October 1987

Mulroney with Soviet leader Mikhail Gorbachev in Moscow,
November 1989

Mulroney with South African leader Nelson Mandela in the House of Commons, June 1990

Luncheon meeting of G7 leaders in Houston, July 1990

Mulroney confers with President George H.W. Bush following Saddam Hussein's invasion of Kuwait at the Bush family compound at Kennebunkport, August 1990. "Don't use the long bomb and see King Hussein."

Mulroney conferring with Prime Minister Laurent Fabius of France at 24 Sussex Drive at a breakfast interrupted by Mulroney's son Nicholas, November 1990

Mulroney meeting with US Secretary of State James Baker in Ottawa prior to the onset of the Gulf War, January 1991

Mulroney Conferring with External Affairs minister Joe Clark during a Gulf War cabinet meeting break, January 1991

Mulroney with German Chancellor Helmut Kohl during his May 1991
visit to Germany

NAFTA Signing ceremony, October 1992. Seated at the table: Jaime Serra,
Mexican Secretary of Commerce & Industry; Carla Hills, US Trade
Representative; and Michael Wilson, Canadian Minister of Finance.
Standing behind: President Salinas de Gortari (Mexico); President George
H.W. Bush (United States); and Prime Minister Brian Mulroney (Canada).

Mulroney, of course, was careful to take soundings in the region about Canadian permanent membership in the OAS before making his final decision. He spoke to both the Mexican and Venezuelan leaders, with whom he had developed good friendships. He also consulted with U.S. senator George Mitchell. Formal cabinet approval was finally given on October 4, 1989.[256] On October 27, 1989, Mulroney announced at the Meeting of Hemispheric Leaders in San José, Costa Rica, that the Canadian government "has concluded that the time has come for Canada to occupy the vacant chair at the Organization of American States that has been reserved for us all these years" and that Canada was "prepared to sign and ratify the Charter of the Organization." "In an age of interdependence," the prime minister went on to say, "the well-being of the peoples of this Hemisphere is indivisible." As the *Globe and Mail* reported, Mulroney "also dismissed other fears about participation, saying it is 'fundamentally silly' to assume that Canada will play a role subservient to U.S. interests. He cited Canada's continued relations with Cuba and Nicaragua as examples of independent foreign policy. He also rejected suggestions that Canada will be involved in narrowing the gap between Nicaragua and the United States. 'As the new kid on the block,' he said, Canada is not interested in playing intermediary between those adversaries."[257]

Two months later, the first real test of the government's endorsement of the OAS landed with a thud on the prime minister's desk. The United States had just invaded Panama to depose its leader, General Manuel Noriega, who was not only threatening the lives of U.S. personnel but was heavily involved in drug trafficking and money laundering throughout the region. As a stalwart ally of the United States, the Canadian government endorsed the U.S. invasion, a decision that did not sit well with the opposition and various interest groups. Liberal MP Christine Stewart accused the prime minister of putting Canada "way out of line in Latin America with his hasty endorsement. . . . There is no country in the world that wouldn't claim special circumstances in intervening. That's why the principle has to be absolute non-intervention."[258]

There was also a lot of fumbling by Canada's newly appointed ambassador to the OAS, Jean-Paul Hubert, who, as a *Globe and Mail* editorial sarcastically noted, reportedly shied "away from the suggestion that Canada supported the U.S. invasion; it had merely understood the U.S. reasons for military action." The editorial went on to ask whether "anyone [has] brought President George Bush up to date on our position since last Thursday, when he telephoned Prime Minister Brian Mulroney to thank him for Canadian support at the United Nations and elsewhere over the invasion? Where did Mr. Bush get the idea that we were supportive? It might have come from Mr. Mulroney, who went to considerable lengths in the Commons to catalogue the misdeeds of former Panamanian leader Manuel Noriega and to affirm his belief that 'the United States acted correctly in these particular circumstances.'"[259]

In joining the organization, Mulroney and his government faced a dual challenge. As John Graham wryly observed, the task was "[to improve] the Canadian public's view of the OAS [and its] image of somnambulance and irrelevance, as well as . . . demonstrat[e] that Canada was not joining a tropical version of the Warsaw Pact which would rubber stamp unattractive U.S. policy actions."[260]

There is little doubt that we rose to this challenge in spite of some early stumbles. One of the first things Canada did was to propose and then fund the creation of a special Unit for the Promotion of Democracy (UPD) with a mandate "to provide a program of support for democratic development which can respond promptly and effectively to member states, which in the full exercise of their sovereignty request advice or assistance to preserve or strengthen their political institutions and democratic processes. Canada was also a vigorous advocate, the following year, of Resolution 1080 (the Santiago Resolution) "designed to confer on the OAS the means for leveraging states back into constitutional democracy 'in the case of any event giving rise to the sudden or irregular interruption of the domestic, political institutional process of the legitimate exercise of power by the democratically elected government in any of the Organization's member states.'"[261] The resolution called for the suspension from the OAS by a two-to-three vote of any member whose democratically elected government is removed by force; it was the basis for OAS action following the coup against Aristide in Haiti.

LESSONS

Under Mulroney, Canada joined two major international organizations— one, La Francophonie, with global reach, the other, the OAS, a continental organization that was founded to promote regional solidarity and cooperation among the states of the Western Hemisphere. Both decisions were in most respects long overdue for a country that prides itself on its international memberships and longstanding commitment to the norms and principles of multilateralism. In taking the decision to join these bodies, Mulroney showed leadership and decisiveness. He was also prepared to take on issues that his predecessors had struggled with and on which bureaucrats had fought to a permanent stalemate, as in the case of both the OAS and the La Francophonie memberships. Mulroney understood that sometimes you have to cut the Gordian knot. In the case of La Francophonie, the problem was that Canada's French-speaking provinces wanted their own representation in such a body. Trudeau didn't want to touch that proposition, but Mulroney decided that it could be fixed with a formula that gave concessions to Quebec without sanctioning its separatist tendencies. He negotiated that formula with Quebec's premier, Pierre Marc Johnson, in a way that was mutually beneficial and was respectful of both Quebec's interests and those of Canada.

Another sign of an effective leader is that he knows his own mind. That was certainly the case with Mulroney's decision to join the OAS. As a candidate for Progressive Conservative leader, he had already made up his mind that it was time for Canada to take its rightful place as a country of the Western Hemisphere. OAS membership had been a hot (or cold depending on your point of view) chestnut in the Department of External Affairs for more than thirty years. Canadian officials feared that if Canada joined the organization it would become the ham in the proverbial sandwich, caught between an assertive United States and the other countries in the region that were deeply resentful of U.S. hegemony. When Mulroney decided to take the plunge, his government very quickly found itself confronting a major crisis, the U.S. invasion of Panama, in which we were indeed the ham in the sandwich. However, Mulroney did not shy away from supporting the United States in its actions. His close relationship with the U.S. president would also yield important dividends in the OAS's handling of the military coup against Haitian leader Jean-Bertrand Aristide a year later. Mulroney was able to lean on President Bush to make the U.S. government "come clean" about its position and eventually work alongside other OAS members—instead of undermining them—to restore democracy to Haiti. Mulroney understood better than some of his predecessors that choosing to sit on a fence is not a policy but a prevarication. You don't solve problems by ducking them.

SEVEN

Never Take No for an Answer—Acid Rain

"I believe you clean up your own act first before you can expect
major concessions from someone with whom you are bargaining.
The Government of Canada will be assuming its own responsibilities
so that we can go to the table with clean hands."

—BRIAN MULRONEY

O N A COLD OTTAWA EVENING IN MARCH 2012, Canada's then foreign minister, John Baird, stood before a group of distinguished guests on the elegant ninth floor of the Lester B. Pearson Building, the home of Canada's foreign ministry, to welcome and introduce his former boss, Brian Mulroney. Generally effusive and self-confident, Baird appeared more than a little nervous. He had begun his political life working as a young staffer in the Mulroney government as a protégé of Perrin Beatty, who was Mulroney's minister of defence. The purpose of the occasion was to celebrate the twenty-first anniversary of the sign-ing of the Canada–U.S. Air Quality Agreement. Normally, anniversaries are celebrated in milestone years. However, the twentieth anniversary had passed quietly without mention until somebody remembered. Better late than never, especially in this case because decades earlier, the problem of acid rain had dominated headlines.

In the 1970s, two Canadian scientists, Harold Harvey, a University of Toronto ecology professor and his graduate research assistant, Richard Beamish, were the first to discover what was silently killing lakes and trees on both sides of the Canada–U.S. border. The problem, as they determined, was caused by sulfur and nitrogen emissions carried in water droplets (and dust) that eventually landed in the lakes and bays of eastern Canada and the states of New England. Coal-fired electricity generation plants in Ohio, Michigan, Pennsylvania, Illinois, and much of the industrial heartland in the U.S. Midwest were the main culprits as they spewed their toxic emissions high into the atmosphere. So too were steel foundries, pulp and paper mills, and even cars. But it was not just Americans who were the guilty party. Canada's own pulp and paper plants and cities around the Great Lakes were also contributing to the problem, as were the coal-belching nickel smelters in Sudbury, Ontario, which rose almost a three hundred metres into the skies, spreading their deadly discharge hundreds of kilometres downwind.

The issue disappeared from the headlines because Canada was eventually able to reach an agreement with the U.S. on an aggressive action plan to curb emissions of acid rain–causing gases. It was, in the words of Canada's ambassador to the United States at the time, Derek Burney, "a very sweet victory," no less because "the acid rain issue literally disappeared from the bilateral agenda . . . becoming a model for progress on other environmental issues in North America."[262]

Much of the credit for this "sweet victory" fell on the shoulders of Canada's prime minister, Brian Mulroney, who coaxed and cajoled U.S. leaders to address the problem. Officials in Canada's foreign ministry and Environment Canada also deserve credit because it was they who handled the nitty gritty of negotiations. The Canadian Coalition on Acid Rain (CCAR), led by Adèle Hurley, also did a lot of the lobbying and helped sensitize Americans to the problem. The CCAR understood political power better than anyone else in the Canadian environmental NGO community, and they pursued that all the way to Washington. Hurley was ceaseless in her efforts (aided by the Canadian embassy) to mobilize those states that were most affected by other states' acid rain. One of the reasons for the U.S. decision to move eventually on the issue was the determined effort of the downwind acid rain states to get the administration to move. By the end, the domestic opposition to acid rain in the

U.S. was at least as important a force as anything that Canada itself could do. But as Professor Harold Harvey himself said in an interview with CBC Radio's Peter Gzowski just before the agreement was signed, Canada was "blessed with politicians who could see the seriousness of the problem and rose to it magnificently."[263]

BACKGROUND

Acid rain is caused when sulfur dioxide and nitrogen oxide emissions—created by burning fossil fuels, vehicle emissions, manufacturing, oil refineries, and other industrial activities—react with oxygen and water in the atmosphere to form sulfuric and nitric acids, and then fall to earth as acid precipitation. Although "acid rain" is the most common term, this process could also create acid snow, fog, hail, or dust. Sulfur dioxide and nitrogen oxide emissions can be transported by wind or air currents over a distance.[264] This is why American industrial pollution was such a big problem for Canada: an estimated 50 per cent of the acid rain that fell in Canada originated in the United States. However, Canadian smelters ranked first, second, and fourth on the list of North America's biggest polluters.

The issue was of growing concern to Canadians when Brian Mulroney won the leadership of the Progressive Conservative Party of Canada. By the early-mid 1980s, "[t]wenty percent of Eastern Canada's 50,000 lakes [were] thought to be acid-damaged. . . . Acid rain [was] a major issue in Canada, as the industries at risk (tourism, fishing, agriculture) account[ed] for almost 10 percent of the nation's gross national product."[265]

As Canada's new Opposition leader, Mulroney decided to go to Washington in June 1984 to meet with President Ronald Reagan. Acid rain, an issue that Mulroney heard much about as he travelled around Ontario, was very much on his own mind and those of some of the members of his caucus. Stan Darling, a Conservative MP, wrote to Mulroney just before his trip, urging him to bring up the problem with Reagan and secure his commitment to resolve it. "This is a high-priority problem facing Canada," Darling wrote, "and we will be on the side of the angels if we get onside rather letting the present government be seen as saviours of the environment. To date they have done bugger all as far as legislation is concerned."[266]

From the moment Mulroney became leader, every conversation he had with an American politician, from the lowest to the highest level, seemed to begin and end with acid rain. Some were receptive, others were not, especially President Reagan, who, as the well-known columnists Jack Germond and Jules Witcover noted, was an acid rain skeptic: "In the 1980 presidential campaign, candidate Reagan claimed that the volcanic Mount St. Helens caused more air pollution in a few months than automobiles in 10 years, that 'growing and decaying vegetation' caused most air pollution, that anyway it had been 'substantially controlled,' and in fact some noxious materials in the air 'might be beneficial to tubercular patients.' Breezes off the Santa Barbara Channel from an oil slick at the turn of the century, he said on another occasion, 'purified the air and prevented the spread of infectious diseases.'"[267]

The domestic political situation in the United States vis-á-vis acid rain was not much better. The politics in question were seen to be regional rather than partisan: Midwest/Ohio Valley/industrial states (including those with strong coal, energy, and auto industries) were strongly opposed to acid rain legislation, while New England states, where acid rain was falling and damaging the environment, supported it. But the numbers in Congress were tipped against the New England states. "'It is as simple as this,' [said] one senior Canadian bureaucrat who . . . argued Canada's case in Washington. 'Ohio has 22 congressmen; New Hampshire has one.'"[268]

During his first meeting with Reagan at the White House, Mulroney told the president that he could "capture the imaginations of all Canadians and Americans" if he were to reduce U.S. emissions by 50 per cent over the next decade.[269] As reported in the Canadian press, "The buoyant Opposition Leader emerged after 40 minutes spent with the President to report that the talks had gone well. 'I think he was quite taken with my enthusiasm for the proposition—I hope he was, anyway,' Mr. Mulroney told reporters congregated at the entrance to the White House."[270]

Those hopes were dashed when Mulroney returned to Washington on September 23, 1984, shortly after his own election as prime minister, to meet with the American president. His trip was not without controversy because relations between Canada and the United States had deteriorated badly under Pierre Trudeau, and many anti-American critics, including officials in the Department of External Affairs, felt that such a visit coming so early in Mulroney's tenure would send the wrong message to Washington. But Mulroney believed the visit was necessary to rebuild relations and put them on a firmer footing. In that, he was strongly supported by Canada's ambassador to Washington at the time, Alan Gotlieb, who welcomed the prime minister's decision.

In his meeting with Reagan, who was facing his own re-election in November, the prime minister discussed many issues. The meeting was warm and friendly because the two men clearly enjoyed each other's company. In Mulroney's own words, it helped him "firm up" personal relations with the U.S. leader. Mulroney also got Reagan's agreement to meet annually—a first in bilateral relations.[271] But on the issue of acid rain there was little progress. As reported at the time, Mulroney raised the issue of acid rain "only briefly" with Reagan and appeared much less enthusiastic after the meeting: "Brian Mulroney, Canada's new Prime Minister, said today that he made no progress this week in persuading President Reagan to move swiftly to curb acid rain. Mr. Mulroney . . . told reporters . . . that 'I can't tell you in fairness that I detected any major departure in his attitude.'"[272]

"CLEAN HANDS"

After he returned to Ottawa, Mulroney realized that he would have to take a different tack to elevate the matter with the Americans. First, he knew that he would have to keep the problem on the president's overcrowded agenda. He did that by getting Reagan to agree to the appointment of "special emissaries" to study the issue. But he also realized Canada would need to come to the negotiating table with "clean hands." That is to say,

Canada would have clean up its own act before asking Americans to do the same. Canadians couldn't be hypocrites and ignore their own contribution to the problem. This was an essential part of the pitch to action Mulroney made to powerful Congressional opponents like Senator Robert Byrd of West Virginia, who suspected that Canada's demands were simply a plot to help it sell more coal to the United States.

Mulroney also called on the provinces to make their own sacrifices in order to encourage the U.S. to act. At a news conference on February 1, 1985, he publicly stated, "[W]e did not go to any bargaining table on acid rain with clean hands. In point of fact, we are behind the Americans in emission control in many significant areas. I believe you clean up your own act first before you can expect major concessions from someone with whom you are bargaining. The Government of Canada will be assuming its own responsibilities so that we can go to the table with clean hands."[273]

The deal the federal government hammered out with the provinces was ambitious and far-reaching: Manitoba, Ontario, Quebec, and the four Atlantic provinces agreed to nearly halve their sulphur-dioxide emissions by 1994. (Combined, these seven provinces emitted a total of 4.5 million tonnes of sulphur dioxide a year, which would fall to 1.89 million tonnes a year.[274]) The cost of the program was not small—$1.5 to $2 billion over the next decade—but it was to be shared by the federal government, the provinces, and industry. Auto-emissions standards would also be tightened to bring them into alignment with tougher U.S. standards. Further, the federal government announced that it would spend $150 million to reduce air pollution from five smelters in Manitoba, Ontario, and Quebec.[275] Even the *Globe and Mail*, which was not always generous towards Mulroney, praised the prime minister for his leadership, noting, "Mr. Mulroney has resolutely headed for the high ground with a declaration that Canada will get its act together before further preaching to the United States. . . . Direct grappling with the problem, rather than waiting for agreement with the United States on a combined attack, was a sound move for a number of reasons. It is work that inevitably must be done (unless we plan to turn our backs completely on acid rain) and is unlikely to become less expensive. It also pulls the rug out from under an argument much favoured by those who lobby against any costly commitment to fight acid rain in the United States—that Canada's domestic effort is too feeble for its preaching to be taken seriously."[276]

SHAMROCK SUMMIT, QUEBEC CITY

In the lead-up to the March 17–18, 1985, so-called Shamrock Summit in Quebec City between Mulroney and Reagan—the first in an annual series of get-togethers during the years Mulroney would serve as prime minister—Canadian and U.S. officials agonized "over how to prevent a stalemate" on acid rain between the two leaders. U.S. officials, in particular, considered it to be "the dangerous issue." The administration wanted to make a "friendly gesture" to Mulroney because he was perceived as being more supportive of U.S. policies than his predecessor, Pierre Trudeau. They also were keenly aware that he had recently brought in tough new policies in Canada to curb emissions. The problem as they saw it was how to agree "on a joint statement that sends out positive signals on the issue without suggesting a significant shift in the U.S. position."[277]

One of Canada's congressional allies on acid raid was the veteran senator Robert Stafford. According to a Canadian Press report at the time, Stafford understood the Herculean task Mulroney had before him: "'The President is one of the most difficult people to say 'no' to that I've ever met,' he said. 'That covers seven presidents.' On the other hand, Mr. Stafford said he [understood] that Mr. Mulroney is a 'pretty charming guy' whose persuasive powers might rival those of the President."[278] Canadian officials were just as gloomy. A senior Canadian government official said at a press briefing on March 7, "the odds are very heavily against the Canadian government, particularly in view of budget constraints in the United States, regional and political divisions on the issue of acid rain in contrast to the unanimity of opinion in this country and the deep philosophical obstacles on the issue within the administration itself. . . . In the face of those odds we are not looking for a dramatic breakthrough."[279]

Less than two hours after Reagan arrived in Quebec City on Air Force One on a blistery cold "spring" day, the two leaders announced they were appointing a "high-level special envoy" from each country to hold consultations and make recommendations on acid rain before the next Mulroney–Reagan summit in spring 1986. The Canadian envoy was William Davis, former premier of Ontario; the American envoy was Drew Lewis, former federal transportation secretary. Each was given a symbolic salary of one dollar for the role. Officially, according to a joint communiqué, the envoys' tasks were to "'pursue consultation' on laws that relate to acid rain pollutants, 'enhance co-operation' in research efforts, 'pursue means to increase exchange' of scientific information, and 'identify efforts' to improve the Canadian and U.S. environments."[280] Unofficially, there were hopes that these two prominent, well-connected figures had the political clout and access to power players to end the deadlock. According to one senior Canadian official, "These two men are artists in politics and the acid rain problem requires artistry in politics."[281] But both White House and Ottawa officials attempted to temper expectations. White House spokesman Larry Speakes asserted, "The president has not changed his basic views on acid rain."[282]

Public reaction to the announcement was decidedly lukewarm. Michael Perley of the Canadian Coalition on Acid Rain said, "I do not want to comment on the individuals, but I think the concept of an envoy and continuing review or study is not what we need from the United States. . . . This is a clear message that the United States is not willing to address the problem."[283] Joel Sokolsky, a political scientist at Dalhousie University, observed that appointing envoys is "mostly symbolic. . . . But it does raise expectations, and it commits Reagan publicly to a high level of interest in the acid rain question."[284] Opposition parties slammed the agreement as an empty public-relations gesture. NDP leader Ed Broadbent put forward a non-confidence motion that was easily defeated in the House, 156 to 56.[285] Ontario NDP leader Bob Rae mocked the appointment, saying, "It's ironic they would choose Mr. Davis. This man was premier for thirteen years and was in a position to do an awful lot about acid rain, when in fact very little happened."[286]

In December 1984, Mulroney's environment minister, Suzanne Blais-Grenier, told senior U.S. and European environment officials at a meeting in London that acid rain was a "bilateral" issue rather than an international one, so it wasn't necessary for Canada to raise it at every international forum. But she was soon set straight on the matter by her boss. Questioned in the House of Commons, Mulroney confirmed that "serious bilateral negotiations" were needed to solve the problem, but he wouldn't disregard international solutions because "the matter is so serious that we will seek help and solutions anywhere we can."[287]

Blais-Grenier represented Canada at negotiations in Helsinki in the summer of 1985, where countries hoped to agree to a protocol to reduce sulfur dioxide emissions by 30 per cent from 1980 levels by 1993. Canada and nine Nordic and Western European nations had agreed to the goal in March 1984.[288] In an interview in April 1985, Blais-Grenier said she would encourage the United States to sign the protocol.[289] But at the meetings in Helsinki that July, the U.S. argued it should be exempt from the protocol because it had already reduced sulfur dioxide emissions by about 30 per cent since 1970, and Blais-Grenier defended their stance: "[T]he U.S. position is that they have already accomplished quite a bit of reduction [in air pollution] and I think the percentages that they've given today . . . are quite convincing." Predictably, critics pounced on this.[290] Canada and eighteen other countries signed the agreement on July 9. The U.S., the U.K., and Poland did not.[291]

THE ACID RAIN ENVOYS

On the bilateral front, the acid rain envoys met for the first time on April 19.[292] Throughout the spring and summer, they met with politicians, environmentalists, industry representatives, researchers, and labour unions, among others, and took field trips to power plants to see the "scrubber" technology used to reduce sulfur pollution from smoke-stacks.[293] But environmentalists remained skeptical about the whole process. Bill Davis acknowledged that he couldn't expect to go as far as they wanted, noting that any recommendations had to be "credible in this environment"—i.e., the political environment of Washington.[294] However, there were early encouraging signs when Lewis told a meeting of New England governors, "I will recommend the Administration acknowledge there is a problem. . . . Saying [sulfide] doesn't cause acid rain seems to me the same as saying smoking doesn't cause cancer."[295]

Lewis and Davis presented their forty-page report ahead of schedule on January 8, 1986. The report recommended the U.S. spend $5 billion over five years to study and implement new "clean coal" technologies; half ($500 million per year) would come from the federal government, and half from industry. The report explicitly linked industrial emissions in the U.S. to acid rain in Canada and the U.S. northeast. However, it did not recommend emission-reduction targets or specific measures, which the prime minister clearly wanted. Nor did it set any timelines.[296] The report also recommended that "a U.S. panel be set up under a senior cabinet official to oversee the $5-billion fund to demonstrate emission-control technologies."[297] The idea behind matching government funds to industry funds was to incentivize industry to find less expensive sulfur-reducing equipment, which would eventually reduce emissions. At the time, it cost more than $200 million to install a scrubber in just one smokestack.[298]

President Reagan released a statement thanking the envoys but reserved judgment, promising only to discuss the matter with Mulroney at their upcoming March meeting in Washington.[299]

Defending the report in the House of Commons on January 13, 1986, Canadian environment minister Tom McMillan said, "In the best of all possible worlds, it's not an ideal report—but it's not an ideal world."[300] However, a *Montreal Gazette* editorial was scathing: "In effect, the report would issue a licence to U.S. industry to keep dirtying the continent for another five years—at least. That's intolerable . . . on this important issue Canada—in the person of Mr. Mulroney—is being played for a sucker."[301]

On March 14, 1986, a few days before the prime minister went to Washington for his annual bilateral meeting with Reagan, the U.S. National Academy of Sciences released its "strongest scientific statement to date," establishing a "causal relationship" between sulfur dioxide emissions and acid rain.[302] Mulroney told the *New York Times* in an interview in Ottawa before his meeting with the president, "'In Canada one would have to be desirous of not knowing and not seeing to fail to observe the damaging effects of acid rain. . . . I mean, it's killing an important part of our environment. And just as surely as summer follows spring, it will ruin the environment unless we act. And Canada cannot act by itself." But the prime minister was careful not to put the problem in a way that would sour his good personal relations with Reagan: "'I doubt we will ever encounter a better or a fairer friend than Ronald Reagan,' he said. 'He's a great friend of Canada.'"[303]

Not much progress on acid rain came out of the prime minister's March 17–20 state visit to Washington, however. President Reagan and his administration were preoccupied with the situation in Nicaragua. Although the president gave his "full endorsement" to the envoys' report and, for the first time, acknowledged that emissions were tied to acid rain, he also said that "serious scientific and economic problems remain to be solved."[304] Nevertheless, at the state dinner that President Reagan held in Mulroney's honour, it was all smiles. As one reporter wrote, "Reagan— calling the Prime Minister 'my good friend Brian'—affectionately wished Mulroney a happy 47th birthday [March 20]."[305] "At my age" Reagan joked, "what can I say to a prime minister who is so young? Well how about good luck kid!"[306]

WASHINGTON VISIT AFTERMATH

After Mulroney returned to Ottawa, he and McMillan emphasized that Canada still wanted an accord on acid rain and had much work to do on that front, but he still considered President Reagan's endorsement an important milestone. As reported by the Canadian Press, Mulroney told the Commons, "'I never said our position and results on acid rain were a triumph. . . . They just appear to be a triumph given the lack of progress by the Liberals over five years. What we said is that there was substantial progress made.' . . . Mulroney said he had asked Reagan to cut American emissions of acid rain pollution but 'I can't persuade the unpersuadable.'"[307]

On April 29, U.S. energy secretary John Herrington told a congressional hearing that the U.S. might never fully implement the report's recommendations, and that the administration had submitted no budget proposals for the $5 billion commitment.[308] The *Globe and Mail* reported that Mulroney "is confident that Mr. Reagan will 'deliver the bacon' when it is time to live up to promises to clean up acid rain. 'I am in no way perturbed' by Mr. Herrington's comments. Mr. Reagan has promised an 'acid-rain program that is in place and a commitment which will be honored,' the Prime Minister said."[309]

Meanwhile, Washington was riveted by an investigation into lobbyist Michael Deaver, a former White House deputy chief of staff whom Canada had hired as a consultant on acid rain issues. The main question was whether Deaver began his lobbying efforts while still working in the White House. There were concerns that the connection to Deaver would taint Canada and the acid rain debate: "'The whole acid-rain issue is being smeared,' laments one U.S. environmentalist, reflecting on the exposure given Mr. Deaver's work for Canada on the subject. 'There's a sense the average citizen thinks there is something off-color about the acid-rain debate.'"[310] Deaver was eventually convicted of perjury.

PLAYING HARDBALL

When Reagan released his 1987 budget on January 5 it included only $287.1 million for acid rain mitigation.[311] Disappointed by the budget, the Mulroney government decided to play hardball. Environment Minister McMillan's reaction to the budget was swift and scathing. "The Canadian government must rethink its belief that U.S. President Ronald

Reagan cares about acid rain," he said.[312] Then, as if to rub salt into an open wound, the U.S. government announced it would sign an acid rain agreement with Mexico that would control air pollution within one hundred kilometres of the border on both sides, and would shut down a copper smelter in Arizona that was a major source of sulfur dioxide emissions.[313] External Affairs Minister Joe Clark wrote a biting confidential letter to U.S. secretary of state George Shultz that was leaked to the press: "The 'continued quibbling' by U.S. officials with ample scientific evidence of the problem's gravity, combined with 'lack of specific action' in the U.S. to clean up the sources of pollutants, 'calls into question the sincerity of the Administration' to live up to President Ronald Reagan's commitments, Mr. Clark wrote. . . . 'While the United States will be spending a great deal of money on clean-coal technology research and development, there is simply no information or evidence that this will produce significant reduction in transboundary pollution in the foreseeable future.' In addition, he said Canadians are baffled by Washington's recent announcement of a pollution agreement with Mexico when there is 'such reluctance to deal with a more serious problem on your northern boundary.'"[314]

GEORGE BUSH'S VISIT TO OTTAWA

Mulroney also decided to work on the vice-president, George H.W. Bush, who he thought, from some of his earlier meetings with him, might be an ally on the issue. He invited the vice-president to Ottawa for a meeting on January 20, 1986. According to a report at the time, "As a senior External Affairs official later conceded, the meeting was meant to catch the attention of U.S. President Ronald Reagan. 'We did not have any expectations of results or solutions during the meeting.' Insiders at the meeting said Mulroney and several senior cabinet ministers did most of the talking, claiming the U.S. administration had broken its commitment to combat acid rain and expressing a deep dissatisfaction with the low priority it is giving free trade negotiations. While Mulroney insisted he had no intention of lobbing 'verbal hand grenades' at the U.S., he was unusually tough in his criticism of the Reagan administration. A chilled Bush, who was obviously ill-dressed for the Ottawa winter [other reports describe him wearing a light raincoat and no gloves], conceded that on the issue of acid rain, 'I think I understood his position pretty well. And, yes, I got an earful.'"[315] Bush clearly had some influence. On March 18, Reagan committed the U.S. government to fund the full $2.5 billion specified in the envoys' report on technology to reduce acid rain. He also announced he would set up a bilateral advisory panel to oversee the U.S. acid rain program, and would launch a review of federal and state regulations to ensure further emissions reductions. This was widely seen as a conciliatory move toward Canada ahead of the president's pending annual meeting with Mulroney in Ottawa in April.

OTTAWA SUMMIT

On Sunday, April 5, before President Reagan landed in Ottawa, Mulroney told CNN, "[W]e need that kind of enforceable treaty to make sure that the damage that is so devastating is arrested and stopped. . . . Canada is ready and is in the process of cleaning up our act, but we can't do it alone. . . . [Acid rain] comes right from the heart of the United States. And either you stop it or our environment is going to be gravely affected. . . . And now what kind of a friend and neighbor would the United States be if confronted with this kind of evidence and it failed to act? Of course you have to act."[316]

The prime minister raised the idea of an acid rain treaty with Reagan at least three times during their first thirty-five-minute meeting, on April 5. The treaty would "lead to targets and schedules for a reduction of emissions on both sides of the border." It would be non-partisan and endorsed jointly by Parliament, the government, the White House, and Congress.[317] A Canadian official reporting on the exchange characterized it as follows: "The prime minister said 'Look, Ron, like it or not, a lot of people gauge the measure, the depth, of our relationship on matters like acid rain.

We're not asking for much—just say you'll consider it; that's all.'"[318] For the very first time, the U.S. president admitted that U.S. sources were responsible for 50 per cent of the acid rain in Canada.[319]

Reagan was to address a joint session of the Commons and Senate on the afternoon of Monday, April 6. In his speech, in material not included in his prepared remarks but written separately on two small sheets of paper,[320] he finally agreed to consider a bilateral accord on acid rain. Notably, he used the word "accord" instead of "treaty"—signalling a less formal agreement that, unlike a treaty, would not require Senate ratification.[321] Reagan decided to add the reference to the treaty after a "vigorous discussion" with Mulroney during a sixty-five-minute meeting in Mulroney's Parliament Hill office earlier that morning that was followed by a working lunch at the prime minister's residence at 24 Sussex Drive, where "senior Canadian and American officials exchanged proposals and consulted cabinet members after realizing that Reagan wanted some movement."[322]

THE FRUSTRATION CONTINUES

Mulroney was unexpectedly critical towards the United States in a speech he delivered at the Americas Society dinner in New York City on March 28, 1988, where he received an award for Canada's contributions to relations among countries of the Western Hemisphere: "Friendship has inescapable costs," he said. "One of them is bearing whatever burdens are required to avoid polluting your neighbour's property with destructive wastes."[323] He also told the largely business audience, "You are a major part of the problem and a vital part of the solution."[324] In an interview he gave for U.S. public television, as quoted in the *Ottawa Citizen*, the prime minister also expressed his frustration at the lack of progress on acid raid: "As much as Reagan has done for other aspects of the bilateral relationship, 'I'm not enchanted with the progress in this,' Mulroney said. 'We've cleaned up our act. We're saying as a friend and neighbor of the United States: You've got to have a treaty.'"[325]

At his final bilateral summit with President Reagan in Washington on April 27–28, 1988, Mulroney presented Reagan with an eight-point proposal for an agreement on acid rain. Secretary of State George Shultz was asked to study it and discuss it with Canada's own foreign minister, Joe Clark, "as a matter of priority."[326] However, a senior U.S. official downplayed the likelihood of reaching an agreement, saying only that Reagan agreed to "take another look" at Canada's position: "We have not bridged the gap on different views. . . . We have difficulty finding a basis for moving forward. . . . There will be no action on acid rain while President Reagan is in office."[327]

When Mulroney addressed a joint meeting of Congress (House and Senate) on April 27, only the second time a Canadian prime minister had been asked to do so (Prime Minister Pierre Trudeau was the first in 1977), he pressed the issue on his Congressional audience:[328]

> We invite the Administration, and the Leadership of Congress, to conclude an accord whereby we agree on a schedule and targets for reducing acid rain that crosses our border. The cost of reducing acid rain is substantial, but the cost of inaction is greater still.
>
> Canada will continue to press fully its case to rid our common environment of this blight—and we shall persevere until our skies regain their purity and our rains recover the gentleness that gives life to our forests and streams.
>
> I ask you this: What would be said of a generation of North Americans that found a way to explore the stars, but allowed its lakes and forests to languish and die? It is our view that economic development and environmental protection are not mutually exclusive, but are mutually reinforcing.[329]

Reaction to the prime minister's speech was positive. House Speaker Jim Wright was lavish with praise: "'This guy's a salesman, I'll tell you that,' the Texas Democrat told reporters. 'It was almost scriptural—he was a stranger and he took us in. What a personality he is. What a friendly person.'" Wright went on to say that Mulroney "'could teach lessons' on politics to Congressmen. Asked if that meant Congress would pass legislation to reduce acid rain, Wright replied, 'Well, I can't forecast what will happen, but he did a magnificent job representing the view of his country.'"[330]

During the G7 summit in Toronto in June, Mulroney and the other leaders discussed acid rain on the opening day of the meeting.[331] It also got a mention, along with other environmental concerns, in the summit communiqué.[332] But the prime minister, alas, had reached the end of the line with President Reagan. On September 14, 1998, after a four-hour meeting with Secretary Shultz, Joe Clark confirmed that the Reagan administration "refuse[d] to budge" on an acid rain agreement, and refused to consider a firm timetable or targets on reducing emissions.[333]

THE CANADIAN ELECTION—NOVEMBER 21, 1988

The environment became an election issue in Canada after a toxic warehouse fire in Quebec on August 23, 1988. The warehouse in St-Basile-le-Grand, just south of Montreal, was illegally storing 117,000 litres of the toxic chemical PCB. The evacuation displaced 5,200 people from their homes and the cleanup cost more than $30 million.[334] Although the 1988 election campaign was dominated by the issue of free frade, polls revealed that Canadians were increasingly concerned about the environment, particularly with its effects on their health. One Gallup poll showed "Canadians consider the environment to be a more pressing issue than the free trade-deal with the U.S."[335] Some two weeks after the PCB fire, on September 4, Mulroney called for a "national vision" on the environment in a French-language radio interview. (His exact term in French was "projet de société," which is used in Quebec to describe various society-wide goals, visions, and commitments.)[336] Environmentalists and election rivals suggested this was campaign-season opportunism. Mulroney's Liberal opponent, John Turner, called it a "deathbed repentance."[337] Commenting later that fall, NDP leader Ed Broadbent noted,

"While our lakes and rivers and streams were being destroyed by acid rain, the Prime Minister continued to put faith in his friend Ronald Reagan who did nothing about it."[338] For his part, Turner staged a campaign event at a maple-sugar camp in the Beauce region of Quebec, where trees had been killed off by acid rain.[339] All three party leaders ended up pledging they would negotiate a clean-air deal with the U.S.[340]

The election result was a landslide. Mulroney's Progressive Conservatives won 169 seats, compared to 83 for the Liberals and 43 for the NDP. This was down from the 203 seats the PCs had held in the previous Parliament, but was still a healthy majority. The Tories got 43 per cent of the popular vote.[341] Environment Minister Tom McMillan lost his seat in the election, but environmentalists were encouraged that Mulroney replaced him with Lucien Bouchard, a political heavyweight, long-time friend, and member of his inner cabinet. "Traditionally we've had [environment] ministers who haven't had any real seniority or importance in the government," said Michael Perley of the Canadian Coalition on Acid Rain. Bouchard travelled to Washington in the first days of President George H.W. Bush's term to meet with Senate Majority Leader George Mitchell and the new head of the Environmental Protection Agency (EPA), William Reilly.[342]

When the newly elected President Bush, who had just won his own election a few weeks earlier, called to congratulate Mulroney on his election win, they floated the idea of an informal meeting before Bush's inauguration.[343] Bush also indicated the week before his inauguration that he intended to continue Reagan's practice of annual summit meetings with the Canadian PM and that he wanted to meet Mulroney "very early" in his term. "We're not going to take for granted our neighbours to the north or to the south," he told a news conference.[344]

BREAKTHROUGH WITH BUSH

On Bush's first Monday in office, the administration confirmed that it would find new money for acid rain controls. "You'll see a new approach to acid rain from this administration," the new secretary of state, James Baker, told congressmen.[345] This was a reversal from Reagan's last budget.[346] William Reilly, the new EPA head, promised in his Senate confirmation hearing that acid rain would be a priority for the Bush administration. He said acid rain controls would be "first out of the box. . . . It's getting very heavy, sustained attention right now."[347] Reilly had previously been a professional environmentalist, including doing a stint with the World Wildlife Fund.[348] But he was also an honest man and became a determined advocate for action within the administration. He also asked the Environmental Defence Fund to develop the cap and trade regime that harnessed the market to deliver the SO_2 reductions promised in the U.S.–Canadian agreement. The regime would eventually produce the highest compliance rate of any EPA regulation before or since, and would become the model for the European emissions trading system and the California/Quebec/Ontario system. Not to mention that the Chinese are implementing a similar system for the whole country, to be in place by 2020.

Bush's first foreign visit as president would be to Ottawa. Bush's summit style was much less flashy than Reagan's. He made it known he preferred low-key meetings, as opposed to nineteen-gun salutes, musical numbers, and other forms of pomp and ceremony. His officials warned they would not be announcing any major agreements on acid rain at the summit, wanting to sort out U.S. domestic policy first. But Canadian officials still intended to push the issue. One senior government official said, "If the Americans don't bring it up the first five minutes, we will." Another said, "'The prime minister will never be satisfied until we have an acid rain agreement' with the U.S."[349] The night before he flew to Ottawa, Bush made a budget address to Congress in which he reiterated his intention to move quickly on acid rain. He offered "significant" cuts by "specific" dates, but no details.

Bush and Mulroney met at a guest house on the grounds of Rideau Hall, before continuing their talks over a working lunch across the street at 24 Sussex Drive, the prime minister's residence. As expected, there were no firm commitments coming out of the meeting, but Bush said he would negotiate with Canada on a bilateral acid-rain agreement and reiterated his intention to introduce a new clean-air bill, as he had told Congress the night before. The Canadian reaction was largely positive.[350] Asked for a timetable, Bush replied, "I had in mind as fast as possible." Canada's prime minister was approving in his own remarks, but his impatience still came through: "I'm like a lot of people who would like it done yesterday."[351] As reported at the time,

> The air of harmony and good humor prevailed earlier at a brief, informal news conference they held outside the Prime Minister's residence at 24 Sussex Dr. when their talks ended.
>
> After Mr. Mulroney proposed in French that they would accept one final question, Mr. Bush quipped: 'C'est fine pour moi,' adding quickly 'it's colder than hell out here,' as the leaders answered questions on a clear, sunny, minus 12-degree day.
>
> In response, Mr. Mulroney joked: "May I introduce my Quebec lieutenant."[352]

Once it became clear that Bush wanted to act on acid rain, Canadian politicians and environmental activists were divided on whether it would be more effective to get a bilateral agreement or to secure U.S. legislation. The Ontario government and many environmentalists emphasized the need for legislation, while the Mulroney government called for an accord to hold the U.S. government to account under international law—something that would be enforceable even if a new government came in and enacted new legislation. In the end, Canada got both.

Progress in the U.S. also came slowly at first as, at least initially, the Bush administration (via the EPA) and Congress each waited for the other to make the first move on acid rain legislation. U.S. officials emphasized that they would not start negotiations with Canada before they got a sense of what shape domestic legislation would take.[353]

MULRONEY'S U.S. TRIP

In his official visit to meet with the new president, Mulroney began his May 1989 trip by first going to Boston, where he met with Michael Dukakis—who had enacted tough acid rain controls in Massachusetts as governor and had also run for the presidency the previous year against George H.W. Bush—and Senator Ted Kennedy. Both offered encouragement to Mulroney's acid rain quest. Mulroney said, "I've been fighting a fight for a long time down here. . . . It's nice to be getting this kind of response."[354] As soon as he got to Washington, Mulroney met with Senate Majority Leader George Mitchell and other senators, who also endorsed his plans to push for an accord. Mitchell said, "In fact, the negotiations on an agreement would help us move legislation (through Congress) and would serve as a stimulus to action by the administration."[355]

When Mulroney met with the American president on May 4, Bush was quick to comment on his counterpart's persistence: "'If there is anything the Prime Minister of Canada has been clear with me about . . . it is this subject,' Bush said. 'He forcefully brings it up and I tell him where we stand.'"[356] However, after the meeting, as Bush and Mulroney spoke to reporters on the South Lawn of the White House, Bush appeared to back off the commitment to a treaty: "There will be great progress made [on reducing acid rain]. Whether the treaty proves to be the vehicle for demonstrating this progress, I don't know and I can't say."[357] A senior Canadian official also sounded a skeptical note in comments to reporters: "'certainly the people we talk to tell us we're going to get what we want.' But, he added, 'until we see it, touch it, sign it, I'm not going to sell tickets to it.'"[358] Both Canadian and American officials hastened to reassure the public that Bush was still on board with a treaty.[359]

Less than two weeks after Bush and Mulroney met in Washington, Bouchard announced that Canada would, in fact, begin negotiating an accord with the U.S. as early as June. In a surprise development, he said he and Reilly agreed to begin negotiations once the EPA bill was introduced, not after it was enacted, as previously suggested.[360] On June 12, Bush unveiled his proposed amendments to the Clean Air Act, which included measures to halve acid rain–causing emissions reaching Canada from 1980 levels by 2000, along with other measures to tackle air pollution. (Sulphur dioxide emissions would be reduced by 40 per cent, and nitrogen oxide emissions by 10 per cent.)[361] The act targeted 107 coal-burning power plants, the bulk of them in Ohio, Indiana, Illinois, and Pennsylvania—considered prime sources for Canadian acid rain. Power plants could reduce sulphur emissions by installing scrubbers, switching to a cleaner power generation method, or engaging in an emissions trading/ credit scheme.[362] Under the act, five million tonnes of emissions would be cut by 1995, which was projected to cut acid rain damage to "sensitive Canadian areas" by up to 90 per cent.[363] "I think we've met Canada's goals and needs," said Reilly.[364]

At a speech at the Canadian Club in Toronto on June 28, Mitchell pressed for a bilateral accord that would ensure compliance from both sides to secure a "permanent" reduction in acid rain.[365] Preliminary bilateral talks on the accord—which officials took pains to describe as not negotiations but "informal discussions" laying the groundwork for future negotiations—were held in Ottawa on July 24.[366]

HOLIDAY IN KENNEBUNKPORT

Bush invited Mulroney and his family for a private visit to his summer holiday home at Walker's Point in Kennebunkport, Maine, over the Labour Day weekend. The leaders enjoyed boating, fishing, and games of horseshoes, but also spent time discussing acid rain, among other bilateral and international policy issues.

In a joint news conference, Mulroney told reporters he would "not be satisfied the issue is resolved until President Bush and I sit down and sign a bilateral clean air accord."[367] According to the *Globe and Mail*, Bush said he could "talk frankly with Mr. Mulroney and described their meeting—their second one-on-one session this year—as 'an unusually productive visit.'"[368] Earlier, Bush commented at a community event, "Foreign policy is not determined on whether a foreign leader likes you or not, but I think it makes a difference if you can develop a good personal relationship."[369]

Beginning in October, a House of Representatives committee agreed to expand California's strict auto emissions standards to the rest of the U.S. California's standards were tougher than those outlined in Bush's proposed Clean Air Act. The move was seen as a milestone that could clear the way for the act—including its acid rain provisions—to become law.[370] In Canada, Bouchard and the provincial environment ministers agreed soon after to bring in the same tough California standards across Canada. Canada had lagged behind the U.S. on auto emissions, a major source of acid rain–causing nitrogen oxides.[371] In his State of the Union address, Bush asked Congress to move quickly to pass the clean-air legislation: "'The American people did not send us here to bicker,' Bush said, citing months of impasse in Congress over the sweeping clean-air bill he sent the legislature last spring. 'There's work to do and they sent us here to get it done.'"[372]

THE "BASEBALL SUMMIT" IN TORONTO

In early April of the following year, Bush and Mulroney met at the SkyDome (now Rogers Centre) in Toronto for a few hours of talks, before throwing out the opening pitches at the Toronto Blue Jays' home opener against the Texas Rangers—a team partly owned by Bush's son, future president George W. Bush. At a news conference with both leaders present, Mulroney said talks on an accord could begin as soon as that summer. As Ross Howard of the *Globe and Mail* reported,

> An adviser to the Prime Minister said later that the plan to begin the acid rain negotiations in advance of the completion of the U.S. legislation was a "real dividend" from the meeting yesterday.
>
> "We were not surprised but very pleased" with Mr. Bush's support for the acid rain accord talks, said the senior diplomatic adviser, who declined to be named. "It is the ninth time the Prime Minister has raised it [acid rain]" in the leaders' meetings.[373]

Mulroney, whose approval rating had sunk to 15 per cent[374] because of the introduction of the goods and services tax (GST) days earlier, was booed heavily by the crowd—but so was Blue Rodeo, the band who sang the national anthem, for including a verse in French during the Meech Lake tensions.[375] The game was a sell-out, with attendance of 49,673.[376] The leaders left before the end of the game, which Toronto won 2–1.[377]

THE HOME STRETCH

In July, Bush and Mulroney reaffirmed their commitment to an acid rain accord at a meeting at Bush's home in Houston before the G7 summit. The accord "would include a joint research and monitoring program, a means of dispute settlement and a joint United States–Canada committee to oversee implementation."[378] As reported at the time, "'President Bush and I have fought long and hard to get where we are today,' Mulroney told reporters. . . . Looking directly at Mulroney, who has described American action on acid rain as a litmus test of his policy of forging closer relations with the United States, Bush said: 'I know this is very important for the Canadian side. And I want to say to you sir, I appreciate your patience and understanding.'"[379]

On July 16, EPA administrator William Reilly met with Environment Minister Robert de Cotret (who had replaced Bouchard after he stepped down following the failure of Meech Lake) in Ottawa. They announced that formal negotiations on the accord would begin August 28. The accord would include controls for various forms of cross-border pollution and emissions, not just sulphur dioxide, and provide a dispute-resolution mechanism. The Canadian negotiators were Robert Slater, assistant deputy environment minister, and Michael Phillips, assistant deputy external affairs minister; the U.S. negotiators were Ambassador Richard Smith and EPA official Eileen Claussen.[380] After a weekend of around-the-clock talks, Congress agreed to a revised Clean Air Act on October 22, 1990. Reilly and de Cotret both predicted the act's approval would pave the way for a bilateral accord. De Cotret said the act's acid rain provisions represented the "breakthrough" Canada had been pursuing for years.[381] Reilly called the act "a promise from us to you—to the people of Canada. . . . The fact that we as a country have been the source of such a large amount of the sulphur dioxide problem in Canada has been a concern to us."[382] After the House approved the bill on October 26, by a margin of 401 to 25, long-time clean-air advocate Representative Henry Waxman said, "That decade of neglect is over."[383] Bush signed the Clean Air Act into law on November 15. Canada and the U.S. wrapped up negotiations on the accord in December.[384] It was initially expected to be signed in January, but with the Gulf War dominating the foreign policy agenda, the event was pushed back to March.

On March 13, 1991, the agreement was signed by the two leaders on Ottawa's Parliament Hill. Both leaders were in a jovial mood. Referring to Mulroney's and Canada's persistent lobbying via Derek Burney, Canada's ambassador to Washington, Bush joked, "He was on me like ugly on an ape. . . . So now, you see I was listening."[385] Mulroney did not hesitate to lavish praise on the American president: "To have moved as you did, the environmental question so quickly within your own borders, so far and to such heights is a tribute to the commitment you made the American people and the government of Canada."[386] Both leaders thanked PC backbencher Stan Darling, MP for Parry Sound-Muskoka, who had been such an early and persistent advocate for acid rain controls.[387]

Canadian editorial reaction was uniformly positive, though there were more than a few swipes at Ronald Reagan. Said the *Toronto Star*, "For years, as Ronald Reagan fiddled in the White House, it seemed that eastern Canada wouldn't have a clean lake or a healthy tree to call its own. But with the coming of President George Bush, the tune changed. Finally, Canadians were able to convince Americans that Reagan was wrong and trees don't cause acid rain. It has taken more than a decade of lobbying, wheedling, whining and posturing—the latter most frequently performed by Prime Minister Brian Mulroney—to bring the Americans to their senses."[388] The *Globe and Mail* opined that "The content of this week's Canadian–U.S. accord on acid rain was largely symbolic, but what wonderful symbolism it was, and how far we have travelled to get to this point. . . . It is too soon to celebrate reductions that have yet to occur, but a toast is in order to all who contributed to this week's happy achievement."[389]

LESSONS

Unlike issues such as the water management levels in the Great Lakes or the Garrison Dam Diversion project between Manitoba and North Dakota, which were largely uncontentious and dealt with through the International Joint Commission, the acid rain problem was deeply political. It pitted the coal producing states of West Virginia and Pennsylvania and the industrial Midwest against the New England states and the provinces of eastern Canada, which were on the receiving end of the problem.

Like climate change, the science of acid rain was also hotly contested and its causes were not well understood. However, the environmental movement on both sides of the Canada–U.S. border was seized by the issue and vociferous about the need for drastic action by the two governments to curtail emissions of so-called "NOx and SOx" gases. Many Canadians, however, took a holier-than-thou attitude and were all too willing to point fingers at the U.S., failing to recognize that we too had dirty hands.

Previous efforts to deal with the issue bilaterally had confronted gridlock in the U.S. Congress and either weak presidents (Jimmy Carter) who couldn't deliver the goods, or strong ones (Ronald Reagan) who simply refused to believe the problem was real. The process of reaching the agreement was a stark lesson in how to effectively manage our relations with our southern neighbour and our most important trading partner, especially when relations have their ups and downs. Its primary takeaway is: never give up, keep your eye on the ball, and, above all, work on key relationships at the presidential and congressional levels. In diplomacy, personal relations do indeed matter.

With Reagan, Mulroney kept the problem bubbling on the stove by getting him to agree to the appointment of "special emissaries" to study the issue, and, more importantly, committing Canada to come to the negotiating table with "clean hands," i.e., agreeing to clean up our own act before asking Americans to do the same. Mulroney may not have changed Reagan's mind on the issue, but he did not let his amicable relationship diminish his persistent efforts to assert Canadian interests and the need for equivalent commitments from the United States.

With the election of George H.W. Bush, Mulroney saw that he had an opening. Unlike Reagan, Bush was keenly aware of the problem because he was an avid outdoorsman and had a summer home in Maine. Mulroney worked the file and his close personal relationship with the U.S. president. He also skilfully manoeuvred the issue with key allies in the U.S. Congress and Washington's bureaucracy.

Finally, this serves as an interesting example of how the Canadian federal system can occasionally work very effectively. Both Quebec and Ontario continually lobbied the neighbouring U.S. states and sent delegations to Washington. And Jim Bradley, the Ontario environment minister, was a consistent advocate for action against acid rain. Ontario's Countdown Acid Rain program, aimed at big emitters like mining company INCO, played a critical role in reducing Canada's SO_2 emissions. (Interestingly, there was a rebel group within INCO, led by Vice-President Roy Aitken and Environment Director Charlie Ferguson, who helped to bring INCO along.) Finally, it helped that the old INCO Sudbury smelter was obsolete and due for refurbishment. It was demolished and replaced with new proprietary technology that was far more energy efficient, less polluting, and more profitable. But this set of negotiations would not have turned out nearly as well were it not for the constant nagging by Bradley and his staff.

The whole acid rain episode was a real success story for Canada, and Mulroney deserves a great deal of credit for it. His constant schmoozing of both Reagan and Bush was critical, and there is no doubt that, without his leadership, little if anything would have happened. In Canada–U.S. relations, negotiations are like attrition warfare. You must keep going back to the table and never take no for an answer.

EIGHT

From Baie-Comeau to Rio's Guanabara Bay—
the Road to the Earth Summit

"When I was very young, we went to the foot of Champlain Street
and swam in Baie-Comeau, for which my hometown was named.
Today, there is a park where we used to swim. The effluence from
the paper mill created landfill, where once there had been pristine
waters. Nobody swims in the bay anymore. And that's where my aware-
ness of the environment, and of environmental degradation, began."

—BRIAN MULRONEY

T HE SUMMER OF 1988 WAS A SCORCHER. One of the hottest on
record for the twentieth century.[390] But it wasn't just Canadians
who were feeling the heat. The effects of El Niño were being felt
around the globe—searing droughts on the American (and Canadian)
prairies, massive cyclones that ripped across the Pacific into Asia, and a
succession of major hurricanes that swept into the Caribbean and up the
eastern seaboard of the United States, bringing their own destruction.

Nineteen eighty-eight was also the year that Canada, under Brian
Mulroney's leadership, for the first time put climate change on the agenda
of the annual economic summit of the seven leading advanced industrial
economies of the world, a summit that he hosted in Toronto. It was also
a summit that saw world leaders endorse the concept of sustainable
development following the publication a year earlier of the Brundtland
Commission Report on the environment and development.[391] In those

days, climate change wasn't a partisan issue, and the growing body of scientific evidence on climate change and other environmental issues was taken seriously by Canada's Progressive Conservative government.

The Brundtland Commission had an enormous impact on Canada. Unlike many other international exercises of this kind, the commission had public hearings all around the world, including in Russia, Indonesia, and even the rainforests of Brazil. There were several in Canada as well, which had a major influence on elite and public opinion. Before Brundtland issued its report, the federal and provincial governments had set up the National Task Force on Environment and Economy, which was chaired by the environment minister for Manitoba and included a large number of CEOs. The report concluded that the environment and the economy went hand in hand but that policy could only be advanced if there were national roundtables of decision makers. The recommendation led to the creation of the National Roundtable on the Environment and the Economy. The first National Roundtable, which was chaired by Environment Minister Lucien Bouchard, included cabinet heavyweights like Finance Minister Michael Wilson. Wilson understood that you had to find a way to integrate the environment into the federal budget, and he did so with the prime minister's blessing and concurrence.

It was not only on the issues of climate change or ozone depletion that Canada was a champion and global leader under Mulroney. Canada also led a series of regional and bilateral initiatives to promote environmental cooperation on issues such as the Arctic and the control of acid raid by Canada and the United States. Canadian public opinion in the late 1980s was also changing and becoming far more environmentally conscious. The new national sentiment was perhaps best summed up by John Fraser, the then Speaker of the House of Commons: "For the first time in human history we are looking down the coming decades with the certain reality that if we do not change our ways we are not going to survive."[392]

On April 20, 2006, Brian Mulroney was named the "greenest prime minister" in Canada's history by a jury of environmental activists selected by *Corporate Knights Magazine*. Why so green? Brian Mulroney recognized that public attitudes were changing and the environment clearly made for good domestic and global politics. But his personal commitment to the issue and willingness to take political risks clearly ran deeper than that. In his speech accepting the award, the former prime minister offered some insight into why the environment had been such a priority for him, noting that his own environmental conscience had been awakened as a young man:

> When I was very young, we went to the foot of Champlain Street
> and swam in Baie-Comeau, for which my hometown was named.
> Today, there is a park where we used to swim. The effluence from
> the paper mill created landfill, where once there had been pristine
> waters. Nobody swims in the bay anymore. And that's where my
> awareness of the environment, and of environmental degradation,
> began. We've seen too many such sights in this country, including
> company towns carved out of the wilderness, with little regard for
> the impact on their surroundings. In fairness, it should be noted
> that in those days few of us knew any better. Now we do. We need
> to learn those lessons of careless development, and of neglecting to
> clean up after ourselves. We need to learn it especially in the North.
> The future of this country is going north, and it is time for a new
> Northern vision, one of sustainable development that preserves
> the Arctic wilderness, protects wildlife and sustains a way of life for
> our indigenous peoples. In Baie-Comeau, I once said: "My father
> dreamed of a better life for his family. I dream of a better life for my
> country." Part of that dream was about leaving a more prosperous
> and united country to our children, but a large part of it was also
> about leaving our munificent country environmentally whole.[393]

Although he had been in office barely a year, in May 1985 Mulroney was the leading voice on environmental issues at the eleventh G7 summit in Bonn, Germany, held early that month. As he wrote in his memoirs,

"I was concerned that the Bonn summit give appropriate emphasis to the problems of the environment, and that there be specific reference to acid rain, air pollution, protection of the ozone layer, and the management of toxic and hazardous wastes. It is, in my view, especially significant that a consensus emerged on the idea that governments and private industry have a joint responsibility in preserving the environment and on the proposal that the 'polluter pays' principle should be developed and applied more widely."[394]

INITIATIVES ON THE ENVIRONMENT:
CLIMATE CHANGE AND HAZARDOUS WASTES

When more than twenty thousand delegates convened in Paris in November 2015 to negotiate a new global convention on climate change, those with long memories would recall that the key, foundational elements of an international strategy to address climate change were first hammered out twenty-seven years earlier at the World Conference on the Changing Atmosphere: Implications for Global Security, held in Toronto in late June 1988. Sponsored jointly by Environment Canada, the World Meteorological Organization (WMO), and the United Nations Environment Programme (UNEP), the conference underscored the growing urgency of climate change while also setting out the core elements of a comprehensive global strategy to mitigate the effects of a buildup of greenhouse gases in the atmosphere.

The conference took place right after the June G7 summit of world leaders, which Canada had also hosted in Toronto, presenting a key opportunity to highlight Canada's commitment to the environment and advance a bold new climate change agenda. The chance to put the environment on the agenda of the G7 for the first time was not lost on the prime minister and his environment minister at the time, Tom McMillan. McMillan was an academic turned politician who was close to the prime minister, having served as deputy House leader when Mulroney was the Opposition leader. Though he was low key, he enjoyed the full confidence of the prime minister and served as environment minister until his defeat in the 1988 federal election, which was fought on the issue of Canada–U.S. free trade.

McMillan urged Mulroney to make the environment a priority at the summit, not only because "Canada had been a key player in the development of international protocols on sulphur dioxide, ozone, and nitrogen oxides," but also because Canada would be hosting the World Conference on the Changing Atmosphere a week later, right after the summit. Mulroney agreed wholeheartedly. But it was a hard sell to other G7 leaders because, with the exception of West German chancellor Helmut Kohl, who was facing pressure from the budding green movement in his own country, they all wanted to keep the agenda focused on the state of the global economy.

But the prime minister's persistence paid off. The environment was initially expected to be relegated to informal conversations among the leaders, but it ended up being discussed on the opening day of meetings.[395] With an estimated two thousand protesters marching down University Avenue—"an assortment of peaceniks, environmentalists, Trotskyites, gays, Sandinistas, Canadian Indians, feminists, Irish nationalists, anti-free traders, leftists and social activists"[396]—the leaders hunkered down in the cavernous setting of the Metro Toronto Convention Centre and hashed out a statement on the need for global leaders to cooperate on environmental policy. Mulroney and Kohl had a third ally in the new Italian prime minister, Ciriaco De Mita, and "each of the three pushed hard for more concerted action on such global problems as acid rain, the endangered ozone layer and pollution of the North Sea."[397] Getting acid rain on the agenda was an accomplishment in itself because Reagan was notoriously reluctant to address the issue, and it is unlikely Mulroney could have succeeded without the support of the other leaders.[398]

When the eight-page summit communiqué was released, the environment received three short paragraphs near the end. But for an economic document to have any reference to the environment—let alone the assertion that "Environmental considerations must be integrated into all areas of economic policy-making if the globe is to continue to support humankind"—was considered noteworthy.[399] As Mulroney wrote in his diary afterwards, "I was pleased that the G7 leaders agreed with me that the environment was crucial, endorsing the concept of sustainable development. As a group, we encouraged the nations of the world to sign and ratify the Montreal Protocol on the Protection of the Ozone Layer. The G7 also sent from Toronto the message that further action was needed on climate change, acid rain, water pollution and other ecological issues."[400]

The World Conference on the Changing Atmosphere, held a week later, was a breakthrough of sorts because it laid many of the key foundational elements of a global climate change strategy that would culminate years later in November–December 2015 at the 21st Conference of the Parties (COP 21) in Paris. The Toronto conference was fascinating for a number of reasons. It was the first conference involving both climate scientists and political decision makers, led by Mulroney and Prime Minister Gro Harlem Brundtland of Norway. Three hundred scientists and political figures from forty-six countries and organizations attended. The conference was not an official event, and participants attended in their personal capacity, but the presence of Mulroney and Brundtland, among others, gave it the air of an inter-governmental meeting.

Brundtland and Mulroney got on extremely well. One very memorable moment came when Brundtland was taken to the old Toronto Island airport terminal, where she unveiled a plaque in commemoration of the British Commonwealth Air Training Plan. Many of the free Norwegian Air Force pilots were trained on the island during the war and there is still an area colloquially called "Little Norway." Brundtland was so touched by this simple ceremony, her eyes welled up with tears.

The sense of urgency about the environment was tangible in the prime minister's opening remarks to delegates in their air-conditioned cocoon in the Metro Toronto Convention Centre sheltered from the sweltering streets of the city: "The world is coming to recognize what we believe in Canada to be self-evident," he began, "that economic development and environmental protection are mutually reinforcing, not mutually exclusive. Our economic activity must be increasingly compatible with today's environmental facts of life. We are faced with climate shifts, desertification, flooding, droughts, ozone depletion, acidification." The prime minister warned that "Carbon dioxide from fossil fuel burning and methane from modern agricultural and industrial practices are accumulating in the atmosphere and trapping solar energy reflected from the earth." But he also stressed that climate change and Third World debt were interrelated problems requiring "equitable resolution."[401]

The importance of bridging the North–South divide would be a constant refrain in Mulroney's approach to global environmental problems. But he also recognized that it was in the self-interest of the industrialized world to lend more than a helping hand to developing countries. "If the debtor nations of the tropics stopped stripping their rainforests to generate export earnings to service their debts," he opined, "the industrialized countries would benefit. The slowing of carbon dioxide build-up would give the developed world much needed flexibility in adjusting our energy mix to reduce reliance on fossil fuels." He concluded his speech by stating that the issue was "not just about the atmosphere, it is not just about the environment, it is about the future of the planet itself."[402]

Energized by the prime minister's speech, in the days that followed the delegates thrashed out the key elements of a roadmap to combat climate change. Their final proposals were ambitious, but they raised the bar on what had to be done, including the establishment of

- an international framework convention that would encourage other standard-setting agreement and national legislation to provide for the protection of the global atmosphere;
- a comprehensive global energy policy to reduce emissions of carbon dioxide and other trace gases in order to reduce the risks of future global warming (such reductions would be achieved

through fulfillment of national commitments to greater energy efficiency, conservation, and modifications in supplies);

- a world atmosphere fund, financed perhaps through a tax on fossil fuel consumption, to mobilize the resources necessary to achieve energy efficiency improvements;

- continuing assessments of scientific results and government-to-government discussion of responses and strategies; and

- a worldwide plan to reduce deforestation and increase afforestation by setting up an international trust fund to provide adequate incentives to developing nations to manage their tropical forests and achieve sustainable development.[403]

Reflecting on the Toronto conference some twenty-five years later, Adam Fenech, a delegate to the 1988 conference, one of Canada's authorities on climate change, and an early contributor to the work of the Intergovernmental Panel on Climate Change (IPCC), wrote enthusiastically about its effects:

> "Our Changing Atmosphere: Implications for Global Security," brought together hundreds of scientists and policymakers from across the globe to Toronto with the goal of initiating international action on climate change. . . . While the previous decade had seen discussions of both global cooling and warming, the Toronto Conference was the "perfect storm" of events to launch the issue of global warming onto the international policy agenda. . . .
>
> *The appearance at the Toronto Conference of then Canadian Prime Minister Brian Mulroney ensured that other international leaders would be in attendance and would bring their international media along with them.*
>
> The 1988 conference, hosted by Canada, put climate change on the global agenda and proposed a specific initial target for a global reduction in the emission of carbon dioxide—20% below 1988 levels by 2005—on the way to a much larger ultimate reduction, to be set

following further research and debate. The Conference concluded by issuing a stark warning to the world: "Humanity is conducting an unintended, uncontrolled, globally pervasive experiment whose ultimate consequences could be second only to a global nuclear war."[404]

That dire warning, of course, is one that President Obama would later echo in his 2014 State of the Union address, when he said that "No challenge poses a greater threat to future generations than climate change."[405]

The role of the media in the Toronto conference was also very interesting. They were intrigued by the presence of so many politicians in what was billed as a scientific gathering. NASA scientist James Hansen had alarmed the U.S. Congress by his testimony about climate change. Perhaps most important, many in the press had conflated climate change with the odd climate events of that summer. It was the driest in memory in North America; the Mississippi water levels were so low that barges were stranded on sandbanks, and those that did sail had to proceed with vastly reduced loads. The governor of Illinois had the half-baked idea of diverting even more water from the Great Lakes down the Mississippi. In response to these events, the press gallery was filled with journalists from around the world, who peppered the bewildered scientists with questions about how to deal with the short-term problems.

The Canadian influence on the climate change file would continue well after Toronto. Howard Ferguson of Environment Canada became the secretary-general of the World Climate Conference in 1990, which marked a milestone in the negotiation of what would become the United Nations Framework Convention on Climate Change (UNFCCC). Elizabeth Dowdeswell, as of 2014 the lieutenant governor of Ontario, chaired one of the two major committees that created the convention. And when Maurice Strong became secretary-general of the World Conference on the Environment and Sustainable Development in Rio (discussed at further length below), he decided to change the channel on UN conferences. The UN had pretty much exhausted its traditional formula of two-week conferences on global challenges, starting with the 1972 Stockholm Conference on the Environment, and then moving on to the Population Conference, the World Food Conference, the Habitat Conference, etc. Strong decided that a new format was needed to seize the public's attention and imagination. So, he lobbied the UN to make Rio an "Earth Summit." In addition to the usual grip-and-grin photo ops for heads of state, he wanted some concrete deliverables. Strong pushed the UN to accelerate the negotiations for what became the climate convention and the biodiversity convention. They were done in record time.

In February 1989, Canada went on to host the ground-breaking Meeting of Legal and Policy Experts on Protection of the Atmosphere. Participants from twenty-five countries and eight international bodies sought agreement on principles that would lay the foundations for a global convention on climate change. The meeting examined a variety of different frameworks for, and approaches to, devising a convention on climate change, recommending that an international convention, or per-haps series of conventions, with appropriate protocols to limit carbon dioxide and other greenhouse gas emissions, be adopted as a means to ensure rapid international action to protect the atmosphere and limit the rate of climate change. The meeting concluded by adopting the Ottawa Declaration, which recognized the atmosphere as being "a common pool resource of vital interest to mankind" that should be protected by all states.[406] The declaration was subsequently presented for approval at the Second World Climate Conference in 1990.

Canada was also one of twenty-four signatories to the March 1989 Declaration of The Hague, which called for an international convention on climate change and stronger mechanisms to ensure international cooperation to protect the environment. Although the declaration did not contain any "operational" commitments, it expressed the intention of the participants to take measures to save the atmosphere and called on all countries to do the same. The declaration included three core principles: (1) reinforcement of UN powers and the creation of a new institutional authority (either by the strengthening of existing institutions or by the creation of new ones) for the purpose of protecting the atmosphere; (2) the granting of specific competences to the International Court of Justice in The Hague related to control and enforcement decisions made by the UN; and (3) "fair and equitable aid" to developing countries that might have difficulty complying with the efforts to protect the atmosphere.[407]

By the time the next G7 summit rolled around, in 1989, Canada had more company on what was rapidly becoming an environmental band-wagon. With a growing voter appetite for action on the environment, even laggards such as U.K. prime minister Margaret Thatcher and French president François Mitterrand—the summit host, with whom Mulroney had developed a close personal relationship—were burnishing their green credentials. The new U.S. president, George H.W. Bush, positioned him-self as more progressive on the environment than his predecessor, Ronald Reagan. In fact, Canadian officials complained to reporters that he was stealing Mulroney's thunder as the greenest global leader.[408][409]

The result was that environmental issues dominated the summit agenda. While the environment merited just three paragraphs in the pre-vious year's G7 communiqué, it took up more than one-third of the Paris document (which was largely completed before the leaders met in Paris). World leaders championed "common efforts to limit emissions of car-bon dioxide and other greenhouse gases, which threaten to induce climate change, endangering the environment and the economy." They also pledged to "help developing countries deal with past damage and to encourage them to environmentally sustainable action," while calling for the speedy "conclusion of a framework or umbrella convention on cli-mate change to set out general principles or guidelines."[410]

At the Paris summit, Canada proposed the novel idea of developing a series of "environmental indicators" modelled on the familiar economic indicators (e.g., cost of living indices) to measure environmental change. At Canada's urging, the Organisation for Economic Co-operation and Development (OECD) was asked to follow up with a detailed study of how such a system of indicators might work. Since the early 1990s, the OECD has been doing just that—developing and refining indicators, modelling, and issuing environmental reports on a regular basis.[411] After the summit concluded, Mulroney told reporters he was "gratified" with how much attention had been paid to the environment. "The concept of sustainable development, which we promoted at Toronto and was endorsed there, is amply reflected in today's communiqué," he said.[412]

Prime Minister Mulroney was also one of the key champions of the Langkawi Declaration on the Environment at the October 1989 Commonwealth Heads of Government Summit in Kuala Lumpur, in which leaders from North and South called for cooperation between developed and developing countries to resolve environmental problems. The declaration noted that the Commonwealth leaders, "representing a quarter of the world's population and a broad cross-section of global interests, are deeply concerned at the serious deterioration in the environment and the threat this poses to the well-being of present and future generations. Any delay in taking action to halt this progressive deterioration will result in permanent and irreversible damage."[413]

The trans-shipment of hazardous wastes was also a growing problem that had received worldwide attention when in 1986 the freighter *Khian Sea*, which was carrying a load of incinerator residues, tried to offload its highly toxic cargo in the Bahamas, where it was refused entry. The ship then changed its name and tried to dump its unwelcome cargo in Sri Lanka, Indonesia, and the Philippines, being turned away each time by local authorities. In 1988, the Italian government hired a freighter, the *Karin-B*, in a failed bid to dump a boatload of toxic waste in Nigeria. Eventually, the ship had to return home with its lethal cargo. These and other highly publicized episodes led to the Basel Convention, which was approved in March 1989 by more than a hundred countries, prohibiting the trans-border shipment of hazardous wastes to countries that were not signatories to the convention and detailing ways of disposing of wastes in a responsible manner. Again, Canada was one of the first countries to sign and ratify the agreement.[414]

ACTION ON THE OZONE LAYER

In May 1985, the world was shocked to learn that a hole had been found in the layer of atmosphere that protects life on Earth from dangerous ultraviolet rays. Scientists with the British Antarctic Survey found that ozone levels high above Antarctica were depleted by about 65 per cent, and they blamed synthetic chemicals called chlorofluorocarbons (CFCS).[415] Scientists had been warning since the 1970s that CFCS interacted with atmospheric conditions to deplete the ozone layer and contribute to global warming—and since CFCS could remain in the atmosphere for decades, there was no telling how much damage they could do in the future. Canada, the U.S., and a few other countries banned most CFCS in aerosol sprays in response, but CFC output continued to increase, due in part to its use in other products such as coolants, solvents, and plastic foam.[416] Now the discovery of the ozone hole charged the issue with an added sense of urgency.

Canada was the first country to ratify the 1985 Vienna Convention for the Protection of the Ozone Layer, on June 4, 1986. The convention, which subsequently went into force in 1988, obligated countries to control activities that might have a harmful impact on the ozone layer and to cooperate on the science on ozone depletion. However, the convention itself lacked real teeth and it would take negotiations on a series of binding protocols—finalized in 1987 as the Montreal Protocol on Substances that Deplete the Ozone Layer—to reduce the actual production and use of CFCS.

Negotiations on the protocol started in earnest in Geneva in December 1986.[417] The main divide was between the U.S. on one side, along with Canada, and the Nordic countries and the twelve countries in the European Economic Community (EEC) on the other. Initially, the U.S. was lobbying for a "near-term freeze" on CFC emissions, with an agreement to reduce them almost completely over the long term, while the EEC wanted to freeze CFC production at 30 per cent above 1986 levels.[418] Canada produced a fraction of the CFCS that either the U.S. or the EEC did, but as a northern country likely to be most severely affected by ozone depletion, it had much at stake.[419] The Canadian text presented in Geneva hewed a middle course, calling for an immediate freeze on the production of CFCs and immediate reductions to their use for commercial purposes. The Canadian proposal also included a complex formula for quotas on national emission reductions that would take into account a country's level of economic development and the size of its population. This was important to bring developing countries on board with somewhat less onerous commitments, at least initially. Canada's proposal fed into what eventually became a U.S. draft text that was supported by a broad-based coalition of Nordic countries, along with Egypt, Mexico, New Zealand, and Switzerland.

There were further rounds of talks throughout the spring and summer. Canada continued to play a key role as an "honest broker," according to Vic Buxton, an Environment Canada official who took part in the negotiations.[420] Observers credited Canada with forging compromises to keep the talks from breaking down. "If there is a strong protocol (for controls) out of this, the world will have Canada to thank," David Wirth, a former U.S. State Department lawyer, told the *Globe and Mail*. "The Canadians have been very principled on this and took a very strong stand early on."[421]

As a forerunner in the negotiations, Canada agreed to host the final round of negotiations in Montreal in September 1987, by which time the number of countries participating in the negotiations had grown to sixty. The negotiations were chaired by Mostafa Tolba, the executive director of UNEP, and the conference chair, Winfried Lang, an eminent Austrian diplomat and international lawyer. Tolba and Lang were assisted through the difficult negotiations by a small group of "friends" who were the heads of delegations from a number of key countries that included Canada. It was this group that was responsible for bringing other countries and producing the draft agreement that ultimately became the basis for a final agreement. However, as Elizabeth May, then a policy adviser to Environment Minister Tom McMillan, later wrote, "The Canadian government and our scientists were in the lead. Canadians were prime drafters of what was to become known as the Montreal Protocol. Our scientists were leading researchers and willing to be advocates. Canadian legal experts chaired the group drafting the text."[422]

Talks at the International Civil Aviation Organization headquarters in Montreal went on longer than planned. In a stunning move, the U.S.— a leading proponent of the deal—suddenly asked that any agreement meet the onerous condition of consensus from countries that produced 90 per cent of the world's CFCs. This would give an effective veto to any country that produced at least 10 per cent, including Japan and the Soviet Union.[423] U.S. officials said the move was designed to make sure American companies weren't at a disadvantage if they moved first, as happened when the U.S. enacted the CFC aerosol ban before other countries;[424] Canadian officials, however, suspected a power struggle within the Reagan administration.[425] Canada reportedly sent a letter of protest to the head of the EPA in response to this new demand.[426] Then a group of developing countries, led by Argentina and Brazil, asked to be exempt from restrictions on CFCs so they could continue their economic development.[427] Meanwhile, the U.S.S.R. asked that its freeze not take effect until 1990, when its current five-year plan would expire, and the twelve EEC countries insisted on being treated as one unit to account for their common trade market.[428]

After five days of wrangling, McMillan opened the final round of negotiations with a dramatic speech to the gathered diplomats. "We must not fail, for nothing less than the future of the planet earth is at stake," he said.[429] "The implications transcend national boundaries. Chemical products do not carry a passport or a flag. The vegetable and animal life of each part of the planet is vulnerable. . . . Collectively we have the ability to save our planet and ourselves from destruction. But do we have the political will? It is clear that immediate action will benefit future generations more than ourselves. Should that make us less resolute?"[430]

An agreement finally came the day before the pact was set to be signed. It called for a 50 per cent reduction in CFCs, based on 1986 levels, by the end of 1999; set a series of schedules for both short-term and long-term controls of ozone-depleting substances; and allowed developing countries to increase CFC production for the next ten years. "This is perhaps the most historically significant international environmental agreement," said the chief U.S. negotiator, State Department official Richard Benedick. "For the first time the international community has initiated controls on production of an economically valuable commodity before there was tangible evidence of damage."[431]

The deal was signed by twenty-four countries, plus the EEC. However, it quickly became apparent that the proposed targets were not ambitious enough. Accordingly, in February 1989 the new Canadian environment minister, Lucien Bouchard, announced that Canada would reduce its use of CFCs by 85 per cent by 1999, thus exceeding the targets of the Montreal Protocol. The EEC members went a step further and agreed in March 1989 to ban the production and use of CFCs completely by 2000. The move came amid reports of higher levels of chemicals than expected in the Arctic atmosphere.

In May 1989, as one of the thirty-six initial signatories to the Montreal Protocol, Canada announced at a UNEP-sponsored forum in Helsinki, Finland, that it too would eliminate production of CFCs and other ozone-harming chemicals. Some eighty-six other countries, in addition to the original thirty-six, announced that they would do the same as well. Canada was also one of the champions of a special UN fund to help developing countries industrialize without CFCs, and it joined a working group to elaborate details of how the fund would work.[432] An Interim Multilateral Fund was subsequently established, to which Canada was not only a financial contributor but also a member of its executive committee, which was also composed of an equal number of representatives from the developed and the developing worlds.[433] Many years later, *The Economist* magazine drew a straight line from the successful negotiation of the Montreal ozone treaty to scientific findings in 2016 that the ozone hole in the upper atmosphere over Antarctica was actually beginning to heal. It also pointed out that Montreal was precedent setting for ongoing international efforts to ban the use of hydrofluorocarbons (HFCS), which are a major contributor to global warming.[434]

During Mulroney's tenure, Canada also became a scientific leader in the work of the UN's Intergovernmental Panel on Climate Change (IPCC), whose mandate was to provide a firmer assessment of the scientific basis of climate change. In addition to its work in the IPCC and its various subgroups that were studying the science and impact of global warming and possible policy responses, Canada was the largest contributor of development assistance to the developing world's forestry sector ($120 million annually), including programs aimed at preserving and restoring tropical forests. Canada also worked hard to encourage the World Bank to make the protection of the environment a top priority in its own economic development projects.

REGIONAL AND BILATERAL INITIATIVES

Canada also pursued a number of key initiatives to promote environmental cooperation with its Arctic neighbours (to add to its bilateral agreement on acid rain with the United States, discussed in detail in Chapter 7). For example, Canada worked closely with Finland in support of a special coordinated approach to environmental issues among the Arctic circumpolar states (Canada, Denmark, Finland, Iceland, Norway, Sweden, Soviet Union, and the United States). The eight Arctic countries met at Rovaniemi, Finland, in September 1989 and established two working groups: one to review the state of the environment in the Arctic and develop a course for further action; the second to consider the existing international legal instruments for the protection of the Arctic environment and the possibilities for further cooperation.

As part of its new multilateral approach to Arctic cooperation, Canada also upgraded its bilateral ties to the Soviet Union. During his November 1989 visit there, the prime minister signed the Canada–U.S.S.R. Agreement on Cooperation in the Arctic and North, which contained three programs covering scientific and technological cooperation, economic cooperation, and social and cultural cooperation. There were also several protocols in a separate Environmental Cooperation Agreement calling for greater level of cooperation on environmental matters between the two countries, including agreed exchanges of findings on such issues as Arctic and northern development, protection of marine and freshwater areas, waste management and disposal, and environmental training and education. Two additional Memoranda of Understanding were also signed: one covering cooperation in atmospheric environmental programs such as climate analysis; measurement of ozone, methane, and greenhouse gases; and research and monitoring on acid rain, Arctic haze, climate change, and air pollution. The other covered cooperation on water research on lakes, inland seas, and rivers. The two governments also initiated steps to limit the possibilities of oil spills in the fragile northern environment through exchanges of information on pollution prevention, monitoring, and prevention.

Though modest and perhaps inadequate by some standards, these initiatives helped lay the foundation for more comprehensive agreements and strategies to address the programs of air and water pollution, global warming, and climate change. They also lent credibility and legitimacy to the key leadership role that Canada would later play in Rio de Janeiro at the 1992 United Nations Conference on the Environment and Development (UNCED).

THE EARTH SUMMIT

The road to the "Earth Summit"—as UNCED was less formally called—had begun some thirty years earlier with the first United Nations Conference on the Human Environment, in Stockholm in 1972. That conference had Canadian fingerprints all over it, not least because it was chaired by a Canadian, Maurice Strong. Strong was a self-made millionaire who at the age of thirty-three had become president of the Power Corporation, one of Canada's largest and most important corporate entities, before going on to head Canada's External Aid Office, which was subsequently renamed the Canadian International Development Agency (CIDA) at Strong's urging of Prime Minister Pierre Trudeau. The Stockholm Conference planted the environment firmly on the agenda of national governments around the world, leading to the creation of national environment ministries as well as the United Nations Environment Programme (UNEP), a major UN agency that was located in the Kenyan capital, Nairobi.

Mounting public concerns about the health of the global environment were reinforced a decade and a half later with the publication of the 1987 report of the World Commission on Environment and Development.[435] The idea for the commission had come from Canada's representative to UNEP, who was also Canada's ambassador to Kenya, the highly regarded diplomat Geoffrey Bruce. Although Norwegian prime minister Gro Harlem Brundtland got most of the credit as the commission's chair, much of the commission's work over the course of its three years of existence was funded by Canada. Jim MacNeill was a Canadian public servant who for many years had headed the environment division at the OECD and had also been the Canadian secretary-general of the Habitat Conference in Vancouver in 1976. At the OECD, MacNeill cultivated critical relationships with member-country environment ministers who, after the Stockholm Conference in 1972, when many of their posts were created, lacked a formal organizational constituency. MacNeill organized the first major conference on the link between economics and the environment, where some of the world's leading economists proved that the link was a positive one if properly managed, and would actually create jobs. When the UN General Assembly approved the creation of the Brundtland Commission, they realized they needed sure hands to organize its staff and ideas. MacNeill, who had written one of the first documents on environmental policy in the Canadian government, was a natural fit for the job, especially given his more recent international experience with the OECD.

MacNeill ran the commission, organizing its meetings, hiring consultants, commissioning papers, etc. The final report was drafted by

Lloyd Timberlake, an American journalist who had worked for the International Institute for Environment and Development, a major environmental think-tank that had been founded by David Runnalls, a Canadian journalist who went on to become the head of the International Institute for Sustainable Development based in Winnipeg, and Barbara Ward, a renowned British development economist. It was edited by Linda Stark of the Worldwatch Institute, an organization headed by one of America's leading environmental champions, Lester Brown.

The report moved the concept of "sustainability," which it defined in social and environmental terms, to the centre of the economic development agenda. It also described in graphic terms the looming dangers of the depletion of the Earth's ozone layer and the risks of climate change. Although some of the report's recommendations had a decidedly Malthusian tone—human population growth combined with industrial production are stripping the planet of its non-renewable and renewable resources at levels that are simply unsustainable—its message was clear: drastic global action was required to ensure the survival of humanity and the other species that inhabit the planet. The commission recommended that a world conference be held five years after its publication to take stock of what—if any—progress had been made to implement its recommendations. Almost immediately, the UN General Assembly began to debate the merits of a second global conference on the environment and sustainability before giving its approval to move ahead. The decision came in the form of an authorizing resolution in 1989.

For a second time, the UN turned to Maurice Strong to chair the secretariat and be secretary-general of the Rio conference, but only after Canadian officials lobbied hard on his behalf. It was an open secret that Strong wanted the post, but nobody had done the job twice and Strong had also made his fair share of enemies. However, Strong had a completely disarming manner. In spite of his considerable private wealth, he was unpretentious. In the words of one of his friends and close associates, "he was like a hardware salesman from Manitoba. He wore cheap suits, drip dry shirts and had that terrible mustache. And, as a result, people thought that he was a hick. And by the time they worked out that he wasn't, he had taken your calls, your wallet, and gone out the back door. He persuaded governments that what they actually wanted to do was what he wanted. He was absolutely brilliant."[436]

Strong pressed his candidacy hard on Canada's foreign minister, Joe Clark, who was supportive. At one private luncheon hosted by Clark that was held in the exclusive, private dining room on the ninth floor of Ottawa's Pearson Building, the home of the Department of External Affairs, Strong had Peter Goldmark—a committed environmentalist who had served as executive director of the New York Port Authority and was now president of the Rockefeller Foundation—in tow. The two spent their entire cab ride across town trading stories about commercial real estate prices in Manhattan, but as soon as they entered the ninth-floor dining room, the conversation quickly turned to more weighty, global matters, including the prospect of a second world environmental summit. Strong's candidacy also gained the support of the prime minister, who even went so far as to place a direct call to the UN secretary-general to promote his candidacy, which was very unusual for the Canadian government. In the end, Strong got the job because he knew everyone in the developing world and because he was on their side.

Strong was a firm believer in the importance of bringing civil society directly into the process in order to generate political pressure for actionable recommendations. Non-governmental organizations were directly involved in the marathon preparatory negotiations, and in the case of some countries, like Canada, they formed part of the official delegation. But while the Canadian government organized and funded a committee for environmentalists and other NGOs to participate in the negotiations, some frustrated environmental activists complained that their voices were going unheard.[437] In the months before the conference, they also had serious doubts that Mulroney would go to Rio, given the brewing constitutional crisis at home in Canada. These doubts mounted as the prime minister's office failed to confirm that he was attending, even ten weeks before the conference was scheduled to start.

"He's thinking about it very, very seriously," one aide told the press at the time.[438]

At least one environmentalist, though, expressed optimism that Mulroney would pull through: Elizabeth May, who had become Canada's national representative to the Sierra Club. In a *Globe and Mail* editorial, May noted that pre-Rio negotiations had already been rocky and expressed hopes that "Brian Mulroney would emerge as the conference's hero." She said someone was needed to step up and pressure U.S. president George Bush and other reluctant global leaders to rally around the conference goals, and that Mulroney, with his considerable international influence, was best suited to do it: "Canada is ideally placed to fill the current void of high-level political leadership for UNCED. From Day 1, Canada has supported the conference. At every meeting of the preparatory committee, the Canadian delegation has advanced innovative and progressive solutions for environment-development issues . . . for my money, what we need is Brian Mulroney to don a Captain Planet cape and start doing some super-hero work."[439]

Mulroney's office confirmed his attendance on March 27, but it did little to calm environmentalists' fears that Rio was headed for disaster. Runnalls, a close observer to the negotiations, noted that they were extremely contentious—far more so than they had been at Stockholm when the environment first made its way onto the global agenda. "Much of the acrimonious debate," he pointed out, "centered around the clash of competing agendas. Developing countries were suspicious that many of the issues on the agenda would become the subject of deals worked out between relatively few countries. They therefore insisted that the Preparatory Committee be open to all members of the UN and that no more than two sub-committees of the Prepcom be allowed to meet simultaneously. While this helped to ensure that countries with small delegations could participate in all decisions, it led to a number of marathon negotiating sessions with well over 100 countries participating."[440]

But on the three key issues taken up by the conference—biodiversity, climate change, and forests—Canada was prominent. Runnalls wrote,

"The Canadian delegation to the Preparatory Committee was very ably led by John Bell of the Department of External Affairs. Elizabeth Dowdeswell of Environment Canada [who went on to become Executive Director of UNEP] chaired the critical committee in the climate change negotiating process, while Arthur Campeau, the Prime Minister's Sherpa to UNCED, was one of the crucial figures in the final negotiation of the biodiversity agreement."[441]

The negotiations in Rio did have their lighter moments. The young Canadian environment minister, Jean Charest, had the time of his life. As head of the delegation before the prime minister's arrival for the last three days of the conference, Charest trampled over formal diplomatic niceties. The Canadian delegation (otherwise known as CanDel) meeting, which took place every morning, is the confidential holiest of holy gatherings of officials. Instructions are received from cabinet, and federal–provincial relations are discussed, as is the Canadian strategy for the day's negotiations. Charest broke the mould by spontaneously inviting Elizabeth May, who was the head of the Sierra Club (and who arrived with her stroller-seated daughter in tow). He then grabbed David Runnalls, who was wandering the halls and attending the conference as the political columnist for the *Earth Summit Times*, the conference newspaper. When Runnalls pointed out this potential conflict to Charest, he told him to come along anyway. It was a wise move because delegates could plant stories with the *Times* to move other countries along during the course of negotiations.

Charest did his best to keep the mood light. He told a tale of himself and his wife walking along the shore of Rio's Guanabara Bay. The beach crowd had thought that his beautiful walking companion was the songwriter, singer, and actress Olivia Newton John. (Strong had used his influence to get all kinds of stars to show up at Rio.) The first dinner of the board of the newly created, Canadian-funded International Institute for Sustainable Development was held in Rio. It was interrupted by Brian Wilson of the Beach Boys, who wanted to shake Maurice Strong's hand. Alas, Strong did not know who he was. But as soon as he was quietly informed about his celebrity admirer, he puffed up his small, pudgy frame and announced that he (Strong) had just been mistaken for Arnold Schwarzenegger.

On another occasion, a young staffer who had a habit of showing up in shorts and a T-shirt at the CanDel meetings put on a million-dollar suit and tie when the Canadian prime minister arrived for his first meeting with the delegation. But the young staffer had the misfortune to enter the room late. Charest looked at him sternly and asked him, "How come you look so good today?" The young man blurted out, "I put a suit on Minister because all the important people are here." It was too late to correct his faux pas before a minister of the Crown. He turned sheet white. After a long, embarrassed silence, both Mulroney and Charest laughed so hard they almost fell out of their chairs.[442]

The biodiversity and climate change agreements were the most contentious issues at the conference. Some countries, led by Austria and Germany, wanted to stabilize carbon dioxide emissions at 1990 levels by the year 2000 and to set the targets and timetable in a convention that would be signed at Rio. The International Convention on the Conservation and Rational Use of Biological Diversity, negotiated in Nairobi ahead of the conference, would require biotechnology companies that exploited compounds found in other countries' plants and organisms to compensate the countries where those organisms were harvested. In practice, this meant that if drug companies developed treatments using species found in developing world rainforests, for instance, they would have to give those countries a share of their profits. It required thirty countries to ratify it to take effect.[443]

The Americans were very difficult players on the issues of both climate change and biodiversity. On climate change, they refused an agreement that contained national targets, despite Mulroney's urgings. And the American vice-president, Dan Quayle, was lobbied hard by the U.S. biotech industry not to go along with the biodiversity convention. The former was saved by calling it a framework convention and stripping it of any hard targets. The latter was saved by Mulroney himself. Mulroney's impassioned public plea on biodiversity energized others countries, including the Europeans. Hitherto, the Europeans, and particularly the Germans, had treaded rather softly with the United States. Germany was to host the G7 summit later in the year and wanted American financial and technological support to deal with the catastrophic environmental aftermath of the meltdown of the Soviet-built nuclear reactor in Chernobyl, Ukraine, which had cast a radioactive plume over much of northern Europe. As a consequence, the Germans were not keen to offend President Bush. In fact, the Americans were so unhappy with the way things were going, Bush threatened to boycott the conference entirely. He did not want to risk being scolded on the world stage during an election year, especially as he had been positioning himself as an environmentalist.[444]

This is where the Canadian role and the personal intervention of the prime minister proved crucial, as he repeatedly urged his good friend the American president to show up in Rio along with other world leaders. "Look, George," said Mulroney, "there is a French expression, 'Les absents ont toujours tort.' In other words, if you're not at the table, you're going to get blamed. So, you're much better to be there, to defend your interests, and to speak about your record, and then to make your own mind up whether you're going to sign onto this or not."[445] With three weeks to go before the summit officially opened, Bush agreed to attend.[446]

However, Bush's commitment came only after the global warming agreement was watered down to a set of non-binding emissions targets that rendered the treaty "irrelevant" and "meaningless," according to environmental groups.[447] Then, on the eve of the conference, the United States said it would not sign the biodiversity treaty in Rio. The U.K., France, and Japan were also reluctant to sign.[448] There were serious doubts that the conference would accomplish anything. "It has become increasingly clear that the political will required to make UNCED a success is simply not there," said Robert Hornung of the Ottawa-based environmental group Friends of the Earth.[449] Even the once-hopeful May said, "It's hard to find indicators for optimism."[450] Canada's environmental leaders began the process of expectations management, with MacNeill and Environment Minister Jean Charest framing the conference as part of a "process" to create a roadmap for pursuing sustainable development, rather than a make-or-break moment in itself.[451]

But on June 1, Mulroney became the first head of government to commit to the biodiversity treaty.[452] "I know there have been some countries who have indicated they won't sign these agreements—for whatever reasons—at Rio," Mulroney told students at a museum near Ottawa. "But I want to tell you today that not only will Canada sign these agreements, but Canada undertakes to ratify these agreements within the present calendar year."[453] Speaking to reporters, he went further in distancing Canada from the U.S. stance: "Obviously when you've got an economy as rich as that of the United States, one that consumes as much as the Americans do—some 25 per cent, with only 5 or 6 per cent of the population—they've got a tremendous political impact on events like this. . . . But this is not to say that the world has subcontracted its responsibilities on the environment to the United States of America. It has not."[454] The decision "immediately set the corridors abuzz in Rio," according to one news report, which quoted a government official as saying, "This is the first time that Canada has stood up to the United States on a major issue in years."[455]

The move was a game-changer. Australia and Brazil soon followed Canada in committing to the treaty, and several other countries indicated they would join them. "I think the announcement that Canada was prepared to poke the Americans in the eye and sign the biodiversity convention may well have saved the convention," Runnalls said. "We're now hearing that the Europeans and some of the developing countries who had been wavering at the beginning are now likely to sign it."[456] The *New York Times* published a leaked memo indicating that William Reilly, administrator of the U.S. Environmental Protection Agency, had urged Bush to reconsider and sign the biodiversity treaty, but the administration refused.[457] Mulroney said publicly he would not pressure Bush to sign the treaty, but took a veiled dig at the U.S. president at a signature ceremony. "As a wealthy industrialized country of the North, we cannot have things only our own way," he said. "The developing countries have to see an advantage in ecological preservation for themselves. If the only reason they have development is to pay off interest to Northern financial institutions, then obviously they are going to do quite a job on their own environment."[458]

Canada also succeeded in getting the issue of high seas fishing on the agenda at the Earth Summit. This was an important issue to Canada because of mounting concerns about overfishing on the Grand Banks off Newfoundland by European fishers. The conference passed a resolution committing countries to the "conservation and sustainable use of marine living resources on the high seas." They also agreed to hold a follow-up conference in St. John's, Newfoundland, in 1993 and "to improve the quality of the information on the oceans" and their management.[459]

In terms of foreign aid, Mulroney pledged to forgive $145 million in debt from ten Latin American countries, provided they use the funds for environmental initiatives.[460] However, Canada was not able, at the Earth Summit, to secure support for a global convention to protect the world's forests , as it had so desperately wanted. Many developing countries, like India, China, and Malaysia, opposed such a convention on the grounds that it would infringe upon their sovereignty and their right to harvest their forests. In the end, "[a]ll that survived was a general statement about balancing forest exploitation with conservation and a basic commitment to keep 'forest principles under assessment of their adequacy with regard to further international cooperation on forest principles.' Among the principles articulated were the recognition of the right of states to develop their forests to meet their socio-economic needs, promotion of the transfer of technology to developing countries to help them manage their forests sustainably, and the need for all countries to make efforts to 'green the world' through reforestation and forest development."[461]

In his speech to delegates to the Earth Summit, the prime minister noted that he was "proud" to sign both the climate change and biodiversity conventions, but that Canada also "supports the extension of international environmental law to cover the world's forests." In order to "capitalize on the momentum of Rio," he also advocated five crucial steps that would see every country in the world develop its own plan for "sustainable development" as Canada had done with the government's own "Green Plan" (a $3 billion action plan containing targets and timetables on a wide range of projects); the immediate ratification by all countries of the two conventions they had just signed; the provision of adequate resources to developing countries to implement their own programs (under the Mulroney government, Canada had already spent $1.3 billion for sustainable development assistance in the preceding five years); the creation of standing "sustainable development commission;" and, finally, an "Earth Charter of Environment Rights and Responsibilities."[462]

Mulroney's performance at the summit earned praise from both analysts and environmentalists. Elizabeth May told reporters, "Let's face it, Canada saved the biodiversity treaty. . . . Let's not be modest just because we're Canadians. Brian Mulroney accomplished something really significant by being willing, within hours of Bush saying he wasn't going to sign it, by saying Canada was."[463] But she also suggested that Mulroney shone more brightly because he stood in contrast with Bush's abysmal performance. "The spin doctors in Ottawa should kiss George Bush's feet," she said.[464] Canada was also praised for having a large and diverse delegation (ninety-three strong) that integrated environmental activist groups and business representatives, and for being actively engaged in the issues. According to a *Globe and Mail* analysis, "A lot of governments ran from this process, but many, including Canada, got deeply involved with it. Indeed, one of the fundamental differences among countries at the conference were those whose national delegations were truly engaged with the issues and those who paid them lip service. Prime Minister Brian Mulroney observed in his final press conference that 'I think some governments read prepared speeches and view this as window dressing. Others take it seriously. You don't have to be around long before you can figure out which is which.'"[465]

But as the summit concluded, a clearly emotional Maurice Strong expressed his disappointment: while the biodiversity treaty succeeded, most other deals on the Rio agenda survived only in a severely diluted form, if at all. Strong held back tears as he lamented the lack of concrete commitments made to head off environmental crisis: "I think the conference has established a basis for a far more successful future. . . . But when we had thought we had done this at Stockholm [the 1972 UN conference], we really hadn't. The only difference is that now we don't have another 20 years to squander."[466]

Why did the air go out of the balloon so quickly? Rio had three problems. The first was that the conference was out of sync with the U.S. election, which took place later that year. That was one of the reasons why Bush initially didn't want to attend the conference and did so only after wresting concessions from other countries that there would be no concrete targets in a climate change agreement. The second reason was that the Japanese prime minister, whose government had earlier signalled it would make a major financial contribution to sustainable development, never left Tokyo because the Diet (the Japanese parliament) was debating a major change to Japan's constitution to allow it to deploy peacekeepers in Cambodia. So their vast, extremely well-briefed delegation was leaderless at Rio. The third problem was that the president of Brazil, Fernando Collor, who was also president of the conference, was impeached halfway through it on corruption charges.

However, Rio's *coup de grâce* came from Strong himself in a fatal mistake he made towards the end of the negotiations. A number of countries had urged Strong to put a price tag on Agenda 21, the UN's action plan on sustainable development. Instead of waffling, officials produced a number that was an astronomical $625 billion a year, which Strong endorsed. There was no real scientific basis for the assessment. It was simply a number that came from a group of bureaucrats assigning figures to different targets more or less at random. However, other countries got sticker shock because they realized their modest contribution would be a small drop in the bucket and wouldn't count, so many withdrew from their previous commitments. When the worldwide recession set in several months later, adding to a growing sense of environmental fatigue, the ambitions of Rio faded, though ultimately they were not completely forgotten.

LESSONS

The Rio convention was the high watermark of Canadian influence on international environmental negotiations. To the extent that Rio was a success (and a mixed one, at best), Maurice Strong was once again an international superstar. Mulroney saved the biodiversity convention and played a prominent role in the climate negotiations. And there were many other Canadians who worked quietly behind the scenes in both the NGO community and the government to advance the Rio agenda.

There were three key lessons that Mulroney himself drew from his experience addressing global environmental issues, and not just at Rio. The first was the importance of leadership: "[I]t doesn't really matter what the process is," he observed, "so long as the problem is addressed by leadership; where political will prevails, solutions will follow."[467] The formation of winning coalitions was critical to the multilateral negotiating process on issues like ozone depletion, climate change, and hazardous wastes. But these also had to be coalitions that bridged the North–South divide and were sufficiently flexible to reduce political divisions and confrontation. Canada was a credible and trusted interlocutor when it came to building such coalitions, not least because the prime minister himself was genuinely sympathetic to the development needs of the South and matched his rhetoric with tangible commitments that put real money on the table to help Canada's southern partners.

The prime minister also pressed his environmental agenda in more than one set of international forums, using the Commonwealth Heads of Government Meetings to considerable positive effect, as in the case of the Langkawi Declaration on the Environment. Canadian interventions were credible because Canada had consistently proved we could "walk the talk," and the impact on the country's reputation was cumulative.

Canada punched above its weight on a wide range of environmental issues—ozone depletion, climate change, biodiversity, and hazardous waste, to name but a few. Canada's environmental positions were always backed by strong scientific research, much of it carried out by members of Canada's own scientific community. Canada didn't always succeed in getting its way, as in the case of forestry at Rio, but Canadians were tenacious negotiators, not sore losers, and Canada always negotiated to see another day.

The second major lesson Mulroney absorbed was that it was important and effective for Canada to work closely with the Americans, not against them, to secure agreed-upon outcomes. That did not mean that Canada toed the American line on every issue. Our positions were defined by our own national interests—as in the case of the biodiversity treaty, where Mulroney said he would sign it despite initial U.S. opposition, while encouraging them to do the same. Because Mulroney had a close personal relationship with the American president and was completely trusted, he could speak frankly to the president when the situation called for it. He always played it straight and never went behind the president's back. As he explained, "Taking your closest friend and ally by surprise is no winning formula." Before he announced his intention to sign the biodiversity treaty, Mulroney instructed one of his ministers, Jean Charest, to "get [EPA head] Bill Reilly on the phone and tell him beforehand that Canada [was about] to sign."[468]

Third, Mulroney also understood that it was important "to get the United States to the table" not by "lecturing the Americans on their record" but by encouraging them to see more clearly what was in their own, long-term national interest. What was true then is also true today. The international system only really works when the United States is an engaged negotiating partner and is willing to play a constructive role. When America leads, there is a better chance that others will follow.

NINE

The Right Side of History:
Gorbachev, Yeltsin, and Kohl

"We are not renting our seat in Europe. We paid for it."
—BRIAN MULRONEY

WHEN MIKHAIL GORBACHEV ASSUMED POWER in Moscow in March 1985, and launched *perestroika* (political restructuring) and *glasnost* (economic openness) reforms, neither he nor leaders of the Western alliance had any notion of just how profound those changes would become"[469] Deng's earlier prophecy that Gorbachev was not going to last as leader proved to be correct. Meanwhile, more than thirty years later, the Chinese remain exclusively focused on economic reforms. Apart from concentrating on economic growth, the Chinese leaders are fixated on stability and security. Political freedoms and human rights are always secondary.

In the run-up to the 1990 Houston summit, G7 leaders had tentatively debated what to do with Gorbachev. Some suggested inviting him to the session. Most deferred to the wishes of their American host. The Americans were suspicious that Gorbachev's reforms were more cosmetic than real, and wary about the continuing military threat posed by the Soviet Union. The Japanese had similar reservations. The Europeans were, to varying degrees, more anxious to deepen ties with the most attractive leader anyone had seen from Moscow. For some, that included granting the U.S.S.R. G7 membership. Not surprisingly, the resulting consensus in Houston was quite restrained.

With his *glasnost* and *perestroika* reforms floundering in the Soviet Union, Mikhail Gorbachev came to the G7 summit in London in July 1991 with an urgent plea for help—financial assistance that he desperately needed to help stabilize his deteriorating domestic situation. It was an eloquent, passionate, and almost operatic performance. For more than one hour, Gorbachev explained why it was time for constructive engagement with the West. The G7 leaders were for the most part guardedly receptive. Some, like Germany's Helmut Kohl, who had the most at stake, were more convinced that the reforms underway were genuine, and they were ready to help. Others, like Japan's Kaifu and U.S. president George H.W. Bush (who was strongly influenced by Cold War veterans like Robert Gates and Brent Scowcroft), were less certain, hence less receptive. As Bush acknowledged separately to Brian Mulroney, it would be difficult for him to get congressional support for financial aid to a country that was building nuclear missiles that targeted New York and spending more than 20 per cent of its budget on military expenditures.[470] Some, like Jacques Delors of the European Commission, tended to interrogate Gorbachev almost in a lecturing manner, much to the annoyance of George Bush, who, in any event, disliked the presence of the unelected Delors at the G7 sessions. Bush's view was apparent from his recollection that Brian Mulroney made "equally important points to Gorbachev but in a more collegial tone and without the lecture or scolding."[471]

Brian Mulroney was one of the few leaders to actively engage Gorbachev at the G7 table. When the embattled Soviet leader indicated how difficult it was for him to cut military spending without a modus vivendi of some sort with the West, Mulroney replied that improved relations diminished the threat to Moscow. He described the difficulty George Bush had in trying to persuade Congress to close military bases in the U.S., adding that there were no U.S. troops patrolling the Canada–U.S. border, in contrast to the massive Soviet deployment in Eastern

Europe. Suggesting that more needed to be done in Moscow itself, Mulroney also told Gorbachev that McDonald's restaurant owner George Cohon's efforts to establish locations in Moscow had been "like dental surgery," taking more than seventeen years to complete. Other G7 leaders reserved their response to separate bilateral meetings on the aprons of the summit session.[472]

While the G7 nations' initial response to Gorbachev was cautious, Mulroney subsequently observed that this meeting "signalled the end of the Cold War" and, in that sense alone, made the London summit memorable.[473] Putting matters into perspective, Brian Mulroney observed separately, "If Gorbachev had said in 1985 that he proposed to do all these things [under *glasnost* and *perestroika*] and asked whether we would help if he did, I believe all of us would have hurried to write a cheque with our contribution."[474]

Some G7 leaders, including Mulroney, were torn between their personal desire to help Gorbachev and the need to tread carefully on the strategic upheaval in play. For instance, in talks with Helmut Kohl in Germany in 1991 Mulroney indicated that he planned to announce the scale-back of Canadian troops in Europe because he "owed it to Gorbachev to show tangible gains to his domestic reforms."[475] On the other hand, at the All-Star baseball game in Toronto (July 1991) Bush told Mulroney that there would be "no miracle or blank cheque for Gorbachev. Our readiness to assist will be linked to fundamental commitments by him to real reform in the U.S.S.R."[476]

Mulroney played a tangential role in bringing Bush and Gorbachev together. Following his own visit to Moscow in November 1989, he reported to Bush that Gorbachev wanted to establish trust with the U.S. president when the two met in Malta in December. As Bush recalled later, Mulroney said the Soviet leader "was expecting no miracles or solutions, nor was he expecting offers of assistance. He simply wanted to get to know me better."[477] The departmental record of Mr. Mulroney's briefing to President Bush following his visit to Moscow states, "The Prime Minister appealed strongly to the President, as leader of the Alliance, to be guided by his own gut instinct but to seize the historic moment and extend a hand to Gorbachev, especially on arms control. It was evident from President Bush's statement on leaving Washington the next day that the Prime Minister's message, even his exact words, had registered."[478] This White House dinner was a classic example of the exercise of influence at the most senior level.

At the same time, Mulroney "lobbied hard for the U.S.S.R. to be granted observer status at the GATT as well as for progressive integration of the Soviets into the International Monetary Fund, the World Bank and other international financial institutions."[479] The Americans, notably Bush, Baker, and Scowcroft, remained skeptical, particularly because of continuing Soviet support for Cuba.

Gorbachev's dramatic performance in London stood in sharp contrast to the stolid, unemotional, and unyielding style of his immediate predecessors—Brezhnev, Andropov, and Chernenko—the latter two dying shortly after taking office. In personality alone, Gorbachev was a breath of fresh air. But Gorbachev was riding a whirlwind of internal forces that rapidly spun out of control. His vibrant persona and his plea for assistance in London did not spare him from a coup attempt in Moscow later in August of 1991—an event that galvanized a more considerate response from the West, especially from the U.S.

Before anyone really knew what had happened in Moscow, notably the fate of Mikhail Gorbachev, George Bush convened an unusual international telethon from his Maine summer residence. He invited Brian Mulroney to join him in making calls to each of the other G7 leaders to establish a firm, common response repudiating the actions of the coup organizers and demanding the immediate return to power of Gorbachev.

At the time of the coup, Brian Mulroney clashed sharply with the cautious "wait and see" advice from External Affairs. Because his principal concern was Gorbachev's well-being, the prime minister quickly served notice that Canada's financial assistance would be suspended until more was known about Gorbachev's status.[480] At the same time, Boris Yeltsin was leading public protests in Moscow aimed at curtailing the attempted coup. Gorbachev returned to Moscow unharmed thanks in large part to the intervention by Yeltsin. His dramatically defiant role saved Gorbachev temporarily but eventually catapulted Yeltsin himself into power in Moscow. Just as Deng had predicted, Gorbachev was swept aside. Events moved abruptly out of his control.

If the coup against Gorbachev had succeeded, Moscow's response to the sudden political upheaval spreading across its former empire might have been much less compliant. That is why Yeltsin's personal courage in mustering massive street protests was determinant. He took advantage from a public thirst for change that the coup plotters could not comprehend. Their positions of personal privilege within the Soviet system shielded them from the deprivations imposed on the citizenry they once ruled.

More than anything else, these calamitous events demonstrated that actions on the ground rapidly overwhelmed conventional thinking, coordinated planning, and the status quo. Gorbachev's striking reforms in the Soviet Union ultimately sparked the collapse of the Soviet Union, the fall of the Berlin Wall, the unification of Germany, and the liberation of Eastern and Central Europe—the most transformational changes the world had witnessed since 1945. For a brief, shining moment, the world saw the prospect of a "new world order" with the spread of greater political liberty in Central and Eastern Europe and a more hopeful, albeit tentative, environment for global peace. Actions that unshackled authoritarian regimes in East Germany, Poland, Czechoslovakia, Hungary, and the Baltic States initiated political changes that many assumed could not be easily reversed. The newly liberated countries of Eastern and Central Europe rapidly joined both the EU and NATO, while remnants of the U.S.S.R. established varying degrees of linkage with an increasingly isolated mother Russia.

The leading personalities of the day—including Brian Mulroney, primarily on the strength of his position of trust with many of the others— were instrumental in steering events without bloodshed or rancor. But the relatively smooth way events transpired following Gorbachev's participation in the London summit is essentially a tribute to the astute, disciplined, and diplomatic leadership of George H.W. Bush. Equally notable was the unusual candor and trust Bush displayed with Mulroney, whom he consulted frequently and often spontaneously because, as he observed, "Brian understood the political pressures on me in the U.S. on these issues more than the others. He also had no real historical blinkers that prevented him from looking around the corner and getting on the right side of history."[481]

Bush's national security advisor, Brent Scowcroft, described what was perhaps the most vital ingredient of all—interpersonal relations. "President Bush invested an enormous amount of time in personal diplomacy and, in my opinion, it was indispensable to the success of our foreign policy. . . . As a result, foreign leaders tended to be there when we needed them."[482] Bush's own take was as follows: "While most countries respect the U.S., they want to know and trust that the U.S. also has great respect for them, for their ways and their sovereignty. . . . If you have confidence in someone, confidence built through personal contacts, you can get a lot more done."[483]

Mulroney kept a clear focus on these remarkable world events even though a domestic constitutional crisis was developing as a result of last-minute opposition to the Meech Lake Accord. At one point in August 1991, he was approached privately by the U.S. president to see if he would be prepared to serve as secretary-general of the UN. Bush expressed confidence that Mulroney's nomination would gain support from all G7 leaders, as well as from Gorbachev—a clear sign of Mulroney's good standing in the international community. While distinctly honoured by the overture, the prime minister decided that he could not accept. His primary responsibility lay in Canada, trying to salvage a new consensus from the setback over Meech Lake. Nonetheless, this invitation was a tangible example of the relationship of trust he had established with the U.S. president.

Yeltsin's less cerebral, more colourful personality, in comparison to Gorbachev's, proved initially to be more compelling to several G7 leaders, including Mulroney, who turned his personal charm (and hunting skills) up several notches in sessions with Yeltsin both in Ottawa and Russia, and made tangible financial commitments to Russia (e.g., $222 million, "a wise investment in peace"). Mulroney also nimbly chaperoned a wary Yeltsin through his first meeting with the newly elected president, Bill Clinton, at the Vancouver summit in April 1993. Yeltsin had established a very close relationship with George Bush, whom he had expected to win. Much to the consternation of Clinton's aides, the initial contacts with Yeltsin in Vancouver were stiff, with little semblance of dialogue. Apprised of the issue, Mulroney volunteered to "work on it." On the second day, and despite a heavily lubricated dinner the night before (for all except Mulroney, who does not drink alcohol), Yeltsin appeared much readier to conduct business with his new best friend "Beel." According to Mack McLarty, Clinton's chief of staff, "without Prime Minister Mulroney's fine and skilled experienced hand . . . I do not believe we would have reached that initial rapport."[484]

However, Yeltsin was soon overwhelmed by internal frustrations and rapidly deteriorating economic conditions back home, exacerbated even further by gross corruption that involved some of his associates and his own family. Despite cosmetic attempts to hold portions of the former U.S.S.R. together, the disintegration into separate republics only made matters worse, stirring deep resentment over the way the Russian Federation was being humiliated in the global, public eye.

The events Mulroney took part in during the 1990s had far-reaching consequences. Russia's endemic economic and political difficulties fuelled the rise of Vladimir Putin, who, to this day, is taking provocative actions intended to restore respect for Russia in the world and to instill pride in Russia at home. Putin was more than willing to turn to his political advantage the resentment over what had become, in his view, a "Western takeover" of much of the former Soviet Empire in Europe. He brazenly seized Crimea and moved to destabilize Eastern Ukraine. The annexation of Crimea prompted the expulsion of Russia from the G8, a group of leaders it had attended as a guest since 1994 and as a formal member since 1998. The move also triggered a wave of economic sanctions from the West against Russia, reigniting tensions not seen since the Cold War. Under Putin, Russia tacked strategically by providing lethal military support to President Assad in Syria and by cultivating closer ties with countries like Iran and Turkey to consolidate a stronger foothold in the Middle East and help fill the vacuum left by the United States. Assad's actions in Syria, backed by Russia, led to a massive refugee exodus and generated instability throughout the region. That may well have been part of Putin's motive.

An unintended consequence of the collapse of the Soviet Union was that the glue that held the Western alliance (NATO) together gradually began to atrophy. The rationale for NATO suddenly had less purpose, and the post 9/11 menace of terrorism was less of a motivation for cohesion. "Coalitions of the willing" became embroiled in inconclusive wars in Afghanistan, Libya, and the Middle East that sapped the U.S.'s willingness to lead and compounded the challenge for alliance cohesion.

GERMAN UNIFICATION

Speaking to a committee of the Bundestag (German parliament) in November 1993, German chancellor Helmut Kohl declared that "Germans will always remember three foreign leaders for their work in assisting their nation's quest for unity. Looking back, I must name three people who really helped us. I am referring only to Heads of State and Government. There was George Bush, who did not hesitate for one minute when it came to German unity. There was Brian Mulroney. And there was Mikhail Gorbachev."[485] Kohl's observation fell on deaf ears in Canada. Not one media source picked it up. And yet it underscored a central tenet of this book—the extent to which Brian Mulroney's careful cultivation of relationships with key foreign leaders allowed him to play a significant role in the most momentous world issues of his time.

Kohl had, at least since 1985, been confident that the Berlin Wall would come down and thought that the event would be a catalyst for unification. Over a G7 lunch in New York that year, Kohl told Mulroney that television commercials from West Germany would demonstrate what West German consumers had available to them, in stark contrast to the limited selection of goods in the East. "When the East Germans have had their fill of the stultifying system called communism" he declared, "the Wall is going to come down."[486] Acting on cue and with an acute sense of time and space, President Ronald Reagan gave the prospect a provocative nudge in June 1987. Standing at the Brandenburg Gate, and ignoring the more cautious entreaties of his own State Department, Reagan declared, "Mr. Gorbachev, tear down this wall!"

Few, if any, could have predicted just how quickly the tide of history would move ahead in Germany, or the peaceful way the cataclysmic events would unfold. Having cultivated a close personal relationship not only with presidents Reagan and Bush but also with dominant European leaders like Prime Minister Thatcher, Chancellor Kohl, and President Mitterrand, Brian Mulroney played a tactful supporting role, working closely with George Bush to help overcome the hard memories of two world wars and gravitate to "the right side of history."

There were huge obstacles to overcome. When Gorbachev visited Ottawa in May 1990—the first visit to Canada by a Soviet leader since 1971—he expressed an "extraordinarily visceral fear of German reunification, exacerbated by the speed at which events were unfolding" after the collapse of the Berlin Wall. Brian Mulroney counselled him to accept the idea of a united Germany in NATO and not to publicly express his opposition during his subsequent visit to Washington. "Bush," he advised, "cannot and will not relent and you will wind up humiliated."[487]

After the fall of the Berlin Wall and as political freedoms surged throughout Eastern Europe, the details of Moscow's authoritarian rule exposed scars of a different nature and inevitably cast the collapsing Soviet Union in an even more unfavourable light. Nonetheless, just before Mulroney was to visit Moscow and shortly after the Berlin wall had come down, George Bush urged the prime minister to assure Gorbachev that he would not "milk the fall of the wall at Gorbachev's expense." In Mulroney's view, Bush was "mindful of the dangers of instability in the Soviet Union and respectful of Russian pride. He kept his own counsel and this was one of his finest moments as president."[488] This message also underscored Bush's innate sense of decency and class, attributes that made him unique as the leader of the Western allies but that escaped notice at home at election time.

Even if he had to accept unification, Gorbachev was determined to keep a unified Germany out of NATO. He also wanted to retain a presence for the Soviet military in Eastern Europe, including Eastern Germany. Thatcher and Mitterrand also had grave reservations about German reunification. In fact, Margaret Thatcher had such deep misgivings that she had great difficulty appearing with the German ambassador in London on the eve of formal reunification in October 1990, and had to be cajoled to do so by her key advisers. She also told the American president that she would not appear at a special ceremony that the German chancellor was organizing on October 3. Thatcher worried openly that a united Germany would dominate Europe, and so great was her fear that she even convened a secret meeting of British historians at Chequers, the official country residence of the British prime minister, to discuss whether Germany had recovered from its Nazi past.[489] The scars of two world wars and the lessons of that history were uppermost concerns for Britain and France. But they had little leverage over events on the ground.

Discussions among the allies were often emotional and rancorous. There were serious concerns about the consequences that a united Germany would bring to Europe, and no ready consensus on the suddenly stronger role it might play, especially in NATO and the EU. The Germans, especially Foreign Minister Hans Genscher, adamantly insisted this was an internal issue primarily if not exclusively for Germans to decide. Mulroney had told Bush that "the minimum price for German unity should be full German membership in NATO, full support in all western organizations and for American leadership of the alliance."[490] When Genscher challenged the propriety of Canada having any position on the issue, Mulroney retorted bluntly, "We are not renting our seat in Europe. We paid for it. If people want to know how Canada paid, they should check out the graves in Belgium and France. NATO got us this far. Solidarity in the alliance will get us further." This intervention pleased Bush. "Brian," he wrote later "was right on target."[491] Bush had an underlying strategic view of the advantages of reunification for the western alliance and for Western values, particularly in light of the upheaval occurring in the Soviet Union, but he was also under enormous pressure from the British, French, and Russians to oppose it.

Paul Heinbecker, who was chief foreign policy advisor and speechwriter to Mulroney (and would later serve as Canada's ambassador to Germany and then the United Nations), wrote, "Mulroney intervened with Bush, whose views would be decisive in NATO, arguing that, after decades of assuring Germans they would be united one day, it would be unfair and potentially dangerous to renege on what was widely understood by the German people to be a promise. It did not take an especially long memory to realize that disappointing the German people was not a good idea. Mulroney made the same argument to Gorbachev, Mitterrand, and Thatcher."[492]

However, close consultative relations at the leadership level did not always translate into the same kind of cooperation when it came to meetings among foreign ministers. On the aprons of a NATO foreign ministers meeting convened by External Affairs Minister Joe Clark in Ottawa in February 1990, the "Two Plus Four" agreement was crafted privately at the Rockcliffe residence of the German ambassador as a fig leaf of sorts for selective alliance consultations—the two being the two Germanys, the four being the U.S.S.R., the U.S., Britain, and Europe—the major World War II allies who served as occupying powers in the post-war period. The agreement was intended primarily to temper French and British, as well as Russian, anxieties. Given Canada's exclusion from the Two Plus Four talks at the residence, Derek Burney had a more jaundiced, or less diplomatic, take on the "private" accord struck in Ottawa. As Canada's ambassador in Washington at the time, Derek Burney complained bluntly to National Security Advisor Brent Scowcroft that "Even the piano player in a whore house knows what is going on upstairs." Burney added in his memoir that "Scowcroft winced but clearly saw larger priorities than the perennial lament about Canadian sensitivities." U.S. secretary of state James Baker wrote a note to Mulroney in appreciation of a breakfast the prime minister hosted for him and Soviet foreign minister Eduard Shevardnadze at that time, saying that "what happened in Ottawa could have real historical significance."[493]

Events on the ground rapidly outpaced any plans or private Two Plus Four consultative umbrellas involving outside powers. Under the bold leadership of Helmut Kohl, the two Germanys merged abruptly in October 1990, warts and all, and at a pace and in a successful manner no one could have planned less than a year after the collapse of the Berlin Wall. There is no way to interpret this stunning event as other than a severe setback for an already crumbling Soviet Union. The most extraordinary consequence is that the situation unfolded without military engagements of any kind, or civil revolt. The collapse of the Berlin Wall unleashed a shock wave of public demonstrations that reverberated throughout Central and Eastern Europe. Memories of brutal putdowns by Soviet troops in Hungary in 1956 and Czechoslovakia in 1968 had not faded. As it became evident that Gorbachev had no intention of suppressing protests with the force of arms, the communist governments throughout the region were toppled unceremoniously and without violence, inspired by courageous leaders such as Lech Wałęsa in Poland and Václav Havel in Czechoslovakia. Helmut Kohl seized the initiative in Germany in what Mulroney indicated to his foreign minister was a "takeover, not a merger." It was a cataclysmic change openly supported by most of those directly affected.

For Brian Mulroney, it was simply a case of being on the right side of history.

ASSISTANCE TO RUSSIA AND EASTERN EUROPE

During his time as prime minister, Mulroney stood out as someone who understood that the battle for human rights and democracy was most directly engaged in Russia and the countries of Central and Eastern Europe. In 1991, for example, Mulroney proposed doubling the capital base of the European Bank for Reconstruction and Development (EBRD), a proposal that raised many eyebrows. Pushing the aid packages for Russia and Eastern Europe through the system at a time when the budget deficit was off target (and soon to be more so) took a lot of effort. Russia was already in arrears on payments owed in respect of Canadian Wheat Board and export development credits. Russia today is not a pretty picture as it descends into authoritarian rule, and the West is often blamed for not having done more to ensure that democracy took firm root there, though Canada under Mulroney was perhaps an exception.

Canada was one of the first countries to endorse the 1989 Paris Sommet de L'Arche Declaration calling for international assistance to support "freedom and democracy" in the newly independent states of Central and Eastern Europe. As Jeanne Laux points out, under the directive of the prime minister, Canada was "quick to mobilize emergency aid," putting together a $72 million dollar package of programs for Poland and Hungary while establishing a new mechanism, the Task Force for Central and Eastern Europe, to coordinate Canada's bilateral assistance.[494] The assistance program was highly innovative and did not necessary involve the allocation of "new" money: "For example, in Poland, a 'counterpart fund' was created from the proceeds of food aid (food sold on concessional terms) and the task force was permitted to redirect that local currency to support its projects. Humanitarian aid, such as milk powder for Bulgaria, was donated from surplus stocks by the Department of Agriculture. Canada took part in the debt forgiveness plan for Poland, agreed upon by the Paris Club creditor governments, but foregoing interest on half the debt owed, a gesture worth some $1.6 billion to Poland but not adding to Canada's current deficit."[495] In addition, Canada provided food credits and technical assistance to the newly sovereign Baltic states. Along with these initiatives, Canada was a founding shareholder in the EBRD. One of the most innovative programs was the Canadian Nuclear Safety Initiative, which was established in June 1992 to improve nuclear reactor safety in the territories of the former Soviet Union to ensure that there would never be another Chernobyl-type disaster.

But as the late John Halstead, who served as Canada's ambassador to NATO and Germany, judiciously observed, "Unfortunately, the deeds of Canada's defence policy did not match the words of Canada's foreign policy. While Canada's interest in Europe was strongly reaffirmed following a foreign policy review carried out in early 1990, the defence policy review . . . seemed to be heading in the opposite direction."[496] Although the government committed itself to stationing 1,100 troops in Germany in its 1991 budget and the prime minister promised the German chancellor that Canadian troops would remain so long as they were "needed and wanted,"[497] in the spring of 1992 the government did an about face. As the *New York Times* reported, the decision did not sit well in Washington or with NATO: "Reflecting eased East–West tensions and Canada's severe budget constraints, Prime Minister Brian Mulroney's Government has announced that it will pull out all its combat forces from Europe by the end of 1994. The decision, which was disclosed late Tuesday in the Government's newest budget, a fiscal blueprint for the coming 12 months, has stirred angry reactions from the Bush Administration and NATO headquarters, mirroring fears that it will increase Congressional pressures for faster American withdrawal and unravel the 43-year-old North Atlantic Treaty Organization. A State Department spokesman said Washington was 'very disappointed' and would have 'greatly preferred a continuing Canadian presence within the NATO force structure in Europe.' The NATO secretary-general, Manfred Wörner, noted Ottawa's action 'with considerable regret, given the political and military importance of the presence of Canadian forces in Europe,' according to a statement issued from his office in Brussels."[498] However, the government defended the decision because the troops were needed in Bosnia, which was true (see Chapter 10).

UKRAINE

Following the aborted coup against him in August 1991, Gorbachev, in a last-ditch effort to save the Soviet Union, moved to set up the Union of Sovereign States. In the meantime, Ukraine declared independence on August 24, 1991. Mulroney had been staying with President Bush at the president's summer compound in Kennebunkport, Maine. Early in the morning, on getting the news, Mulroney immediately called his ambassador to Washington, Derek Burney, who was staying in a motel nearby. He told him what he planned to do and instructed him to get a press release prepared in Ottawa. Burney asked Mulroney if he had discussed his idea with President Bush, who might not want to be surprised by such an announcement being made from his front lawn. The prime minister said he would, but asked his ambassador to check as well with Brent Scowcroft on arrival at the compound later in the morning. Scowcroft was puzzled, but Burney explained "there were more than a million reasons why we wanted to be among the first."[499]

Mulroney had told Mikhail Gorbachev that he would recognize Ukraine as an independent, sovereign nation even before the United States did. Mulroney explained that he owed it to Ukrainians and those fighting for their freedom: "I told (Gorbachev) directly and bluntly that the forces of freedom were burning in Ukraine. . . . And I was going to encourage them, not extinguish them. . . . We did what we believed was right, and I believe history may prove that we were."[500] The prime minister's decision was swift (even though some members of his cabinet favoured a more cautious approach) and came right after Ukrainians formally voted on their independence in a public referendum on December 1, 1991, which was observed by three members of the Canadian Parliament and Alberta's chief electoral officer. On December 2, 1991, Canada formally recognized Ukraine and initiated the establishment of diplomatic relations. It was the first country to do so, followed by Poland.

Although the decision was clearly precipitated by domestic political considerations—most critically the presence of more than a million Canadians of Ukrainian decent—that was not the only factor that drove it, as Mulroney's foreign minister at the time, Barbara McDougall, explained many years later: "Ukraine is of enormous strategic significance. It was then, and it is now. In 1991, it was the epicentre of the Soviet Union's nuclear capacity: By declaring independence, it was a potential nuclear power. On its soil were more than 1,800 nuclear warheads, more than those of Britain, France, and China combined. As a condition of recognition by virtually every Western country, the newly independent Ukraine agreed to sign the Nuclear Non-Proliferation Treaty. Further, the U.S., Russia and Ukraine worked out a deal to destroy all the aging, rusting nukes in the country. It's hard to emphasize the importance of this, given it was just five years after the nuclear power disaster at Chernobyl—just 132 kilometres from Kiev."[501]

LESSONS

More than four decades of sharp division between the U.S.-led Western alliance and the Soviet Union's Warsaw Pact coalition had witnessed a period of acute tension, with the imminent threat of nuclear devastation. The fall of the Berlin Wall precipitated the end of the Cold War and transformed both the political face of Eastern and Central Europe and the balance of power in world affairs. As Mulroney himself acknowledged, "Of all my nearly nine years as prime minister, those two months— November and December 1989—were among the most exhilarating I was to experience. The world was literally changing in front of our eyes, and Canada and Canadians were being asked to play a significant role on history's stage at a vital moment."[502]

The upheavals in 1990–91 left the U.S. as the sole global superpower. Remarkably, all these monumental changes were achieved in a relatively stable manner. It was a period of epic, even convulsive change in world affairs—the consequences of which continue to reverberate. The process was bumpy at times, and there are uncertainties and repercussions that resound to this day, notably in the remnants of the Soviet Union, but there was little bloodshed. The seeds of democracy remain fragile and the attraction of authoritarian rule is still an undercurrent in pockets of the former Soviet Empire, including Russia itself. A humiliated Russia did become increasingly resentful at being reduced to regional rather than global power status. And a much darker mood in Russia now feeds support for Putin and his anti-Western actions, including provocative measures taken in 2016–17 to influence elections in the United States and across Europe.

The non-triumphant and steady hand of George H.W. Bush was the most critical element throughout, helping to preserve stability and cohesion during the tumult, and yet his stewardship failed to resonate with American voters, who soon after denied him a second term in 1992. And the optimistic prospects of a "new world order" faded as quickly as Bush's electoral fortunes. (As Winston Churchill discovered even more emphatically in July 1945, electorates in democracies give little credit to foreign policy success.)

The task now facing the Western alliance is to manage the tensions stemming from a revanchist Russia without compromising the principles of freedom and liberty unleashed in Eastern and Central Europe. Putin's background as a KGB officer gave him not only insider knowledge but also a network of tough-minded associates able and experienced in exercising authority. The KGB was one of the few institutions that remained intact in post-Soviet Russia. By exercising nationalist appeal to Russian pride and using the U.S. and the West as a scapegoat for all that had gone wrong in the Soviet Union and Eastern Europe, Putin established a position of absolute control little different from that which preceded Gorbachev's rise to power. But Putin's aspirations for the nation's past superpower glory are hampered by an economy that is sputtering under ramshackle, if not kleptocratic, management that primarily benefits a few oligarchs as well as Putin himself. Russia's military muscle cannot be discounted, but the horrendous record of attacks against civilians in Syria leaves little room for honour or pride.

As significant as the events leading to the end of the Cold War were, what was unusual was the degree to which Canada participated in the transformation of the world order. By dint of his interpersonal skills and the position of trust he had established with two American presidents and several key European leaders, Mulroney ensured that Canada was an active player, not a bystander, in the most dramatic and consequential events of the past fifty years. Influence in foreign policy requires more than good intentions—of which Canada has a vast quantity but which often reveal more posture than substance and few tangible dividends. Mulroney demonstrated that candid, trusted interpersonal relations can be influential, if not pivotal, in helping to shape unanticipated events. As Bush recorded in his memoir, "Brian demonstrated that it was possible to be both a strong leader of Canada and a true friend of the United States. When we had disputes on trade or environmental issues, he never backed away from placing Canada's interests first. But when we had differences over policy, our personal relationship helped us talk about them frankly, and allowed us to try to resolve them privately, without public posturing."[503]

The period immediately following the Second World War is often celebrated as the "golden age" of Canadian foreign policy. Yet, even though Canada emerged from the war with the fourth largest army, a world-class navy, and a highly effective air force—arguably a military more consequential during the war than, say, that of France[504]—our political leadership during the war was generally detached from critical deliberations about the conduct of the war and the situation in Germany in the immediate post-war world. Despite the "golden" self-appraisal of Canada's role in the creation of international institutions, we rarely assumed a role commensurate with our earlier military effort on major, strategic post-war political issues, not least of which was the occupation of Germany. Canada arguably played a bigger role in the war effort than France but was not granted occupying power status—a point seldom mentioned by anyone, least of all Canadians.[505] Unlike South Africa under Prime Minister Jan Smuts, who was in regular dialogue with Winston Churchill throughout, Canada was something of a bystander. Both during and immediately after the war, Canada was treated essentially as a colony of Britain and not as a sovereign power in its own right.

During each phase of the enormous upheaval in world affairs that occurred from 1985 to 1992, Canada was a distinctive player, engaged directly in positive outcomes on events few had foreseen. Canada's role hinged on the unique position of trust and confidence that Brian Mulroney established through his systematically close, personal relations with presidents Reagan and Bush, Chancellor Kohl, and Prime Minister Thatcher. This is not "made in Canada" conjecture, as were verdicts about the "golden age." It is confirmed by judgments rendered publicly and in memoirs by other global leaders from Mulroney's time in office.

Reflecting on the job and the influence of a Canadian prime minister in world affairs, and as recorded by his former chief of staff, Hugh Segal, Mulroney stated, "It is not because of who we are or where we are in the geopolitical framework but because of how hard we work to make sure we get noticed. That's what few people understand. It is not because of membership in institutions but because of interpersonal relations. Without that, we just do not count, certainly not in terms we would like to count."[506] This was the driving force or catechism for Brian Mulroney's effort to influence major world affairs, and remains a key lesson for Canada's leaders even today.

TEN

Safeguarding the New Global Order:
The Gulf War and Peacekeeping

"Some Security Council members have opposed intervention
in Yugoslavia where many innocent people have been dying on
the grounds of national sovereignty. Quite frankly, such invocations
of the principle of national sovereignty are as out of date and offensive
to me as the police declining to stop family violence simply because
a man's home is supposed to be his castle."

—BRIAN MULRONEY

O N AUGUST 1–2, 1990, UNDER THE COVER OF DARKNESS, the armed forces of Saddam Hussein, the dictator of Iraq, stormed into Kuwait, seizing control of the small country and its capital, Kuwait City. They encountered little resistance, quickly overwhelming the country's defences and its equally surprised population. The emir of Kuwait, and most of the members of his government, quickly fled the country, leaving their citizens to fend for themselves. Thus began one of the first major crises of the post–Cold War era—one that would reshape the map of the Middle East but also test the mettle of U.S. president George H.W. Bush, who was just entering the mid-term of his presidency. It was also a crisis that would test the resolve of Canada's prime minister, who faced a public and an official opposition that were deeply skeptical about any kind of military action against Iraq.

Almost as soon as the crisis erupted, President Bush reached out to his good friend, Brian Mulroney, for guidance on how to deal with it. He asked Mulroney to fly down to Washington on August 6 for an off-the-record discussion over dinner in the family quarters of the White House. Mulroney was accompanied by Canada's ambassador to Washington, Derek Burney and Stanley Hartt, his chief of staff. When they arrived at the White House, Burney was surprised to see that Barbara Bush had been invited to the intimate dinner, which also included National Security Advisor Brent Scowcroft. Burney apologized for not having arranged for Mila Mulroney to accompany the prime minister to the dinner. "No worries," said the prime minister, "You know why Barbara is here, Derek. It is because she is the keeper of the flame. She is the one person in the room if George is going to war that he can trust implicitly."[507]

Bush had just returned from Aspen, Colorado, where both he and British prime minister Margaret Thatcher had been invited to deliver speeches at the fortieth anniversary conference of the Aspen Institute, a major U.S. think-tank. During their meeting at the conference, Thatcher had urged the president to take swift and decisive military action against Saddam Hussein. With her characteristic overbearing manner, she went on to tell the president privately, "Remember George, I was almost to be defeated in England when the Falkland conflict happened. I stayed in office for eight years after that." When the president equivocated, Thatcher replied that she had his back, urging him, at the same time, to show resolve: "Don't go wobbly on me George, don't go wobbly"— a comment that Thatcher's communications director quickly conveyed to the British press to boost her own sagging poll numbers.[508] (In November, she would find herself unceremoniously forced out of office by members of her own party.)

Over dinner at the White House, Mulroney put two questions to Bush and Scowcroft: how would the U.S. plan to deal with Iraq if Saddam Hussein took Americans who were living in that country, including diplomats, hostage? Memories of the Iranian U.S. diplomatic hostage crisis were still fresh, and any kind of hostage-taking crisis could hinder a forceful American response. Mulroney was assured that any potential hostage crisis would not be allowed to stand in the way of military action. The second question had to do with how the United States planned to lay the political groundwork for military action against Saddam Hussein. Mulroney's advice on that matter was clear and pointed. He urged Bush to build a broad international consensus that would include the support of both the UN and NATO before any kind of action was taken. "You must have consensus and you, a former ambassador to the United Nations, are perfectly situated to achieve just that," he said. Mulroney made it clear to the president that without a UN resolution, Canada "could not support this initiative."[509] His advice clearly ran contrary to what some of the president's military advisers were urging. It also ran contrary to the advice the president had received in Aspen from Margaret Thatcher, who had little patience with the UN.

Mulroney urged Bush to reach out to French president François Mitterrand right away, stressing that it wasn't good enough to consult only with the British prime minister if he wanted to bring the Europeans onside. Bush immediately picked up the phone and asked the White House switchboard to place a call to the French president as soon as Mitterrand got to his office the next morning. The fact that the American president was up at 3 a.m. to place a 9 a.m. call (Paris time) was not lost on the French president, nor was the fact that the president, again on Mulroney's advice, was consulting with Mitterrand about his proposed course of action. Mulroney had developed close relations with Mitterrand through the two leaders' cooperation in the creation of La Francophonie. He knew that Mitterrand was sensitive and status conscious. By calling him at the beginning of the crisis, Bush was sending a clear signal that he needed Mitterrand's support, which he got right away.

As the dinner ended, Bush handed Mulroney the raw CIA files on Iraq and the top-secret brief he had just received from the U.S. envoy to Iraq, April Glaspie, to read on his flight back to Ottawa. His gesture was a remarkable sign of the trust and respect the American president had for his friend, the Canadian prime minister, as U.S. presidents are not generally predisposed to hand over top-secret files to the leader of another country.

Over the course of the next several weeks, Mulroney provided counsel to the U.S. president on a wide range of issues. He tried to ease tensions between Bush and King Hussein of Jordan, who the president believed was too cozy with Saddam Hussein. During a visit to the presidential summer compound at Kennebunkport, Maine, Mulroney suggested that the president meet directly with the king to hear out his concerns and better understand his position. The meeting took place a few weeks later. Bush shared with Mulroney the pressure he was coming under from hawks within his own administration and members of his own party in Congress who wanted him to take swift military action. "When you're up 72–0 it is not time for the long bomb" (i.e., a surgical strike), Mulroney advised Bush. At Kennebunkport, Mulroney also made his strongest pitch that Bush should get UN Security Council approval before taking any kind of military action. He also made it crystal clear that a UN resolution authorizing the coalition's action was essential."[510]

Bush also asked Mulroney to call Egypt's president, Hosni Mubarak, to draw the Arab world—a first—into the international coalition he was forming. Mulroney, who knew Mubarak, did so right away. The Egyptian leader was wary about getting too close to the Americans, even though he disliked Saddam and was deeply worried about the consequences for the Arab world of one Arab state seizing the territory of another. He told Mulroney that Saddam had promised Egypt billions of dollars from the Kuwait treasury if Egypt threw its support behind the Iraqi leader. Mubarak asked Mulroney pointedly if Canada was worried about the casualties it might incur if military action became necessary. Mulroney replied that he was worried about Canadian planes being shot down by the Iraqis. The Egyptian leader told Mulroney not to worry because the Iraqis had the worst air force in the world. How did he know? He knew because, as he joked with Mulroney, the Egyptians had trained them!

As a non-permanent member of the UN Security Council at the time, Canada also had ringside seats at the drama that was playing out in New York. With strong Canadian backing, in late November of 1990, the Security Council passed Resolution 678, drafted with the assistance of Yves Fortier, a distinguished Montreal lawyer whom Mulroney had appointed to head Canada's mission to the United Nations. The resolution essentially delivered Iraq an ultimatum: withdraw from Kuwait before January 15, 1991, or the council would reserve to itself the right to use "all necessary means" to force Iraq out of Kuwait after the deadline. The resolution passed by twelve votes. The only holdouts were Cuba and Yemen, which voted against it, and China, which uncharacteristically did not vote against it but chose instead to abstain. Some believed this was because China was trying to curry international favour to secure an easing of the sanctions imposed after the 1989 Tiananmen Square massacres.

The prime minister knew that he also had to lay the domestic political groundwork for the military action against Iraq that would almost surely come sometime early in the new year if Saddam did not do the Security Council's bidding. Innately suspicious of American intentions, neither the Canadian public nor the political opposition favoured military action, preferring to let sanctions take their course in the hope that Saddam Hussein would back down. Public opinion polls showed that Canadians were willing to support military action against Iraq if it took place under UN auspices and in support of UN objectives. One poll showed that 53 per cent of Canadians wanted Canada to play only a defensive role in the conflict.[511] Canadian peace groups—including the Canadian Peace Alliance, women's and labour groups, and the United Nations Association (UNAC)—were strongly opposed to military action.

The opposition parties wanted Parliament to be recalled when the government announced on August 10 that Canada was sending three ships (two destroyers and a supply ship) to the Persian Gulf to help police the economic embargo against Iraq. However, the order-in-council placing the ships on active service was only passed on September 15, well after the ships had crossed the Atlantic and entered the Mediterranean—but in time to meet the ten-day requirement for informing Parliament when it reconvened on September 24. In mid-September, Mulroney also ordered a squadron of CF-18 fighters to support the UN mission. Parliament gave its approval but only after a raucous debate on the government's Active Service Cabinet Order, which put the armed forces on a "war footing."[512]

Mulroney had stuck his political neck out with both deployments, a move that did not go unnoticed by other world leaders. Margaret Thatcher wrote to him to say, "I just wanted to let you know how much we appreciated your decision to send aircraft to the Gulf, to join Canada's ships there. That is very welcome indeed. It is so important that we should all be seen to be present alongside the United States. That is the best hope of convincing Saddam Hussein that there is no way out except withdrawal from Kuwait."[513] Thatcher obviously wasn't aware that not only was Canada there with its military to support the Americans, but that Mulroney was also providing constant counsel to the U.S. president on the diplomatic course he should follow.

On September 24, the House of Commons was asked to approve a motion calling for the "dispatch of members of the Canadian Forces to take part in the multinational military effort in and around the Arabian Peninsula." The motion was subsequently amended to include a resolution asking the government to "present a further resolution to this House in the event of an outbreak of hostilities involving Canadian Forces in and around the Arabian Peninsula."[514] The amended motion was approved on October 21.

Parliament convened early in the new year, on January 15, 1991, in an emergency session to discuss the recommendations of an ad hoc cabinet committee that was dealing with the escalating crisis in the Gulf. The prime minister moved a motion that the "House reaffirms its support of the United Nations in ending the aggression by Iraq against Kuwait."[515] But the newly elected Liberal leader was having none of it. Jean Chrétien proposed an amendment to the government's resolution, which urged "the continued issue of economic sanctions" and excluded "offensive military action by Canada at this time."[516] Chrétien also recommended that Canadian naval forces that were doing patrols in the Gulf to enforce the embargo against Iraq be withdrawn if war broke out. The New Democratic Party (NDP) also voiced its strong objections to any kind of military action and to giving the government a blank cheque to engage in military hostilities. However, Chrétien quickly discovered that his own Liberal caucus was deeply divided on the matter. John Turner, the former Liberal leader, sided with the government, as did many Liberal MPs. The House of Commons eventually approved the government's motion on January 22, with 217 for and 47 against.

The U.S.-led invasion, known as Operation Desert Storm, began on the night of January 16–17, 1991, to rout Saddam Hussein's forces out of Kuwait. At 7 p.m., as he was returning home in his car, Mulroney received a call from President Bush telling him the attack would be launched in two hours. The operation commenced with an aerial bombardment against a wide range of strategic targets in Iraq, with Canadian aircraft providing "sweep and escort missions."[517] Saddam Hussein retaliated by firing SCUD missiles into Israel in the vain hope that the Israelis would attack Iraq and thus draw Arab countries to his defence. It didn't happen. The war against Iraq was short and swift, and the thirty-five-member-strong coalition suffered few casualties as they engaged Saddam's army. As one observer of the war wrote, "Before dawn on 3 March the multinational coalition launched a ground assault to liberate Kuwait, Operation Desert Storm. In a swift and decisive campaign, lasting 100 hours Iraq's armed might was destroyed. Kuwait, ravaged by the Iraqi occupiers, was restored to independence."[518] It had taken a little over a month from start to finish to rout the Iraqi invader. It was a remarkable achievement diplomatically and militarily by any standard, and one in which Canada had played an important role on both counts.

Nevertheless, the government faced public criticism that it had simply been doing the bidding of the United States. (If the public and the media had been privy to the private communications between the prime minister and the U.S. president in the run up to the war, they might have come to a different conclusion.) Mulroney and External Affairs Minister Joe Clark felt the need to go on the political defensive. They gave speeches on post-war planning for the Middle East, recommending a regional security structure similar to the Conference on Security and Cooperation in Europe (CSCE), which would guarantee borders and provide for dispute resolution and confidence-building measures. They also urged a negotiated settlement to the Arab–Israeli conflict and a "world summit on instruments of war and weapons of mass destruction."[519] Many of these ideas were passed on to the UN secretary-general, although they did not find much favour with Canada's key allies, including the United States.

ENFORCING THE PEACE

During the fall 2015 federal election, the Liberal Party, led by Justin Trudeau, made much of the fact that it would restore the lustre to Canada's UN peacekeeping credentials and thus "bring Canada back" into the world, especially when it came to Canada's participation in UN peacekeeping missions. The long slide downwards in Canada's peacekeeping commitments did not, however, begin with the Harper government, as alleged by Trudeau. It started under the government of Jean Chrétien, which began to draw down the number of Canada's overseas peacekeeping deployments, although it was the Mulroney government that made the initial decision to pull out of Canada's commitment in Cyprus. Canadian troops had been there for over twenty-five years, the parties were not showing signs of reaching an agreement, and there were other countries that Canada believed should take their turn contributing peacekeepers. The longstanding Canadian mission in Cyprus formally ended in 1995.

There are many reasons why Canada decided to get out of the peace-keeping business, at least in a major way. Some missions, like the UN mission in Bosnia, were large and consumed much of our military capacity and attention. Later, Canada's participation in the NATO-led International Security Assistance Force (ISAF) mission in Afghanistan taxed the capacity of Canada's armed forces, greatly limiting the ability of Canadian defence forces to do much else. It was also a mission, as the Manley Commission reported, in which Canada took on a role for which our armed forces were not properly equipped—hence the large number of casualties. Weak political oversight of our military contributed to the dangerous assignment of our forces in Kandahar, which is not where NATO wanted us. It knew better.[520]

Developing countries now provide the bulk of the troops assigned to UN peacekeeping missions, especially those that are deployed in sub-Saharan Africa. They can do so far more cheaply than most developed countries, including Canada. Many of these missions are also "double-hatted," which is to say they began as missions led by regional or sub-regional organizations such as the Economic Community of West African States (ECOWAS) or the Organization of African Unity (OAU) before they received their official blessing from the UN Security Council.

Looking back at the historical record, no charge of neglect towards the UN or NATO can be levelled at the Mulroney government. Canada was an active participant in all sixteen UN peacekeeping missions that took place while Mulroney was in office, contributing more than 10 per cent of all troops assigned to the UN, whereas two decades later Canada's contribution had fallen to less than 0.1 per cent. Part of the reason was that Canada's defence budget in the early 1990s stood at 2 per cent of GDP, versus roughly 1 per cent in 2017, which clearly allowed Canada to make a more robust contribution to global security. However, we were not simply "present" when it came to UN peacekeeping; we actively shaped the overall strategy and purpose of those missions, especially as the nature of peacekeeping began to change in the immediate post–Cold War era from a more passive to a more active role that included peacekeeping "enforcement," which itself was not without controversy.

The main lesson of this period in Canadian diplomacy and defence policy is that Canada was effective because it acted in line with its commitments to NATO and the UN and with its capabilities. Canada had influence on both organizations because of the unusual network of respect the prime minister had cultivated with the key players at the time. Canada's commitments were shaped by its interests and its values, which were completely aligned. The origins of Canada's leadership on what subsequently came to be known as the Responsibility to Protect doctrine—which received its fullest expression under the leadership of Foreign Minister Lloyd Axworthy within Jean Chrétien's Liberal govern- ment—was initially developed and articulated during the Mulroney era. In various statements and speeches delivered at the UN, American univer- sities, and other forums, the prime minister and his foreign minister at the time, Barbara McDougall (who succeeded Joe Clark), implored the international community to take forceful action to protect innocent civilians because state sovereignty should be conditional, not absolute, when innocent lives are threatened.

THE BALKANS CRISIS

Confronted with the deteriorating situation in the former Yugoslavia in the early 1990s, the political environment on both sides of the Atlantic was one of intellectual and policy paralysis. For one thing, it was extremely difficult to diagnose the Yugoslav conflict. Many, particularly in Western Europe, held the view that it was a civil war and that it would therefore be best to steer clear of it. Instilling resolve into policy-makers was also difficult because they and the public were still gripped by a classical defi- nition of peacekeeping and could not bring themselves to accept that it was outmoded. Partly as a consequence of this limited perspective, UN peacekeepers were poorly equipped for war fighting. In Canada, the public did not want to see Canadian lives put at risk. There was a lot to be said for being cautious.

At the same time, a continuation of the prevailing situation was intol- erable, a widespread feeling that Mulroney and McDougall captured in their speeches. McDougall was frustrated by the failure of the European

Community and the Clinton administration to keep the pressure on the parties to come to the table. She opposed lifting the embargo on providing arms to the combatants, but she also wanted to keep the option of using force alive, and hinted at the possibility of more forceful peacekeeping. McDougall was also a major proponent of the International Criminal Court (ICC).

Mulroney was the first world leader to call for strong international action to deal with the rapidly escalating crisis in Bosnia. In a speech he delivered at Stanford University in the fall of 1991 at the invitation of former U.S. secretary of state George Shultz (a Stanford alumnus who had served under Ronald Reagan), Mulroney urged the international community to act decisively to avert further human rights atrocities against innocent civilians who were being butchered in the conflict. "Some Security Council members have opposed intervention in Yugoslavia, where many innocent people have been dying, on the grounds of national sovereignty. Quite frankly, such invocations of the principle of national sovereignty are as out of date and offensive to me as the police declining to stop family violence simple because a man's home is supposed to be his castle."[521]

Mulroney was seized with "the fact that in the early 1990s in the heart of Europe there was a bloodbath."[522] He believed strongly that Canada could not simply, in his own words, "sit around, do nothing and not provide leadership." In the case of the Americans, Mulroney observed "they didn't have to move and could make a virtue of it." But Canadians did not have that choice as a medium-sized power that had a major stake in maintaining a strong, rules-based international order. Mulroney also believed that Canada "could not simply make speeches, we also had to do something." He found that there was a lot of inertia in the Department of External Affairs when it came to taking any kind of action to avert the rapidly escalating conflict in the Balkans, which is one of the reasons why he and his foreign minister spoke out as strongly as they did. As Mulroney later explained, "Our traditions and the values we stood for were exportable Canadian products; it is one of the reasons why we did what we did."[523] There is little doubt that Mulroney was also influenced by his wife, Mila, who was of Bosnian-Serbian origin and had many friends in the Montreal community who were Bosnian, Croatian, Muslim, and Christian alike. They were all appalled by the mounting violence and death toll in the Balkans.

After the Serbian–Croatian ceasefire was negotiated under UN auspices by Cyrus Vance in early January 1992, Canada contributed 1,200 personnel to the 13,000-strong United Nations Protection Force (UNPROFOR) for Croatia. At the same time, Canada recognized Croatia and Slovenia as independent states and opened its wallets to provide humanitarian aid to those who had been uprooted by the conflict. Canadian brigadier-general Lewis Mackenzie was appointed UNPROFOR chief of staff, a post he filled with great distinction despite the many challenges that the mission faced. Although UNPROFOR was initially set up to be an interim force to help stabilize the situation in Croatia, it soon evolved into a humanitarian support mission in Bosnia and a preventive deployment mission in Macedonia (with the aim of preventing the war from spilling over into that country). To ensure safe havens for civilians, NATO, at the request of the UN Security Council, implemented plans for the military enforcement of a no-fly zone. UN peacekeepers were also given a mandate to use force if necessary to defend themselves.

But it soon became apparent, with the continuing escalation of the conflict in the Balkans, that the international community had to do more if there was to be any hope of stopping the violence. The Mulroney government called for a toughening of economic sanctions against Serbia and was equally strident in its call for the international community to do more on the ground. "The UN and its member states must be prepared to intervene earlier and stronger in the future to prevent such disasters," the prime minister told delegates to an international youth conference in May 1992. He lamented, "What kind of signal does it send when the world turns a blind eye to the carnage? Bosnia and Herzegovina followed the rules established by the UN. . . . They took the world's word, but they were left to fend for themselves against heavily armed opposition. The result has been, in the words of the Bosnian foreign minister, 'a disgrace for humanity.'"[524] At a speech he delivered in December 1992 at the John F. Kennedy School of Government at Harvard University, the prime minister implored the UN to use "all instruments available" to bring peace to the Balkans. As the *Harvard Crimson* reported, "In a question-and-answer session after his speech . . . Mulroney said the UN should follow the example of initiatives in the Persian Gulf and the Korean War to make peace." The article also pointedly noted, "Several of Mulroney's comments veered from the current U.S. position on foreign policy—most notably on Bosnia, where the U.S. has been more cautious—a point Mulroney was sure to communicate."[525]

Barbara McDougall, Canada's foreign minister, also beat the drum for greater UN involvement to stop the killing. As Nicholas Gammer writes, she delivered a "stinging address to the forty-seventh session of the United Nations General Assembly in September of 1992 epitomizing the Canadian government's frustration with the UN's role in the Balkans. She vented her anger at the Security Council for forcing Canada to pay a disproportionately high share of peacekeeping costs in the UN instead if spreading the growing costs of peacekeeping in Yugoslavia among all the members. . . . McDougall once again stressed Canada's commitment to the concept of peace enforcement by noting that 'recent events demonstrate that the use of force may be a necessary option, and we urge full consideration of the Secretary-General's view in this regard.' It is not difficult to deduce from the Minister's statement that her view of Canadian foreign policy included a Canada prepared to lead a movement among states that was willing to challenge, and where feasible, expand the boundaries of peace enforcement."[526] (Such views, as Gammer further notes, were consistent with some of the ideas espoused by the UN secretary-general at the time, Boutros Boutros-Ghali, in his major report *An Agenda for Peace*, to protect and promote human rights and prevent escalation in civil-conflict situations).

The fullest expression of what would come to be known as the Responsibility to Protect doctrine came in the 2001 report of the International Commission on Intervention and State Sovereignty,[527] which argued that the UN should use military force to prevent massive human rights atrocities in civil conflicts and that state sovereignty is conditional. The same principles were subsequently embraced by the UN General Assembly in 2005 and in successive resolutions of both the Security Council and the African Union. However, the enunciation of the core principles that underlie the doctrine had clearly come during the Mulroney government. In her speech on May 17, 1993, Barbara McDougall asserted a radically new view about the limitations to state sovereignty: "We have to reconsider the UN's traditional definition of state sovereignty. I believe that states can no longer argue sovereignty as a licence for internal repression when the absolutes of that sovereignty shield conflicts that eventually could become international in scope. Some standards are universal: human rights must be respected; democratic institutions must be safeguarded; judiciaries must be free and independent; national sovereignty should offer no comfort to repressors, and no protection to those guilty of breaches of the common moral codes enshrined in the Universal Declaration of Human Rights."[528] The prime minister and his foreign minister repeatedly "called on [UN] members to meet the changing face of international conflict." Although they were the first to admit that "clearly defined criteria for enforced intervention had not been methodically and carefully worked out," they also championed "a bolder and more muscular intervention role for the UN" to "make peace, since attempts to keep it were built on outmoded thinking."[529]

However, it would take three more years for the UN to do what Mulroney and McDougall had urged its members to do. As Edwin Smith, a distinguished international lawyer at the University of Southern California, explains, "The culmination of the war in Bosnia came with the decision of France and the United Kingdom, the principal contributors to UNPROFOR, in the summer of 1995, to move from classical peacekeeping to a robust use of force to ensure compliance with UN mandates. Their diplomacy, the situation on the ground in Bosnia, and domestic factors in the United States also finally convinced the Clinton administration to engage diplomatically and militarily to end the conflict. NATO air strikes on Serb forces in Bosnia in mid-1995, flown principally by the U.S. Air Force, were used to bring pressure on Belgrade to come to the negotiating table. In the Dayton Accords, signed in October 1995, the parties to the conflict accepted the ad hoc Implementation Force (IFOR) created by the agreement."[530] One can only wonder how many lives would have been saved, and how much carnage averted, had the UN and the international community chosen to act forcefully sooner.

The same might be said about desultory international efforts to prevent genocide in Rwanda in 1994, when nearly one million members of the minority Tutsi tribe were slaughtered by members of the Hutu majority government following the collapse of the Arusha accords. As the distinguished Canadian philosopher and founder of York University's Centre for Refugee Studies, Howard Adelman, discovered during the course of his own research, when tensions between Hutus and Tutsis mounted in the early 1990s, "Brian Mulroney was the only international leader of a government to—not just once, but twice—write President Habyarimana of Rwanda before the massive murders even began in 1994. . . . In his letters, he asked Habyarimana to look into the human rights violations and targeting of Tutsis in Rwanda."[531] However, Mulroney left office in June 1993, well before the assassination of Habyarimana and Burundian president Cyprien Ntaryamira on April 6, 1994, when their airplane was shot down as it tried to land in Kigali, triggering the genocidal killings.

CONVENTION ON THE RIGHTS OF THE CHILD

Less well known, though no less substantial, is the important contribution the Mulroney government made to getting other countries to ratify the International Convention on the Rights of the Child and adopt a concrete plan of action to promote the survival, protection, and development of children at the first United Nations World Summit on Children. The convention had been adopted by the UN in November 1989 after ten years of negotiations in which Canada was a strong supporter. The first World Summit for Children, which also aimed to get countries to sign and ratify the Convention on the Rights of the Child, was held on the edges of the annual gathering of world leaders at the General Assembly in New York the following year. Six countries were involved in initiating the summit—Canada, Egypt, Mali, Mexico, Pakistan, and Sweden. Mulroney was co-chair of the conference along with Moussa Traoré of Mali.

According to Stephen Lewis, Mulroney's support for the convention and the role he subsequently played at the summit were "absolutely critical. Together they have formed international fabric around the protection of children and the Convention has become the most ratified instrument in the world [ratified by 196 states with the sole exception of the United States]." Lewis noted further that "the work Mulroney did and the role he played was exemplary. [The declaration] saved the lives of millions of kids. It set concrete targets for governments to reduce the number of infant deaths and guarantee access for children to clean water and basic education."[532]

PEACEKEEPING AND STATE-BUILDING

With the rapid growth in the late 1980s and early 1990s of UN peacekeeping operations that were considerably more complex and "multi-dimensional" than previous ventures, Canada's concerns about the operations' conditions, mandates, and financing grew. Nevertheless, Canada remained an enthusiastic participant, providing everything from commanders to logistics support, engineers, civilian police, and election monitoring. Canada was active in some of the major UN operations of the decade, including the United Nations Transitional Authority Group (UNTAG) in Namibia, the United Nations Transitional Authority in Cambodia (UNTAC), and the United Nations Observer Group in Central America (ONUCA).[533]

In late December 1988, high-level representatives of Angola, Cuba, and South Africa formally signed two agreements (the Tripartite and the Bilateral) in New York, establishing the basis for a peaceful transition in Namibia, the cessation of hostilities between South Africa and Angola, and a timetable for withdrawal of Cuban troops from Angola. The

Tripartite Agreement called for South Africa to reduce the size of its forces in Namibia from 25,000 to 1,500 troops. Under the terms of the agreement, Namibia would also become a fully independent state in April 1990 following the holding of free and fair elections for a Constituent Assembly the previous year that would draft the country's new constitution and organize its new government. The Bilateral Agreement between Angola and Cuba set the terms for the withdrawal of Cuban troops from Angola.

Canadian civil society had been a vocal and active champion of Namibia's independence for many years, and a longstanding participant in UN peacekeeping missions—a commitment that did not waver under the Mulroney government. It therefore came as no surprise that Canada committed itself to playing an active role in the UN's mission to Namibia, which had to oversee not only the withdrawal of South African forces and the demobilization of rebel troops, but also the political process that would accompany Namibia's transition to becoming a free, independent democratic state.

At a series of workshops that were organized by the Canadian Institute for International Peace and Security (a government-funded think-tank), with the support and active engagement of civil society and government officials, a whole-of-government engagement strategy was mapped out for Namibia's transition, including the role that Elections Canada would play in the country's subsequent elections. In the end, Canada contributed $15 million in budgetary support for the UNTAG mission, as well as almost three hundred personnel to the peacekeeping force. Additionally, the Royal Canadian Mounted Police fielded one hundred monitors to help oversee the local security situation and train local police. Canada also provided four thousand ballot boxes and a raft of experts to help manage the election, as well as contributing money and expertise for the repatriation of refugees.

At the time, there was a fair amount of criticism about the management of the transition and the subsequent electoral process amid charges that South Africa was trying to manipulate the process for its own political ends. The Canadian government was accused by some of its NGO critics of being duped by the South Africans and being insufficiently supportive of the South West African People's Organisation (SWAPO), the rebel group that had been fighting for South Africa's independence, as it struggled to transform itself from a guerrilla group into a viable political party. However, notwithstanding the many road bumps along the way, the mission was ultimately a success. Elections for the Constituent Assembly gave SWAPO a majority of the votes, though it fell well shy of a two-thirds majority so it was not able to impose a one-party state even if it had wanted to. The elected Constituent Assembly successfully drafted a new constitution for the country. White Namibians were encouraged to remain and continued to play an important role in the Namibian government and the civil service, including the country's police and military forces. Subsequent elections for the new parliament went relatively smoothly.

The same story played itself out in Cambodia and Central America, where peacekeeping continued to remain an article of faith in Canada's foreign and security policies, and the Canadian contribution included not just money but various forms of peacekeeping, military, development, and electoral assistance.

The one black spot on Canada's otherwise unblemished peacekeeping record, however, was Somalia, where the Canadian contribution to the mission raised troubling questions about the accountability, training, and civilian-military chain of command in Canada's armed forces. Both the Mulroney government and the succeeding Chrétien government's handling of the issue raised troubling questions about the willingness of senior defence officials to accept responsibility for their actions, as was revealed by the Report of the Commission of Inquiry into the Deployment of Canadian Forces in Somalia.

Mulroney's contacts with presidents Reagan and Bush generally led to successful outcomes. However, there was one exception, when a series of telephone calls between President Bush (then in his last weeks of office) and the prime minister led to Canadian participation in the stepped-up Somalia operation. The then undersecretary of state for external affairs,

Reid Morden, was strongly opposed to any kind of Canadian engagement in what he saw as "mission impossible" in the Somalia quagmire, and his view was probably reflected in the department's thinking. Yet it could also have been argued that a critical emergency existed and that Canada was better equipped than most countries to help tackle it.

Decisions by heads of government when the choice is not an easy one can only be taken by a prime minister free of the institutional perspectives of ministers. Under Mulroney, Canada committed itself to deploying 750 peacekeepers to the United Nations Operation in Somalia I (UNOSOM I) in 1992. The contingent sent to join the United Task Force (UNITAF) peace-enforcement mission, later transformed into UNOSOM 2, eventually numbered 1,300. The mission was to safeguard the work of UN relief agencies and other humanitarian NGOs like CARE Canada that were trying to deliver aid to some 1.5 million people who were on the verge of starvation and another 3 million who were in dire straits in a country that had descended into complete chaos and rival clan warfare following the collapse of President Siad Barre's "scientific socialist" regime. Canadian troops were deployed in the northern region of Somalia, which was less populated and generally free of the chaos, famine, and mayhem that wracked the capital city, Mogadishu, and the southern parts of the country. When the UN changed the mission to UNITAF in December, Canada upped its contribution to 900 troops. The Canadian Airborne Regiment Battle Group was assigned to Belet Huen, a city in the Hiran province, 340 kilometres north of Mogadishu. As the CBC reported in its own story of the deployment, headlined "Belet Huen is a Peaceful Place," "Early forecasts aren't optimistic. It's reported that Canadian forces will have to calm trigger-happy gangs, high on narcotics, who rule Somalia fearlessly. But when the Black Hawk helicopters land in Belet Huen, the Canadians are greeted with welcoming cheers. The Canadian soldiers are surprised to find a relative level of calm in Belet Huen. The famine is under control, with almost no one dying of starvation anymore in this replenished region. But over in the Somali capital of Mogadishu, U.S. Marines have shot and killed a Somali during a peace march."[534]

The Airborne Regiment fulfilled its mandate with little or no opposition from local forces. However, reports soon surfaced that some members of the regiment had tortured and murdered a young Somali teenager who was caught trying to steal food from the camp. The behaviour of Canadian troops "highlighted for Canadians, the difficult situation in which the troops were operating, as well as the differences between usual peacekeeping operations and the enforcement mandate in Somalia." Moreover, for "a mission with a mandate such as Somalia, military training had to be supplemented with cultural sensitivity training and knowledge of the local situation."[535]

But the problems with the mission ran a lot deeper than that within the military chain of command. As the CBC also reported,

> Two internal government reports written before the troops were sent to Somalia warned of attitude problems among Canadian soldiers. The Peacekeeping Review stated that "We are seen by some as self-indulgent and not sensitive to the feelings, customs and requirements of others." The Peacekeeping Training Report indicated that "Canadians are known as complainers with an attitude of superiority based in part on a lack of knowledge." This issue later became central to the Somalia inquiry. The question would be asked whether the Canadians should have been sent in at all. . . . Lt.-Col. Carol Mathieu was placed in charge of the Canadian Airborne Regiment in October 1992. He succeeded Lt.-Col. Paul Morneau. During the public inquiry on Somalia, it was revealed that Morneau had recommended that a group of unruly soldiers be removed from the Somalia mission. Morneau was replaced by Mathieu after the Airborne division failed their readiness test before they departed for Somalia. . . . Gen. John de Chastelain was the chief of defence staff when the Canadian soldiers were sent into action in Somalia. He was later criticized for sending the troops despite red flags that the Airborne Regiment was not adequately trained and suffered disciplinary problems. Gen. John Anderson succeeded de Chastelain once the mission

was underway. The media also condemned him for telling the troops in Somalia to maintain a low profile during Kim Campbell's bid for the Conservative leadership."[536]

In 1995, the Liberal government established a commission of inquiry to "look at specific matters relating to the pre-deployment, in-theater, and post-theater phases of the Somali operation." Its terms of reference "obliged" the commission "to conduct an examination of the joint structure, planning, and execution of the Somalia operation by the Canadian Forces and the Department of National Defence."[537] As the commission slowly worked its way up the chain of command to figure out what had gone horribly wrong with the mission, it ran into stiff headwinds from senior officials in the government. Although the Liberal government was clearly happy to see the inquiry delve into the actions and decisions of the previous Conservative government, it grew increasingly concerned as the inquiry dragged on under weak leadership and ever growing expense to the Canadian taxpayer. On January 10, 1997, while Parliament was adjourned, the defence minister announced that cabinet had decided that the inquiry had gone on long enough and that it had to deliver its report with recommendations by the end of June. The government's decision forced the commission to cut off hearings and prevented it from addressing all the matters it considered under its terms of reference. The commission's final report offered multiple recommendations to strengthen the operational readiness of Canadian Forces and their role and responsibilities for subsequent peace operations, although only some of its recommendations were ultimately accepted and implemented.

LESSONS

Canadians have always tended to see their country as something of a moral superpower, and others have sometimes tended to view Canada that way as well, though less generously than Canadians themselves. "The stern daughter of the voice of God" is how Harry Truman's secretary of state, Dean Acheson, once referred to Canada. But it is one thing to take the moral high ground in global affairs, and quite another to practise what we preach by acting on our principles and putting our diplomacy, treasure, and lives behind them.

In the late spring of 2017, the *Globe and Mail* ran a headline stating that the government of Pierre Trudeau had turned a blind eye to reports from its own diplomatic envoys that Robert Mugabe, the autocratic leader of Zimbabwe, was butchering thousands of his own citizens who opposed his rule. In all, an estimated twenty thousand civilians lost their lives between 1983 and 1984.[538] Mugabe was something of a darling in progressive Western circles after he become prime minister in what had been white-ruled Rhodesia, and Canada was no exception in embracing his leadership.

As the *Globe and Mail* reported, Robert McLaren, Canada's envoy to the newly independent country, "tried to raise the alarm. Before his death in 2015, he told a friend, veteran diplomat Jeremy Kinsman, that he had repeatedly informed Ottawa about the brutal attacks by the Zimbabwean military, but there was little interest." Even the World University Service of Canada (WUSC), a prominent NGO, had pulled its teachers from the area where the massacres were taking place, out of a well-founded concern about the safety of its workers, many of whom had personally witnessed the killings. Nonetheless, there was no attempt by Ottawa to pull the plug or cut back on its substantial development assistance program to Zimbabwe to protest the killings. Nothing was said publicly or even privately through diplomatic channels to signal Canada's displeasure. Several months after reports of the massacre, Trudeau invited Mugabe to visit Canada, where "he was wined and dined from Saskatchewan to Nova Scotia" and met with "ministers, premiers and yes, the prime minister, without a word being said about these atrocities." The visit was subsequently declared by the Department of External Affairs to have been a "success" because it avoided stirring "tensions" in Zimbabwe.

In the age of the Internet and social media, it is more difficult for governments today to hold their nose and look the other way when confronted with direct evidence of flagrant human rights abuses by the government of another country—as Prime Minister Justin's Trudeau's government discovered with the sale of Canadian-made armoured vehicles to Saudi Arabia, which were reportedly being used in a non-combat role against Saudi citizens in violation of Canada's export control and human rights laws regarding military equipment.[539] In the 1980s, though, it was clearly easier to keep unflattering diplomatic reports under wraps and bury the evidence in a file drawer. But there was also another, political, logic that was at play. Canada generally tended to shy away from commenting on or interfering in the domestic affairs of another sovereign country even if the government of that country was killing its own citizens. In the abstract, of course, as a signatory to the UN Charter on Human Rights, Canada saw itself as a champion of human rights norms. In practice, for reasons of political expediency and *raison d'état*—in the case of Zimbabwe, the stability of a newly formed, black African–led government—it was perhaps easier to turn a blind eye.

A decade later, under the government of Brian Mulroney, Canada had no such reservations while much of the rest of the world sat on its hands as the former Yugoslavia disintegrated into a bloody, internecine conflict among its different religious and ethnic factions. Canada's leaders were among the first to sound the alarm and call for forceful international action to stop the killing. Mulroney and his senior cabinet members believed that our moral principles should not stop at the water's edge and that Canada, along with the rest of the international community, had an obligation to act when innocent lives were threatened. That principle, which came to be known as the Responsibility to Protect, was eventually enshrined in 2005 in a declaration of the UN General Assembly, although it continues to be imperfectly applied, as global inaction over Syria's brutal, ongoing civil war attests.

"First to pay" was another innovation of the Mulroney government when it came to supporting Canada's memberships in international organizations. Mulroney informed the bureaucracy that Canada should immediately pay its annual UN assessments when they became due. There was to be no delay or hesitation. We were to set an example for the rest of the world. Word quickly spread not just around Ottawa but also in diplomatic circles in New York. It became something of an annual tradition. As Paul Heinbecker, who served as Canada's ambassador to the UN some years later during the Chrétien government, explained, he was under strict instructions to walk Canada's cheque over to the United Nations in early January and formally present it to the relevant UN officials who would gratefully receive it, though not without some bemusement at Canada's promptness.

Mulroney also understood that being true to your values as a nation means that you are prepared to act on them and that you don't wait for others to lead. When it came to our relationship with the United States, Mulroney did not hesitate to tell his close friend the American president that defending a rules-based international order meant that the United States and its allies had to play by those same rules. That meant securing the approval of the UN Security Council before going to war against Saddam Hussein, who had seized the territory of a neighbouring state in violation of the cardinal post-war norm of the sanctity of borders. UN support was essential for the deployment of Canada's troops in any theatre of conflict, including the Persian Gulf. Under Mulroney, Canada was also an active participant in every other UN peacekeeping mission, including that in Bosnia, and played this role without hesitation or equivocation. That is what being a responsible member of the international community entails.

ELEVEN

"I Sure Will"

"Vous avez des ennemis? Mais c'est l'histoire de tout homme qui a fait
une action grande ou crée une idée neuve. C'est la nuée qui bruit
autour de tout ce qui brille. Il faut que la renommé ait des ennemis
comme il faut que la lumière ait des moucherons."[540]
—VICTOR HUGO, *Villemain* (1845)

B RIAN MULRONEY WAS A TRANSFORMATIVE LEADER, and transformative leaders are invariably controversial. As the French novelist and dramatist Victor Hugo once famously wrote, anyone who has done a great deed or created a new idea has enemies. Mulroney perhaps had more than his fair because he profoundly altered the Canadian political and economic landscape. When he came to office in 1984, Mulroney faced major domestic challenges. As Queen's University political scientist Kim Richard Nossal wrote in *Policy Options*, "Domestically, Canada in 1984 was marked by political and economic discontents. The deep fractures left by Trudeau's patriation of the constitution and the refusal of the Québec government to attach itself to the new constitutional arrangements were continuing concerns. Moreover, the country's financial situation was grim: the recession of the early 1980s produced large-scale unemployment, particularly in central Canada; after 16 years of deficit spending by the federal government, the deficit was continuing to spiral upwards."[541] Mulroney's domestic agenda was a very full one and included major constitutional reform and the introduction of a goods and services tax to rectify the federal government's financial situation, which had severely deteriorated under his pre-decessors.

In the normal course of events, these challenges alone would have over-whelmed just about any government. Foreign affairs would have received short shrift or at the very least been treated as a necessary but unwelcome distraction. What is remarkable about the Mulroney era is how active—indeed transformative—his government was on both fronts, the domes-tic *and* the international. Further, the prime minister himself was deeply engaged on both sets of files throughout his tenure. Mulroney's record in foreign affairs, which is the focus of this book, speaks for itself. But it is also a legacy of statesmanlike engagement that continues to the present.

On a soggy, late spring day in 2017, Brian Mulroney stood before a standing-room-only crowd at the annual Canada 2020 conference in Ottawa, a gathering of progressive, liberal-thought leaders, politicians, journalists, academics, and members of the business community. He had been asked to speak about the future of the North American Free Trade Agreement before Canada sat down at the negotiating table in August with the United States, a nation led by a president who during his election campaign repeatedly called the treaty the "worst trade deal in the history of the world."[542] Mulroney's message was a simple one: think big, be bold but also tough when you deal with the Americans.[543] The target of Mulroney's speech was clearly not just the audience that had assembled to hear him speak, but Prime Minister Justin Trudeau and the members of his cabinet and negotiating team.

As Mulroney pointed out, NAFTA has generated unprecedented growth for the Canadian economy and for North America as whole. "It had taken Canada 125 years to generate a GDP of $800 billion. Under free trade, it took only 25 years to double that," he noted. As Mulroney fur-ther observed, "the North American continent with almost 500 million people" has become "the largest, richest and most dynamic free trade area in the world with a combined GDP reaching $20.7 trillion in 2015. With less than 7 percent of the world's population, NAFTA partners in 2015 represented 28 percent of the world's total GDP."

But that is not all. According to Global Affairs Canada, under NAFTA, "Canadian merchandise exports to the United States grew at an annualized rate of almost 4.6 per cent between 1993 and 2015. Canada's bilateral merchandise trade with Mexico nearly reached $37.8 billion in 2015. Some 78 percent of Canada's total merchandise exports were destined to our NAFTA partners in 2015. Total merchandise trade between Canada and the United States more than doubled between 1993 and 2015. Trade between Canada and Mexico . . . increased over 8-fold over the same period."[544]

NAFTA's fate at the time of writing rests with a president who won the presidency by aggressively campaigning against the agreement. Canada's prosperity will be affected by the outcome of the negotiations. As the former prime minister underscored, "It will be the challenge of this government, this parliament and this country. It's one for the history books." Regardless of what Canadians think of President Trump and his policies, Mulroney's advice to the government was to "keep our heads down, our mouths shut" and save what we should say for the negotiating table: "It's at the bargaining table where we can make our comments, caustic or otherwise." But perhaps Mulroney's most important piece of advice was that "We can say no. We're not some pushover little country that someone is going to ambush. We're a $2 trillion economy. We have the strength to say no."

The most enduring myth of the Mulroney era is that Mulroney's relationship with two U.S. presidents was a subservient one based on weakness. It was a myth that was propagated by critics who were viscerally afraid of Canada getting too close to the United States. They feared that Canadians could not compete with Americans, that Canada would lose its sovereignty and somehow disappear into the great American melting pot if it opened its markets to U.S. trade and investment. That fear was also tinged with an unhealthy dose of America envy. Many of the harshest critics of free trade and Mulroney's policies were jealous of the more open, prosperous, and competitive society that lay to the south of Canada's border.

Canada did not meld into the United States under NAFTA. If anything, Canadians are now stronger, more prosperous, more competitive, and more confident about themselves as a nation. The defensive, protectionist nationalist sentiments of the 1960s and 1970s have yielded to a more self-assured, mature attitude towards our relations with the United States and the rest of the world. Nevertheless, some of the old suspicions and insecurities of a bygone era still linger. One of the great ironies of the federal election of 2015 is that the Conservative-led government of Stephen Harper was accused of bungling the management of Canada's ties with the United States by Justin Trudeau, who promised a closer, more collaborative relationship. How the tables have turned if you look back to the bitterly contested federal election of 1988 on free trade, when the Liberals, led by John Turner, fought to keep Canada at a distance from the United States.

As a seasoned labour negotiator turned businessman, Prime Minister Mulroney intuitively understood one of the cardinal rules of politics—it is all about persuasion—and if you want to "punch above your weight" as a medium-sized power in the world, you not only need to be crystal clear about your values and interests at the negotiating table, but to create leverage to advance your interests, especially when you are dealing with a neighbour who is a superpower.

Unlike his predecessor, who delighted in tweaking the feathers of the American eagle, Mulroney understood that a good personal rapport and a close working relationship are essential to the management of Canada's relations with the United States. Such qualities can help us get to the front of the line when other countries and interests are clamouring for the attention of the White House. And on those occasions when the prime minister has to secure the involvement of the president to win key concessions and advance negotiations that are stalled or deadlocked, a close personal relationship with the president means that the White House switchboard will answer the prime minister's call.

During the Canada–U.S. free trade negotiations, for example, Canada sought to establish a bilateral dispute resolution mechanism because it realized that conflicting interpretations about the terms of the agreement would invariably arise in the future and that it was not in Canada's interest to allow disagreements to be resolved by U.S. courts or administrative fiat. It was a make-or-break issue that was only resolved when the two leaders talked to each other directly by telephone and agreed to let their senior officials, Derek Burney and James Baker, work out a deal. There was a lot of frank, tough talk between Burney and Baker. The Americans eventually conceded to Canadian demands when it was pointed out that there were bigger issues at stake in the bilateral relationship and that the concessions Canada was trying to secure as a key ally and friend of the United States were a whole lot less than what the Americans were conceding to their Cold War adversary, the Russians, in arms control talks.

Strong relations between the Canadian prime minister and American president also permit a Canadian leader to speak truth to power. When there is genuine trust and mutual respect, leaders can say things to each other that they otherwise wouldn't for fear of being dismissed or misinterpreted. A careful review of the historical record suggests that Mulroney always defended Canada's interests with the Americans and did so vigorously and openly. For Mulroney, there was neither a Conservative nor a Liberal way to negotiate with the Americans, just a Canadian way, which also meant hanging in there but also knowing when to say no.

Mulroney never gave up the fight on acid rain, which was destroying Canadian lakes and forests, even if it meant voicing those concerns directly and repeatedly in the strongest terms to a skeptical American president. (Through his ministrations, he also successfully turned Reagan's vice-president, George H.W. Bush, into an ally on the issue, which paid real dividends when Bush eventually became president.) There was nothing wobbly or weak-kneed about the way Mulroney dealt with the Americans or other world leaders on other issues like free trade, apartheid in South Africa, biodiversity, and climate change. The fact that Canada did not participate in ballistic missile defence research under the Strategic Defence Initiative, an initiative in which President Reagan placed great stock, is yet another example of Mulroney's refusal to cave in to the Americans when Canadian interests were involved.

Mulroney's personal relations with President Bush ran deeper than those he enjoyed with Reagan. He played both confidant and devil's advocate to the American president at a transformative moment in world history. It was a relationship that no other Canadian prime minister, either before him or since, has had with an American leader. When Bush asked for Mulroney's advice about how to deal with Saddam Hussein, who had just invaded Kuwait, Mulroney shrewdly advised him that the United States had to secure UN Security Council approval if it wanted to get other countries, including Canada, on board to support any kind of joint military action. Mulroney also helped the U.S. president build an international coalition by reaching out to key members in the Arab world, such as the leaders of Jordan and Egypt, on the president's behalf, while counselling him on best way to reach out to French president François Mitterrand.

Mulroney was a strong advocate for the reunification of Germany after the Berlin Wall came tumbling down. Through his friendship with German chancellor Helmut Kohl, Mulroney acquired a better understanding than most other Western leaders had of Kohl's views about the vital importance of reunification to Germans. As a trusted interlocutor, Mulroney could articulate those concerns directly to the White House. Had he not done so, the arguments of British prime minister Margaret Thatcher and French president François Mitterrand, who opposed reunification, could have easily won the day. Helmut Kohl was immensely grateful for Canada's support and went out of his way to say so publicly when reunification became a reality.

One of the hallmarks of the foreign policies of the Mulroney era was the deeply principled nature of Canada's engagements with the rest of the world. Confronted with a humanitarian tragedy of epic proportions in the Horn of Africa, the Mulroney government sent shiploads of food, medicine, and other forms of humanitarian assistance while the rest of the world chose to ignore the crisis. Mulroney acted because he believed it was the right thing to do from a moral perspective, and he ordered his officials to ensure that the United Nations also stepped up to the plate. Following the government's lead, Canadians opened their wallets in what was a model public–private partnership in the face of human tragedy.

The prominent role that Mulroney played in the Commonwealth to help bring down the walls of apartheid in South Africa is also an important part of his global legacy. The system of institutionalized racism was an injustice that Mulroney believed deeply to be wrong, and he did not mince his words. Margaret Thatcher, a formidable foe on the issue, did not take kindly to the lectures she received from the young Canadian prime minister, who she thought was "wet" and naive. But she was on the wrong side of both the argument and history. Mulroney vigorously pressed his case from one Commonwealth Heads of Government Meeting to another, to Thatcher's deep dismay and consternation. However, black South Africans found inspiration and succour in Mulroney's strident, unyielding words, as did other leaders in the Global South.

Under Mulroney, Canada was seen throughout the world as a champion for human rights because of its leader's principled stance on apartheid. To be sure, when it came to implementing economic sanctions, Canada's performance fell short of the prime minister's scolding rhetoric. There were major failures in execution because of internal opposition from those who favoured a more cautious course. However, in the end, these shortcomings did not dim the bright anti-apartheid torch that Canada helped to keep aflame, as Nelson Mandela himself publicly acknowledged after he was released from prison.

Mulroney also extended the global reach of Canada's influence and engagement through two important forums. One of these was the Organization of American States (OAS), of which, under Mulroney's leadership, Canada finally became a full-fledged member; the other, La Francophonie, formally came into existence when Canada and Quebec took their respective seats. Mulroney realized that Canada's efforts to deepen its relations with the countries of the Western Hemisphere had been stunted by the nation's longstanding reluctance to become a member of this important hemispheric regional body. Similarly, he believed that Pierre Trudeau's worries about giving Quebec a seat in La Francophonie (as a necessary accompaniment to Canada's own membership) were exaggerated and that it was time for both Canada and Quebec to take their rightful places in the commonwealth of the French-speaking world.

Leadership means giving instructions to "just do it."[545] Once Mulroney made up his mind that he wanted to get something done, he mobilized the right people to get results. This was true on trade, Ethiopia, acid rain, the environment, South Africa, and other major files. When it came to making key appointments, Mulroney was less concerned about partisan affiliations or political leanings than about competence. He always wanted the very best person for the job. For Mulroney, the national interest came first. That is why he appointed Simon Reisman to be his top trade negotiator with the Americans. It is also why he chose David MacDonald to oversee Canada's famine relief efforts in Ethiopia and Stephen Lewis to represent Canada at the United Nations in New York. But just as important, as Si Taylor, former undersecretary of state for external affairs, observes, "Mulroney knew how to get things organized . . . there was a very sophisticated and elaborate machinery that was set up to manage the Free Trade Agreement. The government also held three summits in the space of eighteen months, a Commonwealth Summit, a Francophone Summit, and a G7 Summit. That was a major burden. People outside of the bureaucracy don't think about it. When I look back on it that was a major accomplishment. If the government also had to decide between alternatives they knew how to do that."

Taylor also notes that, for Mulroney, governing was very much a team effort when it came to foreign policy: "While Brian Mulroney and Joe Clark from time to time disagreed on issues, and sometimes Joe Clark took initiatives that Brian Mulroney didn't approve of, by and large (considering that the press was just itching to show disagreement because they had been rivals for the leadership) they worked together well. The government presented a united front. They shared the burden on the Commonwealth file. On others, it was clearly the Prime Minister's business like La Francophonie. Joe Clark had little to do with it because it was more a matter of domestic politics."[546] On Canada–U.S. free trade, the prime minister was clearly in the lead. Under Reagan, Joe Clark's relations with Secretary of State Shultz were important because Reagan was not someone to engage substantively on the issues.[547]

The spirit of bipartisanship Mulroney showed in some of his senior diplomatic appointments is evident today in the strong support Mulroney has given to the Trudeau government as it struggles to define its course with the unpredictable and erratic presidency of Donald Trump. As discussed in Chapters 1 and 2, Mulroney has put his Rolodex and counsel at the disposal of the prime minister and his cabinet—all in the interest of securing Canada's future at a time of great political uncertainty and volatility in Canada–U.S. relations. But there is an interesting personal dimension to this story as well. As the *Toronto Star* pointedly noted, "Mulroney once spent an entire chapter of his memoirs excoriating Pierre Trudeau—his personal nemesis, prime ministerial predecessor, and partisan rival. . . . [But] 'that was then, now is now,' Mulroney said, 'My wife and I have been friendly with the present prime minister—as has my family—for many years. He has always treated us with great courtesy and respect. He's the one I deal with. He sets the tone.'"[548] The relationship that has developed between the younger Trudeau and Mulroney speaks well of both leaders.

During the nearly nine years that he was prime minister, Mulroney transformed Canada's relations with its two North American partners and its relations with the rest of the world. Canadians take for granted the prosperity that came with free trade under the Canada–U.S. FTA and then NAFTA. They are not alone in forgetting that the "new world order" that emerged, albeit too briefly, after the Soviet Union collapsed was not a foregone conclusion. The late 1980s to the early 1990s was a period of instability and uncertainty. The generally peaceful transformation of the Soviet Union and collapse of communist regimes in Eastern Europe could have ended badly if Western leaders and their Russian counterparts had been negligent, bungling, or incompetent. It took more than one set of firm hands to guide the transition, and Reagan, Bush, Gorbachev, Yelstin, Thatcher, Kohl, Mitterrand, and Mulroney all played their parts.

Throughout his tenure in office, Mulroney showed discipline and laser-like focus. He also demonstrated that it is possible to juggle more than one set of priorities at a time without dropping the ball. While handling a complex set of files on the domestic front (the introduction of a goods and services tax and constitutional reform, among others), he also managed to set a bold new course in Canada–U.S. relations while simultaneously pursuing other major foreign policy initiatives. Mulroney also showed that a commitment to continentalism is not at odds with a policy of strong and assertive internationalism. In fact, the two hands, played well, complement each other, especially when the world knows that Canada's leader has the ear of the president of the United States.

Mulroney also showed that there is nothing wrong with Canada being "the stern daughter of the voice of God" when the world has lost its moral compass. But he also knew that Canada had to put its skin in the game if it was to be listened to and taken seriously. Mulroney urged strong international action to avert further bloodshed in the Balkans, but he also made the decision to deploy a large Canadian peacekeeping contingent for the UN mission.

When Chrystia Freeland rose in the House of Commons on June 6, 2017, to deliver what future historians may one day say was the most important address by a Canadian foreign minister in more than two decades, she talked about a new imperative for Canada on the world stage. "International relationships that had seemed immutable for 70 years," she said, "are being called into question. From Europe, to Asia, to our own North American home, long-standing pacts that have formed the bedrock of our security and prosperity for generations are being tested." She is certainly right about that. At the same time, she argued that "it is clearly not our role to impose our values around the world, Mr. Speaker. No one appointed us the world's policeman." But she added, "it is our role to clearly stand for these rights both in Canada and abroad." Further, she noted, Canada "can and must play an active role in the preservation and strengthening of the global order from which we have benefited so greatly. Doing so is in our interest, because our own open society is most secure in a world of open societies. And it is under threat in a world where open societies are under threat."[549] Those same words could just as easily describe the role that Canada played some thirty years ago to preserve and strengthen the values of a global order with its diplomacy, development assistance, and military—from Eastern Europe to Russia, from sub-Saharan Africa to Haiti, from the Balkans to Cambodia—under Brian Mulroney.

Freeland also talked about the changing role the United States now sees for itself in the global order, and its potentially diminished presence: "The fact that our friend and ally has come to question the very worth of its mantle of global leadership, puts into sharper focus the need for the rest of us to set our own clear and sovereign course. For Canada that course must be the renewal, indeed the strengthening, of the postwar multilateral order." "We will follow this path," she said, "with open hands and open hearts extended to our American friends, seeking to make common cause as we have so often in the past. And indeed, as we continue to do now on multiple fronts—from border security, to the defence of North America through NORAD, to the fight against Daesh, to our efforts within NATO, to nurturing and improving our trading relationship, which is the strongest in the world. And, at the same time, we will work with other like-minded people and countries who share our aims."[550]

Canada must always set a "clear and sovereign course" for itself. Bold words but surely the right instinct. Canada must always look out for itself as a nation. That means its leaders have to be true to Canadian values and interests. This was something that Brian Mulroney clearly understood throughout his years in office. It was a sentiment he impressed upon his ministers and senior officials. Though Mulroney recognized the importance of working with like-minded partners to advance Canadian values and interests, he also knew that Canada's influence was enhanced if its voice carried weight in Washington. Though U.S. power and leadership may currently be diminished because of what is perhaps a temporary aberration in American politics, the U.S. will undoubtedly remain the centre of gravity for Canada and other members of the Western alliance for the foreseeable future. Mulroney understood that it is better to work with the United States and its leaders than against them if Canada's interests are to be advanced. What was true some thirty years ago is still true now, although it is undeniable that Donald Trump's presidency presents its own, unique challenges for Canada's leaders.

This book ends where it began—at the Reagan Library in the Simi Hills of southern California. Monday, April 5, 1993, was another overcast day, but the occasion was a celebration, not a funeral. Ronald Reagan, the former U.S. president, had invited Brian Mulroney, who had just announced that he would step down as prime minister, to a special tribute ceremony Reagan had organized for him at the library. After former prime minister Margaret Thatcher and former Soviet leader Mikhail Gorbachev, Mulroney was the third distinguished visitor to the library. He was fresh from a meeting he had hosted the day before between the newly elected U.S. president, Bill Clinton, and the first democratically elected Russian leader, Boris Yeltsin, in Vancouver.

As the *Los Angeles Times* reported, "After the tour of the museum, the two men and their wives strode past a military band and onto a stage in the library courtyard, where about 400 library donors, local leaders and other admirers applauded. [Then,] in separate speeches under cloudy skies, Reagan and Mulroney, ardent foes of communism during the 1980s, each embraced President Clinton's plan to boost economic aid to Russia and the other former Soviet republics." Mulroney praised Reagan, who "presided over a period of unprecedented prosperity and began the dialogue that led to the end of the Cold War." Reagan returned the compliment: "Brian Mulroney would never say that he played a significant role in this remarkable string of events, but I sure will."[551]

NOTES

===

CHAPTER ONE

1   Remarks for delivery at the funeral service of First Lady Nancy Reagan
     at the Ronald Reagan Presidential Library by the Right Honourable
     Brian Mulroney, March 11, 2016.

2   Remarks for delivery at the state funeral service of President Ronald
     Reagan at Washington National Cathedral by the Right Honourable
     Brian Mulroney, June 11, 2004.

3   Ibid.

4   This observation is offered by J.H. Taylor, "Personalities, Policies and
     the Department of Foreign Affairs and International Trade," in Greg
     Donaghy and Kim Richard Nossal, eds., *Architects and Innovators: Building
     the Department of Foreign Affairs and International Trade, 1909–2009*
     (Montreal and Kingston: McGill-Queen's University Press, 2009), 291.
     Also see J.H. Taylor, "The Conservatives and Foreign Policy-Making:
     A Foreign Service View," in Nelson Michaud and Kim Richard Nossal,
     eds., *Diplomatic Departures: The Conservative Era in Canadian Foreign Policy,
     1984–93* (Vancouver: University of British Columbia Press, 2001), 211–19.

5   Si Taylor, Interview with the author, September 12, 2016.

CHAPTER TWO

6   Quoted in Charles McMillan, "How Free Trade Came to Canada:
     Lesson in Policy Analysis," *Policy Options*, October 2007, 26.

7   "Notes of Meeting," Rt. Hon. Brian Mulroney, April 6, 2017.

8   Derek H. Burney, *Getting It Done* (Montreal and Kingston: McGill-
     Queen's University Press, 2005), 63.

9   William Johnson, "Protectionist Policies Harm Canadian Jobs, Mulroney Says in U.S." *Globe and Mail,* June 21, 1984.

10 Brian Mulroney, interview with the author, May 5, 2017.

11 Ibid.

12 Philip Cross, "Trump Is Reviving the Worst of Canada's Left-Wing Anti-American Tendencies," *Financial Post,* August 5, 2016.

13 Brian Mulroney, *Memoirs, 1939–1993* (Toronto: McClelland & Stewart, 2007), 337–38.

14 Thomas Walkom, "Hard Times Renew Appeal of Move toward Free Trade," *Globe and Mail,* January 21, 1985.

15 "Canada's Non-Choice," *Wall Street Journal,* August 28, 1984.

16 Ibid.

17 William Johnson, "Canada Tests Free Trade Waters," *Globe and Mail,* September 25, 1984.

18 Douglas Martin, "Canada's Great Trade Debate," *New York Times,* January 23, 1985.

19 William Johnson, "Mulroney-Reagan Talks Yield Hope for Close Ties," *Globe and Mail,* September 26, 1984.

20 Graham Fraser, "PM, Reagan Would 'Halt Protectionism,'" *Globe and Mail,* March 19, 1985.

21 John Cruickshank and Bruce Little, "Mulroney to Pursue Talks on Freer Trade," *Globe and Mail,* February 16, 1985.

22 Barry Nelson, "Kelleher Calls for Pact with U.S.," *Globe and Mail,* March 27, 1985.

23 Peter Cowan, "Mulroney Hedges on Freer Trade with U.S. after Peterson Warning," *Gazette* (Montreal), July 4, 1985.

24 Walkom, "Hard Times Renew Appeal."

25 "51% Support for Free Trade Is High Point in Economic Rating," *Gazette* (Montreal), June 29, 1985.

26 Denise Harrington and Alan Story, "Avoid Rushing into Free Trade, Peterson Warns Other Premiers," *Toronto Star,* August 22, 1985.

27   Canada, *Report of the Royal Commission on the Economic Union and Development Prospects for Canada* (Ottawa: Minister of Supply and Services Canada, 1985).

28   Southam News, "Commission Endorses Free Trade as Cure for What Ails Canadian Economy," *Citizen* (Ottawa), September 6, 1985.

29   Ibid.

30   Bruce Little, "Macdonald Urges Sweeping Change in Economy, Government, Social Aid," *Globe and Mail*, September 6, 1985.

31   Charles Lynch, "Has Thumper Don Turned Tory Blue?" *Citizen* (Ottawa), September 7, 1985.

32   Alan Christie, "Ontario Backs Free Trade Deal with Safeguards, Kelleher Says," *Toronto Star*, September 24, 1985.

33   Peter Goodspeed, "Free Trade Will Create Jobs: Reagan," *Toronto Star*, September 18, 1985.

34   There are a number of excellent academic accounts of the Canada–U.S. free trade negotiations and the NAFTA negotiations, which succeeded them. See, for example, Michael Hart, *Decision at Midnight: Inside the Canada–U.S. Free-Trade Negotiations* (Vancouver: University of British Columbia Press, 1994) and Maxwell A. Cameron and Brian W. Tomlin, *The Making of NAFTA: How the Deal Was Done* (Ithaca, NY: Cornell University Press, 2002).

35   Wendy Warburton, "U.S. Hails Trade Talk Intervention," *Citizen* (Ottawa), September 27, 1985.

36   Mulroney interview.

37   Allan Fotheringham, "Reisman an Envoy U.S. Will Understand," *Citizen* (Ottawa), November 12, 1985.

38   Mulroney, *Memoirs*, 564.

39   One story involved Reisman flamboyantly crushing out his cigar on Treasury Secretary John Connolly's mahogany desk. When asked whether the story was true, Reisman said, with a mischievous grin, "Some stories are better in the telling!"

40   "U.S. Senate Might Kill Freer Trade," *Gazette* (Montreal), April 12, 1986.

41 David Oxtoby, "Freer Trade in Everyone's Interest, Says Leader of U.S. Negotiating Team," *Citizen* (Ottawa), January 2, 1986.

42 Hart, *Decision at Midnight*, xii.

43 Ibid., 286.

44 Allan Gotlieb, *Washington Diaries, 1981–89* (Toronto: McClelland & Stewart, 2006), 581–82.

45 Private communication with a member of Gotlieb's staff who was with the ambassador after dinner on March 19.

46 Elizabeth Kastor and Donnie Radcliffe, "Slap Flap," *Washington Post*, March 21, 1986.

47 The victim of the slap, Connie Connor, was moved to the embassy's commercial division shortly after the incident. She worked there for seventeen more years until she was let go following a downsizing of the embassy's staff. See Paul Koring and Jane Taber, "Victim of Gotlieb Slap Fired," *Globe and Mail*, July 15, 2003.

48 Bob Hepburn, "Tories Said Planning Slick Free Trade Sales Pitch," *Toronto Star*, September 20, 1985.

49 See Hart, *Decision at Midnight*, 442.

50 Martin Cohn, "Tories on Free Trade Crusade," *Toronto Star*, February 16, 1986.

51 For one cabinet discussion, Flora MacDonald brought comic books from the 1911 election illustrating graphically the dire consequences predicted at that time.

52 "U.S. Senate Might Kill Freer Trade," *Gazette* (Montreal), April 12, 1986.

53 Wendy Warburton, "Freer Trade Survives Big Test in U.S.," *Citizen* (Ottawa), April 24, 1986.

54 The negotiations officially began on May 21, 1986.

55 Mulroney, *Memoirs*, 448.

56 At one point, Secretary Baker advised Derek Burney that "In Texas, sugar is culture!"

57 Robert Lee, "Reagan to Consider Acid Rain Plan," *Ottawa Citizen*, April 7, 1987.

58   Canadian Press, "Tories Pass Trade Bill over Chorus of Opposition," *Gazette* (Montreal), September 1, 1988.

59   See Hart, *Decision at Midnight, p.*

60   Burney, *Getting It Done*, 118.

61   Ibid., 111–12.

62   James A. Baker III, *Work Hard, Study . . . and Keep Out of Politics!* (Evanston, IL: Northwestern University Press, 2008), 458

63   Ibid., 459.

64   Derek Burney, interview with the author, May 6, 2017.

65   From the Liberal Party platform, as excerpted in "Liberal Blueprint for Canada," *Toronto Star*, September 29, 1988.

66   Burney, *Getting It Done*, 130.

67   Cross, "Trump Is Reviving the Worst."

68   Quoted in L. Ian MacDonald, "Opinion: 25 years on, Canada is the clear winner of free trade deal," *Montreal Gazette,* October 5, 2012.

69   Zoellick is on record as acknowledging receipt of a long-distance call when he was in Moscow from Canada's ambassador, Derek Burney, insisting vigorously, no doubt to the amusement of KGB listeners, precisely why Canada had to be included. This episode illustrated vividly how proximity and candour at the very top carried broader dividends for Canada in terms of access and influence.

70   Robert Zoellick, "Trump Gets It Wrong: Trade Is a Winner for Americans," *Wall Street Journal*, August 7, 2016.

71   Ibid.

72   As Zoellick pointedly demonstrated, 60 per cent of U.S. imports are intermediate goods that enable more efficient production of goods in the U.S.

73   Quoted in a speech delivered by Brian Mulroney to mark the twenty-first anniversary of the acid rain treaty with the United States, March 13, 2012.

CHAPTER THREE

74   Geoffrey York, "Somalia on Brink of Another Famine, UN warns,"
      Globe and Mail, February 5, 2017.

75   David Lamb, "Where Death is a Way of Life," *Gazette* (Montreal),
      January 5, 1985. Excerpt originally published in the *Los Angeles Times*,
      "Famine in Ethiopia: Suffering and Grace," December 30, 1984.
      Used with permission.

76   Ibid.

77   Ibid.

78   Michael Valpy, "Toppled Royalty, Continuing War Blamed for Famine,"
      Globe and Mail, November 12, 1984.

79   Paul Taylor, "Cargo Planes Sought to Shift Ethiopian Aid," *Globe and
      Mail*, December 4, 1984.

80   United Nations Food and Agriculture Organization, *The State of Food
      and Agriculture 1984* (Rome: Food and Agriculture Organization of the
      United Nations, 1985).

81   Lamb, "Where Death Is a Way of Life."

82   Alex De Waal, *Evil Days: Thirty Years of War and Famine in Ethiopia:
      An Africa Watch Report* (New York: Human Rights Watch, 1991), 32–35.

83   Ibid., 4.

84   Ibid., 5.

85   Tony Burman, "Ebola: Canada Forgets Its Leadership in Ethiopian
      Famine," *Toronto Star*, November 1, 2014.

86   Ibid.

87   "Alerting the World to Famine in Ethiopia," *The National*,
      November 1, 1984, http://www.cbc.ca/archives/entry/
      alerting-the-world-to-famine-in-ethiopia.

88   Canadian Press, "Lewis Supports African Aid Plan," *Globe and Mail*,
      November 8, 1984.

89   Brian Stewart, "When Brian Mulroney Was Great," CBC News,
      May 15, 2009. Used with permission, http://www.cbc.ca/news/
      canada/when-brian-mulroney-was-great-1.859343.

90   Interview with a senior Canadian official who chose to remain
      anonymous.

91   Ibid.

92   Brian Stewart, email message to the author, July 17, 2017.

93   Canadian Press, "Clark to Visit Ethiopia on Way to Gandhi Rites,"
      Globe and Mail, November 2, 1984.

94   Michael Valpy, "Clark Satisfied Food Getting Through," *Globe and Mail*,
      November 6, 1984.

95   Stewart, "When Brian Mulroney Was Great."

96   Valpy, "Clark Satisfied Food Getting Through."

97   Denys Horgan, "Canadian Relief Workers Already in Ethiopia,"
      Globe and Mail, November 3, 1984.

98   Ibid.

99   Charlotte Montgomery, "Canada to Increase Its Aid to Ethiopia,"
      Globe and Mail, November 7, 1984.

100   Stewart, "When Brian Mulroney Was Great."

101   Jeff Sallot, "Ex-cabinet Minister Appointed New Ambassador to
      Ethiopia," *Globe and Mail*, September 13, 1986.

102   Hugh Winsor, "Ottawa Scrambles to Match Public Aid," *Globe and Mail*,
      January 31, 1985.

103   Canadian Press, "Lewis Supports African Aid Plan," *Globe and Mail*,
      November 8, 1984.

104   Canadian Press, "End Rhetoric and Aid Africans, Lewis Says in 1st U.N.
      Speech," *Toronto Star*, November 7, 1984.

105   Ibid.

106   Ibid.

107   Ibid.

108   Montgomery, "Canada to Increase Its Aid to Ethiopia."

109   Hugh Winsor, "Public Spurs Ottawa to Boost African Aid," *Globe and
      Mail*, November 17, 1984.

110   Canadian Press, "Aid Workers Wondering Where the Axe May Fall,"
      Globe and Mail, November 13, 1984.

111   "The Aid We Promised," *Globe and Mail*, November 14, 1984.

112   Winsor, "Public Spurs Ottawa."

113   Donald Grant, "Canadians Donate $11 Million in Month to Aid
        Ethiopia," *Globe and Mail*, December 8, 1984. Used with permission.

114   Winsor, "Public Spurs Ottawa."

115   Grant, "Canadians Donate $11 Million."

116   Winsor, "Public Spurs Ottawa."

117   Grant, "Canadians Donate $11 Million."

118   Canadian Press, "Some Famine Aid Will Go Astray," *Globe and Mail*,
        December 15, 1984.

119   Grant, "Canadians Donate $11 Million."

120   Tim Brodhead, "If Africa Is the Question, Is NGO the Answer?"
        International Journal 41, no. 4 (autumn 1986): 869–81,
        doi:10.2307/40202413.

121   Canadian Press, "Increase in African Aid Urged," *Citizen* (Ottawa),
        March 27, 1986.

122   Grant, "Canadians Donate $11 Million."

123   Hugh Winsor, "Ottawa Scrambles to Match Public Aid," *Globe and Mail*,
        January 31, 1985.

124   Canadian Press, "Increase in African Aid Urged."

125   Winsor, "Public Spurs Ottawa."

126   Grant, "Canadians Donate $11 Million."

127   Winsor, "Ottawa Scrambles to Match Public Aid."

128   Canadian Press, "PM Praises Canadians in Christmas Message."
        Globe and Mail, December 22, 1984.

129   Janyce McGregor, "Tears (Still) Are Not Enough, 30 Years Later,"
        CBC News, February 10, 2015, http://www.cbc.ca/news/politics/
        tears-still-are-not-enough-30-years-later-1.2949836

130   Liam Lacey and Claire Bickley, "The Northern Lights Sparkle for
        Fans and Famine Victims," *Globe and Mail*, February 11, 1985.

131   McGregor, "Tears (Still) Are Not Enough."

132   Canadian Press, "PM Picks Up Juno for All Canadians," *Gazette*
        (Montreal), August 30, 1985.

133 Canadian Press, "Agency Head Insists Food Aid Being Sold," *Globe and Mail*, December 13, 1984.

134 Ibid.

135 Associated Press, "Canadian Official Finds No Evidence Food Aid Misused," *Globe and Mail,* December 17, 1984.

136 Canadian Press, "Ethiopian Famine Aid to Continue Despite Charges," *Gazette* (Montreal), January 24, 1985.

137 Associated Press, "West Blamed for Extent of Famine," *Globe and Mail*, December 12, 1984.

138 Ibid.

139 Canadian Press, "MacDonald Named Ambassador to Ethiopia," *Citizen* (Ottawa), September 13, 1986.

140 Canadian Press, "Canada Okays Ethiopia Aid," *Vancouver Sun*, February 22, 1988.

141 De Waal, *Evil Days*, 5.

142 Canadian Press, "PM Lauds Lewis for UN's Africa Plan," *Citizen* (Ottawa), June 4, 1986.

143 Canadian Press, "MacDonald Named Ambassador."

144 Dave Todd, "Compassion Fatigue: With the Great Powers Preoccupied," *Southam News/CanWest News*, December 6, 1989.

145 "Diminishing Canada," *Toronto Star*, December 28, 1989.

146 Dave Todd, "Widely-Predicted Deep Cuts in Foreign Aid and . . ." *Southam News/CanWest News*, February 20, 1990.

147 Ibid.

148 Dave Todd, "Canada's Reputation as a Good Samaritan Suffered . . ." *CanWest News*, February 28, 1990.

149 Stewart, "When Brian Mulroney Was Great."

150 Ibid.

151 Harvey Schachter, "A Conversation with Stephen Lewis," *Whig-Standard* (Kingston, ON), April 16, 1986.

152 Brian Stewart, email message to the author, July 17, 2017.

CHAPTER FOUR

153   Terry Pedwell, "Prime Ministers on a Plane: Harper, Predecessors Together for Mandela Tribute," *Toronto Star*, December 9, 2013, https://www.thestar.com/news/canada/2013/12/09/prime_ministers_on_a_plane_harper_predecessors_together_for_mandela_tribute.html.

154   Richard Jackson, "PM Back to Hero's Welcome, Uplands Reception 'Most Affectionate of My Lifetime,'" *Ottawa Journal*, March 17, 1961.

155   Stephen Lewis, interview with the author, August 1, 2017.

156   Mulroney, *Memoirs*, 765.

157   Ibid., 766.

158   Joe Clark, *How We Lead: Canada in a Century of Change* (Toronto: Random House, 2013), 106.

159   Mulroney interview.

160   Linda Freeman, *The Ambiguous Champion: Canada and South Africa in the Trudeau and Mulroney Years* (Toronto: University of Toronto Press, 1997), 55.

161   Ibid., 149–50.

162   Chris Brown, "Canada and Southern Africa: Autonomy, Image and Capacity in Foreign Policy," in Maureen Appel Molot and Fen Osler Hampson, eds., *Canada among Nations 1989: The Challenge of Change* (Ottawa: Carleton University Press, 1990), 218.

163   Ibid., 219–20.

164   Mulroney, *Memoirs*, 433-434.

165   Freeman, *The Ambiguous Champion*, 168.

166   As recounted by Arthur Milnes, who met with Margaret Thatcher in the Tea Room of the House of Lords in London in May 2007. Based on private notes he took at the meeting, which are in his files at the Queen's University Archives.

167   Charles Moore, *Margaret Thatcher: The Authorized Biography, Volume Two: Everything She Wants* (London: Penguin, 2015), 555.

168   Ibid., 559.

169   Confidential interview with a former senior government official.

170   Mulroney, *Memoirs*, 406.

171   Ibid., 407.

172   Si Taylor, Interview with the author, September 12, 2016.

173   Mulroney, private written communication with the author based on his own notes of the meeting with Thatcher.

174   Si Taylor, interview with the author, September 12, 2016.

175   Derek Burney, interview with the author, September 12, 2016.

176   Stephen Lewis, interview with the author, August 1, 2017.

177   David R. Black, "How Exceptional? Reassessing the Mulroney Government's Anti-Apartheid Crusade," in Michaud and Nossal, *Diplomatic Departures*, 183.

178   Ibid., 221.

179   Ibid., 222.

180   See, for example, Audie Klotz, *Norms in International Relations: The Struggle against Apartheid* (London: Cornell University Press, 1995); Philip I. Levy, "Sanctions on South Africa: What Did They Do?" *American Economic Review*, 89, no. 2 (May 1999): 415–20; and Anton D. Lowenberg and William H. Kaempfer, *The Origins and Demise of South African Apartheid* (Ann Arbor: University of Michigan Press, 1998).

181   Alexander Laverty, "Impact of Economic and Political Sanctions on Apartheid," *The Africa File: A Source for Adventures and Commentary in Southern Africa*, June 7, 2007. Used with permission, https://theafricanfile.com/politicshistory/impact-of-economic-and-political-sanctions-on-apartheid.

182   Ibid.

183   Ibid.

184   Clark, *How We Lead*, 65.

185   Ibid., 65.

186   Mulroney, *Memoirs*, 766.

187   Clark, *How We Lead*, 186.

188   Black, "How Exceptional?," 184.

189 Freeman, *Ambiguous Champion*, 5.

190 Letter personally shared with the author by Brian Mulroney.

CHAPTER FIVE

191 This is one of the themes of my co-authored book with Derek Burney, *Brave New Canada: The Challenge of a Changing World* (Montreal and Kingston: McGill-Queen's University Press, 2014).

192 Shintaro Ishihara, *The Japan That Can Say No: Why Japan Will Be First among Equals* (New York: Simon & Schuster, 1991); and Ezra Vogel, *Japan as Number One: Lessons for America* (Cambridge, MA: Harvard University Press, 1979).

193 See Terence Corcoran, "Why Justin Trudeau Shares His Dad's Love of Murderous Communist Despots Like Castro," *National Post*, November 29, 2016.

194 Ibid., 76.

195 Burney, *Getting It Done*, 82.

196 Mulroney, *Memoirs*, 438.

197 Ibid., 439–40.

198 Ibid., 443

199 Minister for International Trade, Secretary of State for External Affairs, Minister for External Relations, Memorandum to Cabinet, *A Canadian Strategy for Canada*, Document 5-0096-87MC (01), March 16, 1987, p. 000003. Document released under the Access to Information Act.

200 Record of Committee Decision, Report of the Cabinet Committee on Foreign and Defence Policy, Meeting of March 25, 1987, Ratified by the Priorities and Planning Committee, Meeting of March 31, 1987, *A Canadian Strategy for Canada*, Document 5-0096-87RD(01)(C), April 1, 1987. Document released under the Access to Information Act, p. 000007.

201 "China—The Way Ahead" and "Future Initiatives," Minutes, The Cabinet Committee on Foreign and Defence Policy, Document 9-89CMFDP, June 28, 1989. Document released under the Access to Information Act.

202 "Notes for PGM Remarks to Cabinet Committee, 19 June 1989," Minutes, The Cabinet Committee on Foreign and Defence Policy, Document 8-89CMFDP, June 19, 1989, p. 000145. Document released under the Access to Information Act.

203 The Cabinet Committee on Foreign and Defence Policy, Minutes, Document 8-89CMFDP, June 19, 1989. Document released under the Access to Information Act, p. 000140.

204 Cabinet Minutes, Document 9-89CBM, June 15, 1989. Document released under the Access to Information Act.

205 Mulroney, *Memoirs*, 796.

206 Ibid., 134.

207 Ibid., 851.

208 Brian Mulroney, speech to the Japanese Diet in Tokyo, May 7, 1986.

209 Mulroney, *Memoirs*, 437.

210 Mulroney, speech to Japanese Diet.

211 Mulroney, *Memoirs*, 436.

212 Ibid.

213 Helmet Kohl had an unfortunate habit of removing his headset (for translation) many times when his Japanese colleague was speaking.

214 George H.W. Bush and Brent Scowcroft, *A World Transformed* (New York: Vintage, 1999), 508.

215 See Norman Paterson School of International Affairs, *Winning in a Changing World: Canada and Emerging Markets* (Ottawa: iPolitics, 2012).

216 Ron Richardson, *Canada Asia Review 2004* (Vancouver: Asia Pacific Foundation of Canada, 2004), 16.

217 See Burney and Hampson, *Brave New Canada*.

CHAPTER SIX

218 Jean-Philippe Thérien, "Co-operation and Conflict in la Francophonie," *International Journal* 48, no. 3 (summer 1993): 496.

219 Ibid., 505.

220 Ibid., 512.

221 Ibid., 510.

222 Lise Bissonnette, "French Smiles Are Nice, but Francs Are Better," *Globe and Mail*, June 13, 1987.

223 Quoted in Mulroney, *Memoirs*, 333.

224 Ibid., 333.

225 Ibid., 334.

226 Ibid., 413.

227 Ibid., 415.

228 Ibid., 417.

229 Bertrand Marotte, "Organizer of Francophone Summit Anxious to Avoid Treading on Toes," *Globe and Mail*, August 14, 1987.

230 Bertrand Marotte and Patricia Poirier, "Expect No Miracles at Summit, PM Says; 41 Francophone Nations Gather," *Globe and Mail*, September 2, 1987.

231 Graham Fraser and Bertrand Marotte, "Francophone Leaders End Meeting with Affirmation of New Solidarity," *Globe and Mail*, September 5, 1987.

232 Mulroney, *Memoirs*, 412.

233 L. Ian MacDonald, "France Salutes Brian Mulroney with Its Highest Civilian Honour," *iPolitics*, December 6, 2016, http://ipolitics.ca/2016/12/06/france-salutes-brian-mulroney-with-its-highest-civilian-honour.

234 Bertrand Marotte, "'Father' of Summit Questions Priorities," *Globe and Mail*, September 7, 1987.

235 Lise Bissonnette, "Dakar Summit Agenda Carefully Routine for Francophonie," *Globe and Mail*, May 20, 1989.

236 Thérien, "Co-operation and Conflict," 502–3.

237 Mulroney interview.

238 Javier Pérez de Cuéllar, private conversation with the author.

239 Barbara McDougall, "Haiti: Canada's Role in the OAS," in Chester A. Crocker, Fen Osler Hampson, and Pamela Aall, eds., *Herding Cats: Multiparty Mediation in a Complex World* (Washington, DC: United States Institute of Peace, 1999), 398.

240 Ibid., 400.

241 Ibid.

242 John W. Graham, "Canada and the OAS: Terra Incognita," in Fen Osler Hampson and Maureen Appel Molot, eds., *Canada among Nations 1996: Big Enough to Be Heard* (Ottawa: Carleton University Press, 1996), 301.

243 Peter McKenna, *Canada and the OAS* (Ottawa: Carleton University Press, 1995), 66.

244 Ibid., 70–71.

245 Quoted in Heath MacQuarrie, "Canada and the OAS: The Still Vacant Chair," *Dalhousie Review* 48, no. 1 (1968), 41–42.

246 McKenna, *Canada and the OAS*, 74–75.

247 Ibid., 76.

248 MacQuarrie, "The Still Vacant Chair," 43.

249 McKenna, *Canada and the OAS*, 88.

250 Ibid., 92.

251 Edgar J. Dosman, "Canada and Latin America: The New Look," *International Journal* 47, no. 3 (summer 1992), 533.

252 Ibid., 534.

253 Ibid., 535.

254 "Canada Joins OAS: Mulroney Pledges New Relationship," *Globe and Mail*, October 28, 1989.

255 Mulroney interview.

256 Dosman, "Canada and Latin America," 536–37.

257 *Globe and Mail*, "Canada Joins OAS."

258 Ross Howard, "Critics Anticipate Diplomatic Problems after Endorsement," *Globe and Mail*, December 22, 1989.

259 "Invading Panama: A Nation Wavers," *Globe and Mail*, January 11, 1990.

260 Graham, "Terra Incognita," 302.

261 Quoted in Graham, ibid.

CHAPTER SEVEN

262 Burney, *Getting It Done*, 163.

263 "Discoverer of Acid Raid Looks Back," *Morningside*, CBC Radio, June 30, 1991, http://www.cbc.ca/archives/entry/ discoverer-of-acid-rain-looks-back.

264 "What Is Acid Rain?," United States Environmental Protection Agency, https://www.epa.gov/acidrain/what-acid-rain.

265 George D. Moffett, "U.S., Canada Confront Acid Rain," *Christian Science Monitor*, March 19, 1985.

266 Mulroney, *Memoirs*, 289.

267 Jack Germond and Jules Witcover, "How Reagan Will Avoid Acting on Acid Rain," *Toronto Star*, January 15, 1986.

268 Susan Riley, "Acid Rain: There's Only One Optimist in Town," *Ottawa Citizen*, April 4, 1987.

269 Mulroney, *Memoirs*, 290.

270 William Johnson, "Cut Acid Rain by Half, Mulroney Asks Reagan," *Globe and Mail*, June 22, 1984.

271 Mulroney, *Memoirs*, 327–28.

272 Douglas Martin, "Canadian Leader Sees No U.S. Shift on Acid Rain," *New York Times*, September 29, 1984.

273 Michael Keating, "Provinces to Assist in Cutting Acid Rain," *Globe and Mail*, February 2, 1985.

274 Rick Boychuk, "Acid-Rain Pact to Cut Emissions in Half by 1994," *Gazette* (Montreal), February 6, 1985.

275 Canadian Press, "Ottawa Antes $300 Million in Acid-Rain Fight," *Gazette* (Montreal), March 7, 1985.

276 "Clean Hands for the Summit," *Globe and Mail*, February 5, 1985. Used with permission.

277 Canadian Press, "Stalemate Feared on Acid Rain," *Globe and Mail*, March 1, 1985.

278 Ibid.

279 Patrick Nagle, "New Acid-Rain Plan Won't Spur U.S. Action, Ottawa Says," *Gazette* (Montreal), March 8, 1985.

280 Jeff Sallot, "Mulroney, Reagan Name Acid Rain Envoys," *Globe and Mail*, March 18, 1985.

281 Benjamin Taylor, "Canada, U.S. Name 2 to Study Acid Rain," *Boston Globe*, March 18, 1985.

282 Brian Butters, "U.S. Doesn't Give an Inch on Acid Rain," *Gazette* (Montreal), March 18, 1985.

283 "Environmentalists Reject Acid Rain Talks," *Globe and Mail*, March 18, 1985.

284 George D. Moffett, "U.S., Canada Confront Acid Rain," *Christian Science Monitor*, March 19, 1985.

285 "Reagan–Mulroney Parley Is Debated," *New York Times*, March 20, 1985.

286 Canadian Press, "I Won't Point Any Fingers over Acid Rain: Davis," *Gazette* (Montreal), March 19, 1985.

287 Canadian Press, "PM Puts Acid Rain atop List for Reagan," *Globe and Mail*, December 20, 1984.

288 Michael Keating, "Canada, 9 Others Sign Acid Rain Pact," *Globe and Mail*, March 22, 1985.

289 Michael Keating, "Blais-Grenier Pressing U.S. Counterpart on Acid Rain," *Globe and Mail*, April 18, 1985.

290 Christie McLaren, "Blais-Grenier Defends U.S. on Acid Rain," *Globe and Mail*, July 9, 1985.

291 Reuters, "U.S., U.K., Poland Balk at Pollution Pact," *Gazette* (Montreal), July 10, 1985.

292 Canadian Press, "Acid-Rain Envoys Hold First Talks," *Gazette* (Montreal), April 20, 1985.

293 Alan Christie, "Costly 'Scrubbers' Cause Problems, Utilities Tell Davis," *Toronto Star*, August 8, 1985.

294 Alan Christie, "Acid Rain Envoys Fight for Credibility," *Toronto Star*, August 12, 1985.

295 "Reagan Aide Urges Action on Acid Rain," *Los Angeles Times*, September 13, 1985.

296 Guy Darst, "U.S.–Canada Report on Acid Rain: U.S. Urged to Speed 'Clean-Coal' Methods," *Boston Globe*, January 8, 1986.

297   Terrance Wills, "Industry Has Acid-Rain Veto: Davis," *Gazette* (Montreal), January 9, 1986.

298   John N. Maclean, "Reagan Holds Back on Acid-Rain Plan," *Chicago Tribune*, January 9, 1986.

299   "Reagan May Reject Study on Acid Rain, Envoy Says," *Toronto Star*, January 8, 1986.

300   Wills, "Industry Has Acid-Rain Veto."

301   "Played for a Sucker," *Gazette* (Montreal), January 9, 1986.

302   Dianne Dumanoski, "Acid Rain Study Asserts Link to Sulfur," *Boston Globe*, March 15, 1986.

303   Christopher S. Wren, "Mulroney Praises U.S.–Canada Ties," *New York Times*, March 16, 1986.

304   Dianne Dumanoski, "Reagan Backs Report on Acid Rain Pollution," *Boston Globe*, March 20, 1986.

305   Larry Black, "Reagan Joshes 'Kid' Mulroney at Dazzling White House Bash," *Toronto Star*, March 19, 1986.

306   Brian Mulroney, written communication with the author.

307   Canadian Press, "PM Admits Summit Pact on Acid Rain 'No Triumph,'" *Citizen* (Montreal), March 22, 1986.

308   Jennifer Lewington, "U.S. May Cut Back on Acid-Rain Fight," *Globe and Mail*, April 30, 1986.

309   Jennifer Lewington and Jeff Sallot, "Mulroney Confident Reagan Will Deliver," *Globe and Mail*, May 1, 1986.

310   Jennifer Lewington, "Canada's Image: Whiner to the North," *Globe and Mail*, May 17, 1986.

311   David Israelson, "Reagan Stance on Acid Rain Leaves Ottawa Concerned," *Toronto Star*, January 7, 1987.

312   Ibid.

313   "Frustrating Week for Canada in Pollution Battle with U.S.," *Toronto Star*, January 10, 1987.

314   Jeff Sallot, "Clark Letter Chastises Shultz over 'Quibbling' on Acid Rain," *Globe and Mail*, January 20, 1987.

315 Ken MacQueen, "In His Five Hours Here, U.S. Vice President . . ." *Southam News/CanWest News,* January 21, 1987.

316 Linda Diebel, "Back Acid-Rain Pact, PM Urges Reagan," *Gazette* (Montreal), April 6, 1987.

317 Christopher Waddell and Jennifer Lewington, "PM Urges Canada–U.S. Treaty to Control Acid-Rain Emissions," *Globe and Mail,* April 6, 1987.

318 Greg Weston, "Reagan Shift on Acid Rain Considered Significant," *Ottawa Citizen,* April 7, 1987.

319 Rob Ludlow, "Ronald Reagan Leaves with a Promise to . . ." *Southam News/CanWest News,* April 6, 1987.

320 Hugh Winsor, "Great Expectations: For Mulroney, Something to Clasp from a Last-Minute Concession," *Globe and Mail,* April 7, 1987.

321 Walter V. Robinson, "Reagan Says He'll Weigh Canada's Bid on Acid Rain," *Boston Globe,* April 7, 1987.

322 Martin Cohn, "Reagan to Consider PM's Pleas," *Toronto Star,* April 7, 1987.

323 Canadian Press, "Friendship at Risk over Acid Rain, PM Warns U.S.," *Ottawa Citizen,* March 29, 1987.

324 "What's Really Offensive," *Gazette* (Montreal), March 30, 1988.

325 Canadian Press, "Friendship at Risk."

326 Les Whittington, "Prime Minister Brian Mulroney, Saying He Doesn't . . ." *CanWest News,* April 28, 1988.

327 Kenneth Freed, "Reagan Rebuffs Mulroney on Acid Rain Plan," *Los Angeles Times,* April 28, 1988.

328 Terrance Wills, "'Salesman' PM Can't Peddle Acid-Rain Cuts," *Gazette* (Montreal), April 28, 1988.

329 Speech by the Rt. Hon. Brian Mulroney, Prime Minister of Canada. Cong. Rec. 27 April 1988: 9135–9136. Accessed through Govinfo. Web. 24 August 2017.

330 Wills, "'Salesman' PM."

331 Bob Hepburn, "Leaders Declare War on Drugs," *Toronto Star,* June 21, 1988.

332 "Leaders Pledge to Help World's Poor," *Toronto Star*, June 22, 1988.

333 Linda Diebel, "Mulroney Calls Bush 'Loyal Ally' on Acid Rain," *Toronto Star*, November 10, 1988.

334 Oakland Ross, "Skeletons in Our Eco-closet," *Globe and Mail*, June 6, 1992.

335 Terrance Wills, "Pall Hangs over PCS' Environment Record," *Gazette* (Montreal), September 10, 1988.

336 Graham Fraser, "PM Proposes Commitment to Environment," *Globe and Mail*, September 5, 1988.

337 Robin Ludlow, "Environment Concerns Raise a Stink," *Ottawa Citizen*, September 17, 1988.

338 Hugh Winsor, "Broadbent Bashes Broken PC Promises," *Globe and Mail*, October 11, 1988.

339 Benoît Aubin, "'Polluter Pays' Basis of New Turner Policy on the Environment," *Globe and Mail*, October 18, 1988.

340 Robin Ludlow, "Dukakis Would Have Been Best but Environmentalists . . ." *Southam News/CanWest News*, November 8, 1988.

341 Mark Kennedy, "PM Eager to Pass Trade Bill," *Ottawa Citizen*, November 23, 1988.

342 Robin Ludlow, "Environmentalists Are Guardedly Optimistic about Lucien Bouchard's . . ." *Southam News/CanWest News*, January 30, 1989.

343 Mark Kennedy, "PM Eager to Pass Trade Bill," *Ottawa Citizen*, November 23, 1988.

344 Jennifer Lewington, "Bush Plans to Continue Summit Talks with Canada," *Globe and Mail*, January 13, 1989.

345 Peter Calamai and Les Whittington, "Bush Plans a Kinder, Gentler Summit with . . ." *Southam News/CanWest News*, January 24, 1989.

346 Jennifer Lewington, "U.S. Acid Rain Move Seen as Possible Setback," *Globe and Mail*, January 10, 1989.

347 "U.S. Rushing to Prepare Acid-Rain Controls, Bush's Man Says," *Gazette* (Montreal), February 1, 1989.

348 Robin Ludlow, "When U.S. President George Bush Visits Ottawa Next Friday, the . . ." *Southam News/CanWest News*, February 2, 1989.

349 Jonathan Manthorpe, "Canada Does Not Expect Any Breakthroughs in . . ." *Southam News/CanWest News*, February 8, 1989.

350 Robin Ludlow, "Without Offering Specific Details, U.S. President George Bush . . ." *Southam News/CanWest News*, February 10, 1989.

351 Timothy J. McNulty and Howard Witt, "Bush's Acid-Rain Pledge Raises Canadian Hopes," *Chicago Tribune*, February 11, 1989. Used with permission.

352 Christopher Waddell and Jennifer Lewington, "Bush Promises Accord on Acid Rain," *The Globe and Mail*, February 11, 1989.

353 Jennifer Lewington, "Pact on Acid Rain Not Likely This Year," *Globe and Mail*, February 20, 1989.

354 Tim Harper, "PM Encouraged by Two Pep Talks on Acid Rain Plan," *Toronto Star*, May 4, 1989.

355 Bob Hepburn, "Acid Rain Talks Endorsed by U.S. Senate Leaders," *Toronto Star*, May 4, 1989.

356 Tim Harper, "Acid Rain Pact Is On, Both Sides Insist," *Toronto Star*, May 6, 1989.

357 Canadian Press, "Bush Balks at Accord on Acid-Rain Pollution," *Edmonton Journal*, May 5, 1989.

358 Jennifer Robinson, "Bush Backs Off Speedy Pollution Pact," *Gazette* (Montreal), May 5, 1989.

359 Harper, "Both Sides Insist."

360 Joan Bryden, "Canada Will Begin Negotiating an Acid Rain . . ." *Southam News/CanWest News*. May 15, 1989.

361 Larry Tye, "Bush, Pledging to 'Clean the Air,' Presents Tough Antipollution Plan," *Boston Globe*, June 13, 1989.

362 Peter Calamai, "While Environmentalists, Legislators and Even Some Industrialists . . ." *Southam News/Canwest News*, June 12, 1989.

363 Robin Ludlow, "Canada Welcomes Bush's Acid Rain Plan," *Southam News/CanWest News*, June 12, 1989.

364 Pater Calamai, "While Environmentalists, Legislators."

365 Jack Nagler, "Acid Rain Far from Solved, U.S. Senator Says," *Globe and Mail*, June 29, 1989.

366 Canadian Press, "Negotiators Just 'Talk' about Acid-Rain Accord," *Ottawa Citizen*, July 25, 1989.

367 Julian Beltrame, "Canada Has Agreed to Join the U.S. . . . ." *Southam News/CanWest News*, August 31, 1989.

368 Jennifer Lewington, "Mulroney, Bush Vow Action on Drugs, Trade," *Globe and Mail*, September 1, 1989.

369 Jennifer Lewington, "Fish, Tennis on Agenda as Mulroney Visits Bush," *Globe and Mail*, August 31, 1989.

370 "U.S. Tightens Emission Law," *Windsor Star*, October 3, 1989.

371 David Israelson, "Observers Gasp at Toughness of Exhaust Rules," *Toronto Star*, October 29, 1989.

372 Peter Calamai, "Bush Urges Sharp Troop Cuts in Europe," *Gazette* (Montreal), February 1, 1990.

373 Ross Howard, "Bush Offers Hope to PM on Acid Rain," *Globe and Mail*, April 11, 1990. Used with permission.

374 Janet Cawley and Storer H. Rowley, "Bush, Mulroney Mix Issues with Innings," *Chicago Tribune*, April 11, 1990.

375 "Mulroney Raps 'No Class' Fans," *Ottawa Citizen*, April 11, 1990.

376 Ibid.

377 Stanley Meisler, "Bush, Mulroney Have a Ball at Baseball Summit," *Los Angeles Times*, April 11, 1990.

378 Rosemary Speirs, "Canada Gets Long-Awaited Promise of Acid-Rain Agreement from Bush," *Toronto Star*, July 10, 1990.

379 Norma Greenaway, "President George Bush and Prime Minister Brian . . ." *Southam News/CanWest News*, July 8, 1990.

380 Tom Spears, "Acid Rain Talks to Begin in August," *Ottawa Citizen*, July 17, 1990.

381 Norma Greenaway, "William Reilly, the U.S. Government's Top Environment Official, Is . . ." *CanWest News*, October 22, 1990.

382 Linda Diebel, "Acid Rain Law Called 'Promise' to Canada," *Toronto Star*, October 23, 1990.

383 Norma Greenaway, "The U.S. House of Representatives Overwhelmingly Endorsed Major . . ." *CanWest News*, October 26, 1990.

384 Colin MacKenzie, "U.S., Canada Complete Talks on Acid Rain," *Globe and Mail,* December 20, 1990.

385 Michael Kranish, "U.S. and Canada Sign Acid Rain Pact Benefiting New England," *Boston Globe,* March 14, 1991.

386 Anne McIlroy, "Accord Attacks Acid Rain," *Edmonton Journal,* March 14, 1991.

387 "People," *Edmonton Journal,* March 15, 1991.

388 "Passing the Acid Test," *Toronto Star,* March 14, 1991.

389 "The Long, Tough Road to the Acid-Rain Accord," *Globe and Mail,* March 15, 1991.

CHAPTER EIGHT

390 Portions of this chapter are adapted from my earlier essay "Pollution across Borders: Canada's International Environmental Agenda," in Molot and Hampson, *The Challenge of Change,* 175–92.

391 World Commission on Environment and Development (WCED), *Our Common Future* (Oxford: Oxford University Press, 1987).

392 Quoted in Hampson, "Pollution across Borders," 175.

393 Brian Mulroney, "Verbatim: A Call for a New Northern Vision," *Policy Options,* June 2006, 5.

394 Mulroney, *Memoirs,* 373–74.

395 Joel Ruimy, "Acid Rain, Ozone Worries Are Raised in Talks," *Toronto Star,* June 20, 1988.

396 Stanley Meisler, "Assortment of Protesters Unified on a Theme," *Los Angeles Times,* June 20, 1988.

397 Joel Ruimy, "Economic Summit's Accomplishments Fleeting," *Toronto Star,* June 25, 1988.

398 Nomi Morris, "Success on Environment for Low-Key Kohl," *Toronto Star,* June 22, 1988.

399 Robert A. Rankin, "Summit Results Mixed," *Philadelphia Inquirer,* June 22, 1988.

400 Mulroney, *Memoirs,* 743.

401 Reproduced in Arthur Blanchette, *Canadian Foreign Policy, 1945–2000: Major Documents and Speeches* (Kemptville, ON: Golden Dog Press, 2000), 276.

402 Ibid., 278.

403 Environment Canada, "Conference Statement," The Changing Atmosphere: Implications for Global Security, Toronto, Canada, June 27–30, 1988.

404 Adam Fenech, "Reflections on the Toronto Conference – 25 Years Later," University of Prince Edward Island Climate Lab, July 2, 2013, http://projects.upei.ca/climate/2013/07/02/reflections-on-the-toronto-conference-25-years-later/.

405 Barack Obama, State of the Union Address, January 20, 2015, https://obamawhitehouse.archives.gov/the-press-office/2015/01/20/remarks-president-state-union-address-january-20-2015.

406 "Protection of the Atmosphere," Statement of the International Meeting of Legal and Policy Experts, Ottawa, February 22, 1989.

407 "Declaration of The Hague," United Nations Conference on the Environment, The Hague, Netherlands, March 11, 1989.

408 Linda Diebel, "Mulroney Already Losing Summit Publicity War to U.S.," *Toronto Star*, July 9, 1989.

409 Don McGillivray, "Politicians Jostle for a Seat on Environment Express," *Edmonton Journal*, July 10, 1989.

410 "Key Sections of the Paris Communique by Group of Seven," *New York Times*, July 17, 1989.

411 See "Environmental Indicators, Modelling and Outlooks," Organisation for Economic Co-operation and Development, Environment Directorate, http://www.oecd.org/env/indicators-modelling-outlooks.

412 James Ferrabee, "Mulroney Winner on Environment," *Calgary Herald*, July 17, 1989.

413 "Langkawi Declaration on the Environment," The Commonwealth, 1989, http://thecommonwealth.org/history-of-the-commonwealth/langkawi-declaration-signed.

414 See Fen Osler Hampson, "Hazardous Wastes," in *Multilateral Negotiations: Lesson from Arms Control, Trade, and the Environment* (Baltimore: Johns Hopkins University Press, 1995), 278–99.

415 Brian Handwerk, "Whatever Happened to the Ozone Hole?" *National Geographic News*, May 7, 2010, http://news.nationalgeographic.com/news/2010/05/100505-science-environment-ozone-hole-25-years/.

416 "Canada Backs Global Chemical Limit," *Ottawa Citizen*, December 12, 1986.

417 This discussion about negotiations leading to the Montreal Protocol for the Protection of the Ozone Layer is adapted from my chapter "The Ozone Accords," in *Multilateral Negotiations*, 256–77.

418 Thomas Netter, "UN Conference Agrees on Need to Save Ozone," *Chicago Tribune*, December 6, 1986.

419 Irwin Block, "U.S. Urged to Soften Its Position on Ozone-Layer Protection Treaty," *Gazette* (Montreal), September 15, 1987.

420 Jim Robb, "Canada Urging Action to Protect Ozone Layer," *Ottawa Citizen*, February 14, 1987.

421 Michael Keating, "Canada Key Player in Ozone Layer Talks," *Globe and Mail*, February 21, 1987.

422 Elizabeth May, "When Canada Led the Way: A Short History of Climate Change," *Policy Options*, October 2006, 51.

423 David Lauter, "U.S. Move May Stall Ozone-Layer Treaty," *Los Angeles Times*, September 9, 1987.

424 Ibid.

425 Dennis Bueckert, "U.S. Stance Could Foil Bid to Draft Ozone Treaty, Delegates to Talks Say," *Ottawa Citizen*, September 11, 1987.

426 Lauter, "U.S. Move May Stall."

427 Canadian Press, "Developing Nations Balk at Curbs, Putting Ozone-Treaty Talks at Risk," *Gazette* (Montreal), September 12, 1987.

428 Block, "U.S. Urged to Soften."

429 Philip Shabecoff, "Ozone Treaty Nears, but Obstacles Remain," *New York Times*, September 15, 1987.

430 Canadian Press, "McMillan Warns Diplomats of Ozone Layer 'Time Bomb,'" *Windsor Star*, September 15, 1987.

431 Philip Shabecoff, "Dozens of Nations Reach Agreement to Protect Ozone," *New York Times*, September 17, 1987.

432 United Nations Environment Programme, "Helsinki Declaration on the Protection of the Ozone Layer," May 5, 1989.

433 Ian H. Rowlands, "The Fourth Meeting of the Parties to the Montreal Protocol: Report and Reflection," *Environment* 35, no. 6: 25–34, http://www.ciesin.org/docs/003-077/003-077.html.

434 "The Montreal Protocol: To Coldly Go: Extending an Old Treaty That Saved the Ozone Layer Could Improve Cooling Technology— and Slow Global Warming," *Economist*, September 24, 2016, http://www.economist.com/news/international/21707531-extending-old-treaty-saved-ozone-layer-could-improve-cooling-technology-and-slow.

435 See WCED, *Our Common Future*.

436 Interview with a former associate of the late Maurice Strong who chose to remain anonymous.

437 Peter Gorrie, "Eco-Summit Losing Lustre," *Toronto Star*, July 23, 1991.

438 John Hay, "Mulroney's Indecision on Environment Summit Is a Complex Calculation," *Ottawa Citizen*, March 24, 1992.

439 Elizabeth May, "Put on Your Capt. Planet Cape, Brian, and Get Busy," *Globe and Mail*, February 7, 1992.

440 See WCED, *Our Common Future*.

441 David Runnalls, "The Road from Rio," in Fen Osler Hampson and Christopher J. Maule, eds., *Canada among Nations, 1993–94: Global Jeopardy* (Ottawa: Carleton University Press, 1993), 137.

442 David Runnalls, interview with the author, July 6, 2017.

443 Canadian Press, "U.S. May Reject Environmental Pact," *Kitchener-Waterloo Record*, May 25, 1992.

444 Anne McIlroy, "Failure of Talks May Make Summit More Worthwhile," *Ottawa Citizen*, April 6, 1992.

445 Runnalls, "The Road from Rio," 137.

446 Norma Greenaway, "Bush to Attend Earth Summit," *Calgary Herald*, May 13, 1992.

447 Peter Gorrie, "Global Warming Treaty 'Irrelevant,' Critics Charge," *Toronto Star*, May 9, 1992.

448 Associated Press, "U.S. Dissent Seen as Threat to Rio Summit," *Kitchener-Waterloo Record*, June 1, 1992.

449 Dennis Bueckert, "A Summit to Save the Earth? Or a Squandered Chance to Act on a Global Warning?" *Hamilton Spectator*, May 30, 1992.

450 Peter Gorrie, "Can Global Summit Help Heal the Earth?" *Toronto Star*, May 30, 1992.

451 Ibid.

452 Dennis Bueckert, "We'll Sign Key Pact On Species: PM," *Gazette* (Montreal), June 2, 1992.

453 "PM Targets Nations That Balk on Pacts," *Vancouver Sun*, June 2, 1992.

454 Geoffrey York and James Rusk, "PM Urges Action to Save Species," *Globe and Mail*, June 2, 1992.

455 Bueckert, "We'll Sign Key Pact."

456 Canadian Press, "Global Effort: Ottawa's Pressure Irritating U.S.," *Kitchener-Waterloo Record*, June 3, 1992.

457 Canadian Press, "U.S. Red-Faced at Earth Summit," *Windsor Star*, June 6, 1992.

458 James Rusk, "Mulroney Signs Ecopact," *Globe and Mail*, June 12, 1992.

459 Stephanie Meakin, "The Rio Earth Summit: Summary of the United Nations Conference on Environment and Development," Background Paper BP-317E (Ottawa: Library of Parliament, Research Branch, Science and Technology Division, November 1992), http://publications.gc.ca/Collection-R/LoPBdP/BP/bp317-e.htm#F.%20The%20Ocean%20Resources%20Meeting(txt).

460 Anne McIlroy, "Canada Forgoes $145M to Third World," *Ottawa Citizen*, June 13, 1992.

461 Meakin, "Rio Earth Summit."

462   Address by Prime Minister Brian Mulroney at the Earth Summit, Rio de Janeiro, June 12, 1992, reproduced in Blanchette, *Canadian Foreign Policy*, 278–79.

463   Rusk, "Mulroney Signs Ecopact."

464   McIlroy, "Canada Forgoes $145M."

465   James Rusk, "Earth Summit Trips over High Hurdle," *Globe and Mail*, June 16, 1992.

466   James Rusk and Isabel Vincent, "Summit Brought Down to Earth," *Globe and Mail*, June 15, 1992.

467   Mulroney interview.

468   Mulroney, *Memoirs*, 909.

CHAPTER 9

469   Ibid., 439.

470   Ibid., 856.

471   Ibid., 863.

472   Ibid., 863.

473   Ironically, perhaps, author Amy Knight claimed that the Cold War began with the defection of the Soviet cipher clerk Igor Gouzenko from the Soviet embassy in Ottawa in September 1945, a defection that was kept from the public until February 1946. (See Amy Knight, *How the Cold War Began*, [London: Carrol and Graf, 2006].) Others have suggested that Winston Churchill's "Iron Curtain" speech in Fulton, Missouri, in June 1946 was a more pivotal event.

474   Ibid., 861.

475   Ibid., 853.

476   Ibid., 863.

477   Bush and Scowcroft, *A World Transformed*, 160.

478   Mulroney, *Memoirs*, 708.

479   Ibid., 707.

480   Writing for the *Toronto Star*, Carol Goar declared that "his approach was exactly right." Quoted in Mulroney, *Memoirs*, 874.

481 Quotation provided from the files of Arthur Milnes, former speech-writer and private researcher for Brian Mulroney.

482 Bush and Scowcroft, *A World Transformed*, 61.

483 Ibid.

484 Russell L. Riley, *With Foreign Leaders: Inside the Clinton White House; An Oral History* (New York: Oxford University Press, 2016), 263.

485 Mulroney, *Memoirs*, 725.

486 Ibid., 405–6.

487 Ibid., 763.

488 Ibid., 699.

489 Christopher Hope and Lydia Wilgress, "Margaret Thatcher Had Deep Misgivings over Reunification of Germany, National Archives Reveal," *Telegraph* (London), December 30, 2016.

490 Mulroney, *Memoirs*, 725.

491 Ibid., 725. Also in Bush and Scowcroft, *A World Transformed*, 250.

492 Paul Heinbecker, *Getting Back in the Game: A Foreign Policy Playbook for Canada* (Toronto: Key Porter, 2010), 80.

493 See Burney, *Getting It Done*, 171.

494 Jeanne Laux, "From South to East? Financing the Transition in Central and Eastern Europe," in Maureen Appel Molot and Harald von Riekhoff, eds., *Canada among Nations 1994: A Part of the Peace* (Ottawa: Carleton University Press, 1994), 185.

495 Ibid., 186.

496 John Halstead, "A New Order in Europe: Evolving Security Systems," in Fen Osler Hampson and Christopher J. Maule, eds., *Canada among Nations 1990–91: After the Cold War* (Ottawa: Carleton University Press, 1991), 161.

497 Alexander Moens, "A New Security Strategy for Europe," in Molot and von Riekhoff, *A Part of the Peace*, 163.

498 Clyde Farnsworth, "Canadian Troops to Pull out of Europe by '94," *New York Times*, February 27, 1992.

499 Derek Burney, interview with the author, June 23, 2017.

500   Quoted in Canadian Press, "Harper Pays Tribute to Former Rival
       Mulroney," CTV News, April 18, 2007, http://www.ctvnews.ca/
       harper-pays-tribute-to-former-rival-mulroney-1.237952#.

501   Barbara McDougall, "History, Not Politics, Drives Canada's
       Support of Ukraine," Globe and Mail, February 27, 2014,
       https://beta.theglobeandmail.com/globe-debate/history-not-
       politics-drives-canadas-support-of-ukraine/article17137053/.

502   Mulroney, Memoirs, 709.

503   Bush and Scowcroft, A World Transformed, 63.

504   France fought ineptly for six brief weeks at the outset of World War II,
       then recovered more valiantly in the final year after being liberated by
       the U.S., Britain, and Canada. For most of the war period, and despite
       Hollywoodish interpretations, France's role involved more collaboration
       than resistance.

505   To be sure, many of our diplomats in the Department of External
       Affairs played an important role in the negotiations that led to the
       creation of the North Atlantic Treaty Organization, the Bretton Woods
       institutions, and the United Nations—but at the political leadership
       level, Mackenzie King and his successor, Louis St. Laurent, were gener-
       ally cautious and passive when it came engaging with the Americans
       and the British on key geostrategic matters. For an adulatory account
       of the post-war "golden age" in Canadian diplomacy, see Andrew
       Cohen, While Canada Slept: How We Lost Our Place in the World, 4th ed.
       (Toronto: McClelland & Stewart, 2004).

506   Mulroney, Memoirs, 874–75.

CHAPTER TEN

507   Mulroney and Burney interviews.

508   Kitty Kelley, The Family: The Real Story of the Bush Dynasty (New York:
       Knopf, 2004), https://books.google.ca/books?id=sQSvBYRoxKUC&pg
       =PT513&lpg=PT513&dq=Margaret+Thatcher+%22george+don't+go
       +wobbly%22&source=bl&ots=yYpNYM3ktQ&sig=olbKorucv8hcI7O8
       TaQVV4fXZuM&hl=en&sa=X&ved=0ahUKEwiLi5efxaTUAhVF6YM
       KHUPCBSgQ6AEIPTAE#v=onepage&q=Margaret%20Thatcher%20
       %22george%20don't%20go%20wobbly%22&f=false.

509   Mulroney, *Memoirs*, 800.

510   Ibid., 801.

511   J.L. Granatstein and David J. Bercuson, *War and Peacekeeping: From South Africa to the Gulf; Canada's Limited Wars* (Toronto: Key Porter Books, 1991), 247.

512   Michel Rossignol, "International Conflicts: Parliament, the National Defence Act, and the Decision to Participate," Background Paper BP-303E (Ottawa: Library of Parliament, Parliamentary Research Branch, Political and Social Affairs Division, August 1992), 21.

513   Mulroney, *Memoirs*, 848.

514   Granatstein and Bercuson, *War and Peacekeeping*, 245.

515   Ibid., 246.

516   Ibid., 247.

517   Martin Rudner, "Canada, the Gulf Crisis, and Collective Security," in Hampson and Maule, *After the Cold War*, 277–78.

518   Ibid., 278.

519   Ibid.

520   *Independent Panel on Canada's Future Role in Afghanistan* (Ottawa: Minister of Public Works and Government Services, 2008).

521   Quoted in Nader Hashemi, "Peacekeeping with No Peace to Keep," in Maya Shatzmillar, *Islam and Bosnia: Conflict Resolution and Foreign Policy in Multi-ethnic States* (Montreal: McGill-Queen's University Press, 2002), 185–86.

522   Mulroney interview.

523   Mulroney interview.

524   Quoted in Nicholas Gammer, *From Peacekeeping to Peacemaking: Canada's Response to the Yugoslav Crisis* (Montreal & Kingston: McGill-Queen's University Press, 2001), 98.

525   Bryan D. Gasten, "Mulroney Urges UN Presence in Bosnia," *Harvard Crimson*, December 11, 1992.

526   Gammer, *From Peacekeeping to Peacemaking*, 100.

527   The report can be found at https://web.archive.org/web/20070731161527/http://www.iciss-ciise.gc.ca/report2-en.asp.

528 Gammer, *From Peacekeeping to Peacemaking*, 100.

529 Ibid., 102.

530 Edwin M. Smith, "Collective Security, Peacekeeping, and Ad Hoc Multilateralism," in Charlotte Ku and Harold K. Jacobson, eds., *Democratic Accountability and the Use of Force* (Cambridge: Cambridge University Press, 2002), 96.

531 Howard Adelman, "Mandela Will Be Sorely Missed," *The Exchange, CJIA*, December 6, 2013. Available at: http://cija.ca/mandela-will -be-sorely-missed.

532 Lewis interview.

533 This discussion draws on Fen Osler Hampson, *Nurturing Peace: Why Peace Settlement Succeed or Fail* (Washington, DC: United States Institute of Peace Press, 1995), 53–169.

534 "'Belen Huet Is a Peaceful Place,'" CBC News, December 28, 1992. Used with permission, http://www.cbc.ca/archives/entry/ belet-huen-is-a-peaceful-place.

535 Nancy Gordon, "Beyond Peacekeeping: Somalia, the United Nations and the Canadian Experience," in Molot and von Riekhoff, *A Part of the Peace*, 292.

536 CBC News, "Belen Huet Is a Peaceful Place."

537 Commission of Inquiry into the Deployment of Canadian Forces to Somalia, *Dishonoured Legacy: The Lessons of the Somalia Legacy, vols. I–V* (Ottawa: Minister of Public Works and Government Services Canada, 1997).

538 Geoffrey York, "How the Pierre Trudeau Government Turned a Blind Eye to Africa Massacres," *Globe and Mail*, May 14, 2017, https://www.theglobeandmail.com/news/world/pierre-trudeau- muted-response-to-zimbabwe-massacre/article34985007.

539 Steve Chase, "Saudi Arms Deal: Trudeau Government Registers Concern with Saudi Arabia over Apparent Armoured-Vehicle Use," *Globe and Mail*, August 7, 2017, https://www.theglobeandmail.com/ news/politics/trudeau-government-registers-concern-with-saudi- arabia-over-apparent-armoured-vehicle-use/article35896121.

CHAPTER ELEVEN

540 "You have enemies? Why, it is the story of every man who has done a great deed or created a new idea. It is the cloud which thunders around everything that shines. Fame must have enemies, as light must have gnats."

541 Richard Kim Nossal, "The Mulroney Years: Transformation and Tumult," *Policy Options*, June 1, 2003, http://policyoptions.irpp.org/magazines/the-best-pms-in-the-past-50-years/the-mulroney-years-transformation-and-tumult.

542 See, for example, Stephen Gandel, "Donald Trump Says NAFTA Was the Worst Trade Deal the U.S. Ever Signed," *Fortune*, September 26, 2016, http://fortune.com/2016/09/27/presidential-debate-nafta-agreement.

543 Notes for an Address by the Right Honourable Brian Mulroney at the Annual Canada 2020 Conference, NAFTA: A Way Ahead, Ottawa, Ontario, June 16, 2017.

544 *North American Free Trade Agreement (NAFTA)*, Global Affairs Canada, http://international.gc.ca/trade-commerce/trade-agreements-accords-commerciaux/agr-acc/nafta-alena/fta-ale/info.aspx?lang=eng.

545 Taylor interview.

546 Ibid.

547 Burney interview.

548 Alexander Panetta, "Mulroney Takes on Role to Help Trudeau Despite Rivalry with His Dad; 'That Was Then,'" *Toronto Star*, April 5, 2017, https://www.thestar.com/news/canada/2017/04/05/former-pm-mulroney-to-brief-liberal-committee-on-us-relations-nafta-perspective.html.

549 "Address by Minister Freeland on Canada's Foreign Policy Priorities," Global Affairs Canada, June 6, 2017, https://www.canada.ca/en/global-affairs/news/2017/06/address_by_ministerfreelandoncanadasforeign-policypriorities.html.

550 Ibid.

551 Phil Sneiderman, "Reagan Joins Mulroney in Backing Aid to Russians," *Los Angeles Times*, April 6, 1993, http://articles.latimes.com/1993-04-06/local/me-19702_1_ronald-reagan-presidential-library.